The Secrets of Lost

The Secrets of Lost

—m—

The Validity of Multi-Dimensional Existence

Rev. Gillian V. Harris M.S.P.

Copyright © 2015 Rev. Gillian V. Harris M.S.P.
All rights reserved.

ISBN: 1515004767
ISBN 13: 9781515004769

At age 13, I was having trouble with math. Dad hired a guy who worked at the lab with him, 21 year old Ken Brenneke, to tutor me every Tuesday afternoon. Cool guy. I remember being a bit smitten by Ken! He was a gentleman and ignored that and I talked about everything I could to stray from the subject of mathematics. I intrigued him with my deep interest and involvement with metaphysics. One day I described to him something I'd seen/experienced many, many times, "there's a guy…" I described a handsome man, Caucasian, in his young 20s. "He's wearing a black leather jacket. He has brown hair. He's walking along a row of bushes, like along a sidewalk". "Oh! Do you know him?" he asked. "No", I answered, "I AM him". My eyes locked with his as I waited for an answer.

I was clear on the FACT this young man in my head was me. -Clear as I am that MY fingers are typing these words. -Crystal clarity. When you look in a mirror and have no question that the reflection is you - I had the same level of absolute knowingness that this man was ME. Or…I was him! Both! And I saw him over and over again, I observed him through a portal of some sort. I certainly didn't understand it and hoped Ken would have an answer for this. All I got was a slight pause as his blonde eyebrows bunched together, then one word, "…Oh!" Knowing that I was counting on him, he added that I should keep investigating to understand it. I did just that from then to the present. And without me really knowing it, along the way, from then to now, I was being lead on a journey of discovery that ultimately answered the question I was trying to ask Ken. "How could I be him?" I sensed him to be far away. East coast or even England. He was dressed very trendily. He was present tense. And he is me. How could this be? Asking that and other similar questions along with sharing the answers is part of my life's purposes. These pages hold what I've learned over the past 40+ years as the information relates directly to the scenes we loved in LOST.

Table of Contents

	To those who have not; STOP HERE!	xi
	Jacob & the black smoke jungle monster	xiii
	Okay, so, what happened was...	xiii
	Acknowledgments	xv
Chapter 1	Intentions	1
Chapter 2	Intentions II "Guys? .....Where are we??"	8
Chapter 3	Victories & Destiny	11
	Flashback	12
	Hit home....	13
	Journal 1	15
Chapter 4	Forward To The Beginning	22
	My haunted hut in the woods	24
	You get what you expect	30
Chapter 5	Written Versus Outcome	32
	Pilot-oscopy	34
Chapter 6	C.U.I.: Creating Under The Influence	37
	Brilliance	38
	Journal 2	40
Chapter 7	Killamystery: The Whispers, Mediumship & Channeling	42
	Journal 3	47
Chapter 8	There Is No Life After Death	49
	Journal 4	50
Chapter 9	Guys, **WHAT** are we?	52
Chapter 10	Cameos.....By Consciousness	65

Chapter 11	It's In The Wind.....	67
	We are unique expressions of omnipotent perfection...	69
	Shawn & torah part 1	71
	Journal 5	72
	Journal 6	73
Chapter 12	Guys? . . . What Time Is It?!	76
	Incarnations & sliding doors.... Guidance & consciousness.....	76
Chapter 13	Petal Hopping	83
	Petal to petal....	84
	The petals of John Locke	85
	Incarnation one:	85
	Incarnation two - a sliding door of incarnation one:	86
	Sliding door three (Because Lock is transitioning from an incarnation)	87
	Quick tangent:	88
	The petals of James Le Fleur	89
	Petal to petal	90
	(Terminal) lucidity...	90
	Petals of kate	91
	INCARNATION 2 is a sliding door of incarnation 1;	91
	What happens when your body dies:	92
	Petals of dr. Jack shepard	93
	SLIDING DOOR #2 (Saved the best for last)	94
Chapter 14	Soul Mates & Spirit Family	98
	Petal to petal	98
	Journal 7	101
Chapter 15	Guidance From ...The Others!	102
Chapter 16	LA X	107
	Airborne	108
	Touchdown!!	110
	Journal 8 -	115
	BTW; the rain in lost -was real!	123
	BTW; the sweat in lost was real!	123
	Native O'ahu	126
	My ho'ukupo	134
	Journal	136
	John & Rey	139

Chapter 17	Lori & Raina	143
	Interview date 9-9-14	143
	Journal 9	165
Chapter 18	Shawn & Torah Part 2	166
	A little reflection on my time with torah:	178
Chapter 19	Flash Forward	180
Chapter 20	CURSING! There is no such thing!	182
Chapter 21	The Hatch	193
	The incident	196
Chapter 22	Panic Attacks	202
	Energy correcting	206
Chapter 23	Lifetime Hallmark	208
Chapter 24	The Island	209
	Journal 10 Sunday February 8	210
Chapter 25	The Point	211
	Duped for the greater good!	212
Chapter 26	Check please!!!	213
	BRB!! (Be Right Back)	213
	I want SECONDS!!!!!	216
	Journal 11	218
	Appendix A Dissolving Contracts	223
	How to kill a contract	223
	Appendix B Bibliography	227

To those who have not; STOP HERE!

Let me fill you in on this series so you understand why I flipped out and just HAD to write this book! LOST is more than just a story of a crashed jetliner full of cool people onto a mystical island. I saw a massive opportunity to use the series as a structure for conversation about Life...and about Life after Life...

But wait! First, in the LOST series, you get to know some beautiful characters;

Kate: Gorgeous felon. - Kind of a murderer! And...kind of an arsonist, larcenist, robber and a bunch of other criminal stuff. Kinda. And she's super sweet, really pretty and very fit!

Jack: the only MD on the scene - proving himself to himself as a result of a childhood that broke him. And then there were the wives... the pills... the beard...and the secret sibling.

Clare: torn about keeping her gestating baby boy, she was on her way from her native Australia to Los Angeles where she would meet the couple who would adopt him. The plane crashes. Prior to the flight, a total quack psychic told her something horrible that she believed so she lived the nightmare out on the island!

Sawyer: a HOT man-mess! -Kind of a cowboy without the hat ...or a horse. Perfect muscles highlighted by sweat attempt but fail to mask his heart. As a child, from under the bed, he heard two gun shots as his Dad took his Mom in a murder suicide. As an adult, Sawyer sought revenge against the man who led his Dad to that dark place. He thought he found him in Australia...

Hurley: The Angel of the island. -The outspoken consciousness of peace and community. Hurley was a humble (lottery win) millionaire. He was also broken as a child with a rolling stone father. So he binged (and forgot to purge) growing an overeating disorder so intense, he gave it a name and personality separate from himself. That and... he's a medium! Yeah. Hurly sees and talks to dead people!

Miles: Dead people talk to him, too, but he can't see them. Miles was sent to the island on a paid assignment to find someone who's "deceased" yet "LIVING" on the island! Yeah, they hired Miles to, literally, do metaphysical reconnaissance & capture.

Charlie: Drummer. Adorable yet troubled heroin addict. Totally high when the plane went down. He did a tango with sobriety while simultaneously doing a samba with addiction. Tempted (big time) then rehabbed on the island. Charlie has a gate keeper, intuitive **Desmond**, who saves him from death repeatedly until finally Charlie is a hero and dies while saving everyone.

Sayid: THIS hot man-mess is a whole lot of whoop-ass meets National Geographic meets Middle Eastern Ken Doll. Sayid was an army 'interrogator' with skills. He's a seasoned torturer. Wracked by guilt for all he'd done and grieving the loss of the love of his life, Nadia, he ends up on Flight 815 and the island where his wicked skills are needed again...for the greater good, of course! ...And the cycle of guilt continues....

Sun & Jin: This beautiful Korean couple was on the verge of break up before flight 815. Jin, the son of a fisherman, was forced to be a corporate thug by Sun's father in order to marry her. So, in a days' work, he'd deliver messages – with his fist. When she figured it out, Sun resented her father for this. Ironically, the organic veggie growing Sun displayed a strong streak of her dad within as she used her airline money to take over her Dads corporation, becoming his boss. She then secretly purchases a gun, handles obstacles and gets back to the island -all in an effort to reunite with Jin who she last saw on a ship as it blew up below her helicopter.

John Locke: He's referred to in these pages as 'Locke'. Orphaned by crazy teen mom. Then as an adult he was pushed out a high rise window by his Dad, on purpose. Locke ...likes knives!
   Paralyzed from the waist down, wheelchair bound and in a deep identity crisis, Locke is determined to do ....a walkabout! That's why HE was in Australia. Plane crashes and suddenly he CAN walk - and run - and hunt with his suit case FULL of shiny knives!

Rose & Bernard: Rose has (had) cancer. Her husband Bernard took her to Australia to see a healer who told Rose, regrettably, he couldn't help her. Bernard didn't know that. On their way back to L.A., the plane crashes on the island. Rose's cancer symptoms vanish. She knows the island has healed her. So, with that being the case - WHY LEAVE?! She n Bernard build a cabin, the jungle is their picket fence. They choose to stay, peacefully, out of the chaos that continues from beginning to end on the island around them.

Jacob & the black smoke jungle monster

In the LOST series, Jacob is called Jacob. His brother is referred to as The Man in Black. I call it like I see it in this book. I reference Jacob's brother as **The Black Smoke Jungle Monster!** Their story is about the fact that what you see is not always as it appears!

A woman I'll call the Island Mother, killed their real mom right after they were born. Knowing this truth (thru a moment of mediumship) and in a rage that Island Mother had demolished his nearly completed lifelong project to finally leave the island, he killed the Island Mother. Jacob came into the scene at the tail end of that killing and didn't understand what was happening so he killed his brother for killing the woman he thought was his mother. Jacob drags his brother to the sacred tunnel that leads to a deep abyss beaming "white light" from the core of the island. He has killed his brother's body. Revenge washes his sibling down a stream, into the tunnel and down into the heart of the island. Moments later, from the mouth of the tunnel, his brother rises up, out and into the jungle as....The Black Smoke Jungle Monster. A very pissed off monster. A monster with an agenda!!

Jacob had an agenda, too. While his bro, Mr. Black Smoke, was stuck on the island torturing people, Jacob freely traveled the world, TOUCHING people. His physical touch... seemed to make them destined to eventually do time... on the island.

Okay, so, what happened was...

They board Oceanic flight 815 in Sydney for a ride to L.A. The plane is terribly off course (like, by about 1000) miles when suddenly, on an island below, somebody (Desmond) forgot to push 'the button' which set off what they describe as "an electromagnetic anomaly" that caused the plane to break apart and crash on the island and into the water around it. This was a deadly crash, make no mistake about it. EVERYONE "DIES"! But...they don't know they're dead cuz after you die you find out death isn't what you thought it was! And so from these opening moments of LOST, we continue forward with 121 episodes of LIFE!

Yeah...

So, here's the thing, all of our bodies will eventually stop working. Yours. Mine. Every person on the planet right now is facing imminent "transition" from this lifetime. In light of this pertinent and urgent reality, with the proper narration - LOST becomes an incredible tool to learn from. -What happens when our bodies die?

For me, as a Meta Physician, I'm using this book as an outlet. The discussion within these pages can bring peace of mind and spiritual realization which enhances our lives, influences our choices and affects the entire human race in a ripple effect of personal transformations.

Rev. Gillian V. Harris M.S.P.

If you have not yet watched LOST you can, of course, still benefit from this book. HOWEVER, if you haven't yet, I DO urge you to simply close this book after reading this section and start watching until the end. Yes it's long but if ya Netflix-it you can do 2 or 3 episodes at a time like I did! - Watch LOST. - Be affected. - THEN open this book up again.

After this page, I will not hold back!

Acknowledgments

Originally, this book was a gift to ...the masses. As I wrote, it became a gift to my parents and with that realization the race to finish became more and more urgent with every unpredictable day. And then life was happening and different friends were going through different challenges, some as serious as cancer or grieving the death of someone else. This made me race even faster. By the time I was done, I realized this book was not just a gift to everyone it is a gift ...to me.

To Roy & Enor, my parents, friends; through all of life's changes, wins and occasional chaos you have been *my constant*. I have anchored deeply in your love. I cherish you both as my parents and I treasure being your daughter. I am so grateful to understand we are in the same Spirit Family...an eternal union. I am comforted to know we are family lifetime after lifetime! That explains why our love for each other is so incredibly rich, so deep, there are no adequate words...

To every friend, teacher, light bearer I've ever had this incarnation just a huge thank you for time we've spent in this lifetime and others; time, love and joy shared which has worked as a beacon of light/life for me. To those who've helped me through tough & scary moments. To those with whom I have frolicked and played. To those who journeyed with me on some pretty *wild* adventures, this is for you. Many names are not coming to me at this moment but right off the top of my heart, my Spirit Siblings Cindy Golden, Diane Martin, Anne Kim, Kim Bowie, Jackie Coleman-Pyles, The Chambers family, Vera Stamenkovic, Linda La Rose, Angie, Angela, Alan, Ellen & Ellen, Teresa Jenkins, Melody McCully, Cheyenne, Wendy White -'The Angel of the Night'! Dominick Garcia, Cliff Isaac, Calvin Scott Calvin, Dugg & Randy, Chris Fisher, Glenn Gilchrist, Jonathan, Kate Jukes, Abie Aguiar, Denise, Denise, Denise and Deniece! Dina & Tovi. Marzella! Auntie Bev! Sonia, Auntie Sheila and Uncle Keith, Brenton, Debbie & June, Stephanie Gibson, Georgia Webb, Lisa Bogenschutz (A.K.A. Lucy, A.K.A Agent Bogenschutz or Agent B), Bill Morgner, Kate Messmer, Rochelle Sherbert, Joli Forbes, Lisa Dinkins, Laura Peterson, Cindy Mason Hein, Dana Echols, Marc Lavin, Jonathan Herbert, David Hall, Steve O'Hara, Gregory Hines, Steve Barry, David Borys, Gene & Bridgette. Kevin & Maria Fleming, Ezell Wiggins, Mark Drummond, Karla w/a K! Karen Sharpe, Johann Beckles, Steve Julian and everyone else from my days in beloved radio. Margaret Lamont, Shawn Randall, Torah, Lori Board Camacho, Raina, Ron & Mary Hulnick, Michael Beckwith, James Von Praagh, Marianne Williamson, Deepok & Oprah. Randy Frakes, Bill Heller, Bill Pruitt, Kathy Ellis, A plethora of Dolls (Employees of Valet Of The Dolls) - more names than I can remember including Samantha Berglund, Siobhan Ridgway Gazur, Mary Pat Farrell, Jennifer Scelsi & her lovely daughters, Katrina Henry, Lynn Helmn, Michelle Rochester, Cari Butler, Sarina Nosal, Jamila Sockwell, Jenson Atwood and literally about 2000 others including literally hundreds of customers who've touched my heart since our start date 3/3/03. My lash lady of 9 years Monique Deptula and my hair hero Joreen Chism. And from more than 40 years ago- Ken Brenneke! OMG, Ken, thank you so much. I was at SUCH an impressionable age and instead of shutting me down, you engaged me and encouraged me to journey deeper into that which is outside the physical! Much gratitude!! Dad! Thank you for FORCING me to have a math tutor! Lol! Special thanks, also to: Graphic artist Stanley Johnson (www.sevenlegs.net) – What an awesome process!!!! Of all our projects, this was by far, the most exciting! You are SO talented! Thank you for hearing me, feeling me and ultimately nailing a kick ass book cover!

I just forgot a bunch of names, friends, family, people, souls, light beams who are so sacred to me I only hope they can feel me, my gratitude and love as they are branded in my heart. Their energetic investment in me is forever imprinted in my history of loving. I hope these pages are as good for you as they have been for me. We are safe... We are vibrant... We are blissfully, busy!
Loving you...
Eternally
Gillian

1
Intentions

So enchanted, was I, with LOST that during the first few seasons, I remember a couple of occasions when I would mention the show to people, "did you see LOST?" In explaining how MUCH I was enjoying it I would say, "It's SO awesome that...I wanna take a plane trip and I want what happened to them to happen to me!" (I hadn't yet reached the episodes where Jack was taking plane flights for the same reason!) MINUS the scary fall, I was serious. AND minus the worry and sadness for my family - the idea of having to cope, adjust, creatively MacGyver life on such a beautiful island with such wonderful people... - REALLY sounded like an awesome idea. I suppose I was, at that time, idealizing that in *real life* it would be at least as wonderful an *escape*, as it was for me to watch it from my house in Woodland Hills, Ca.

Then...we got to seasons 4 and 5 (OMG - what the?! Where ARE we?) and season 6 was like, 'Wait...'. Like a smart pup tryin' to figure it out. -Head tilt to the right, "WHAT?" Forward time, backwards - sideways?! Eloise & Charles begot Daniel & Charlie! What?! Christian and a couple different women on different continents begot Jack & Clare. Sometimes I had to just stop my Netflix. "PAUSE, damn it!" - Sit back. Take a long sigh and then... think.

It's so immaculately written that ya really do need to get to the end to truly understand. And A LOT of what I came to understand, I'm not sure ...the writers fully understood.

I mean no disrespect by that. There are areas where metaphysically, there are explanations. That is what I'm doing here, now. Those parts excited me over and over again. And then, there are definitely some 'TeeVee' moments that I will just allow to be TeeVee! Theatre. But then AGAIN - the bottom line, one that I hope you'll get over and over here, is that we are created in such a way we can create anything we want. And then, some of the 'wackiest' stuff in LOST is based on true multi-dimensional reality - presented via this wonderful and amazing story that took 6 seasons to tell.

And just like choosing which neighborhood you wanna live in or *move from* (lol) after a while, I was feeling like maybe I didn't wanna be on the damn island so much after all. Not NOW. Not after that they'd effed it all up! Blowin' shit up. Killin' people. -That crazy assassin black smoke n' whatnot! I was like wait a MINUTE ... Let's go back to the clip where you're back in the US living off the airline settlement money!!!!

Then we get to the end... The last episode of Season 6 was not the end for those characters which...was one of the biggest points, in my view. I love them (Jeffrey Lieber, JJ Abrams and Damon Lindeloff - Ultimately, head writers were Lindelof and Carlton Cuse but then there were also about 20 other amazing writers. So, when I mention the writers, I mean no disrespect to the others if I only mention Damon and Carlton! I don't know who did what so I'm talking about all of them - I LOVE THEM ALL!)...for allowing themselves to be mediums for the creation and telling of this story! While I sense at least one or two of them in the bunch is extremely Spiritual and Metaphysically minded, I think that even for him (her), there are parts of the story told that were told unintentionally! I hope that within these pages I am able to show them what they missed! I hope to give everyone who saw LOST great big 'Ah Ha' moments that in a beautiful way transform your life. WONDERFUL things! I mean, besides the mastery at telling a story... I don't know that they were/are aware of the gravity - the depth of value provided through LOST. In such a large way they were being of service for the greater good of all concerned. "All" being mankind or at the very least, those who witness the series. And to the degree that I don't believe they were completely aware of the gift they were providing, it is also my humble opinion that the creators of LOST were under the INFLUENCE of their unconscious as well as guides, (a) non-physical source(s) outside of (yet one with) this physical realm. I mean... they didn't even come UP with the idea, ya know!?! A skeleton of it was brought to them by the ABC network.

Lostpedia.wickia.com says the original idea for the show was born in 2003 when an ABC bigwig, Lloyd Braun, pitched the idea for a series with a castaway theme to Jeffrey Lieber. Lieber wrote a pilot and was asked to rewrite it. Braun then went to JJ Abrams who added the Sci Fi vibration to Liebers concept. Apparently it was with Abrams input that the island, as an entity, became a character. Problem was, Abrams was already multi-tasking projects so they added Damon Lindeloff. But then Abrams was so busy with other stuff Damon was overwhelmed. Reports have it that Carlton Cuse talked Damon into staying on the show and joined the staff as an executive producer! All that behind the scenes stuff going on while destiny worked through the team to create this masterpiece. So... this was totally from SCRATCH, yo! And... from everything I've read, from that article to others, I keep getting the strongest feeling that for the most part, they may still be unaware of how their work is a tool from the treasure chest of the Creator (God!).

Remember I mentioned just a bit ago that it does seem that at least one of them has a clue... Www.Eonline.com did a piece March 16, 2014. In this on-line article, Cuse is quoted as saying "No, no, no. They were not dead the whole time." He wants us to believe they survived the initial plane crash then died later and met up in heaven (or wherever that last scene was). Um. No + yes = not quite because that's incomplete. And I feel like saying that, "no, no, no" was either Carlton speaking it the way HE PERSONALLY sees life or maybe he was trying to push back the obvious because it's ... *complicated!*

So... they took a skeleton idea and let the magic of Spiritual community effort begin. -And, how interesting for the person at the network who passed on this challenge to these writers, originally... That person who asked for a series based on a 'cast away theme' was also being influenced in a much larger picture than they even realized they were in. -Probably just anxious to tell a cool ratings winning saga when they planted a seed. I don't think the network would have wanted this show if they knew what *time* it really was!! Better said, not sure the network would have gotten so excited AHEAD OF TIME, had they known where LOST would go - how many dimensions and incarnations it would cross, dabble and frolic in!!! Or ...would they???!! Tis the season, after all.

There is a strong wind in the air of growing, global, Spiritual consciousness. The age of Aquarius was the beginning - we are now deep in a movement of heightened awareness and self/love realization.

Meta = outside of. So understand me when I say LOST was metaphysical from the opening scene. The unfolding of mystical truths didn't just happen over time, they happened from the first few minutes of the series!!

One of the first things I will do in this book is share with you, the differences I found between the written pilot of LOST and the end result - 'aired pilot' that we saw!

You don't HAVE to be a New Age Spiritualist to enjoy the LOST series from a metaphysical perspective but for those of us who live from that place this show was made especially for us! Lindelof is quoted in that same www.Eonline.com article as suggesting the show was a way of answering one of life's mysteries, " what's the meaning of life and what happens when you die?" Hugging you, Damon!!! THAT is my point, exactly! Mostly. And...in showing us an example of "what happens when you *die"* as he put it, they gave more than the last 10 minutes of season 6 - they gave us a full 121 episodes!

At the very end Jack asks his dad how it is that he's ..."here"! His Dad answers by asking him the same question! Now, I want to say Jack had been seeing his Dad, Christian, since

Season 1 Episode 5 @ 4: 50 but of course we learned much later that (on the island) it was actually Jacob's Nameless-Body-Snatching- Black-Smoke-Jungle-Monster brother who had been impersonating or better yet, USING Christian's body to lead Jack on an emotionally torturous chase through the jungle(the same way he used John Locke's and after the murder of Jacob he used Alex's likeness to threaten her kind of adopted father, Ben). But here's the thing - Mr. Jungle Monster wanted to leave the island and couldn't. Jack DID leave the island. AND he saw his Dad again in the lobby of the hospital (Season 4 Episode 10 @ 14:41). Mr. Jungle Monster wasn't there. He was stuck on the island. Now, there are mediums n whatnot who see transitioned people like Jack's father, all the time. But...Jack wasn't really a Zen behavior kinda guy. In fact he was AMA (American Medical Association), with a science based philosophy about how life and 'death' work. And.... granted, again - Jack was kinda wigged out at the point of this vision, as he was feeling the call to go back to the Island which led him to do some serious pill poppin'. The fact an 'island' would be beckoning him was just ... beyond sanity! - So, he lost it!

I believe for Jack, the reason he was so able to see his dad in that hospital scene (season 4 episode 10 @ 29:49) was because his dad was hovering in earth realm and knew his son was in trouble. So, yeah.

Loved ones visit loved ones. If they can, anyway. - More on that later. In this case, Jacks Dad could.

MANY people cross and don't know it. LOST did an excellent job of portraying that in many areas. I look forward to dissecting those moments, here! But ultimately I'm most excited by the multitude of incarnations portrayed and by the time you're done here, you will see the massive gift in this! With the perspective provided, you can more easily grasp the reality of life as eternal.

I'd missed it upon first viewing but the second time through the 6 seasons, I caught Naomi (Season 5 Episode 13 @ 22:27) as she is auditioning Miles for a big paying job that will take him to the island. He's a medium and she needs him to find someone (Ben). She explains that the person he's gotta find is dead. In fact she says the island has a bunch of "deceased" individuals "residing on it". Well that wasn't just Jacob and his nameless brother. It was everybody including the person she was looking for.

I hadn't originally intended to bring this point up in the beginning. I ended season 6 figuring everyone who saw it understood the same thing. Then I learned there's controversy. That there are many who only heard the "No, no, no..." quote and clung to it for dear life. -Even if it didn't make as much sense. But it's the "what if we answered a mystery" quote that hit the nail on the head. And by the way, the very last episode wasn't about what happens when you die, it was about what happens once you've healed enough, released enough, moved into allowance enough to...evolve onward. It was about acceptance and coming into harmony with your transition from the previous incarnation to a new dimension and maybe a new incarnation and in the process grasping, if only for a fleeting moment, how large/grand this life truly is.

In the Esquire article referenced earlier Carlton is quoted as saying "We thought about reincarnation but that was just a step too far". Lol! That makes me giggle! Both writers were reported to have teased that the "reboot" could possibly involve reincarnation. That makes me think they don't get what they've already done. The first 6 seasons were filled with reincarnation experiences!! I look forward to bringing you all up to speed, here! And thank the writers of LOST for teasing me! I look forward to the LOST "reboot", if indeed there is one! Interestingly enough, I went back to see that Esquire article a few weeks later and the page with this interview...was no longer available...

This book is designed to delve into the explanation of what LOST depicted but didn't explain. Such explanation wouldn't have been as ...fun for TV!!?! And also it COULDN'T have explained some of these things because part of being LOST is thinking you don't have the answers. -Speaking of which - was 'New Man in Charge' supposed to help or just ...tease?! I would like to pretend like I didn't follow someone's advice to Google and see that clip! Lol! Only thing cool was it was great to see Walt & Hurley again!

I'm racing to write this book in case there IS a reboot! While I welcome that, please know this book is created with the first 6 seasons of LOST as inspiration. For now, we'll call it 'The Secrets of LOST'. If they do a reboot, I reckon there may need to be a Secrets of LOST Part 2!

So, here's my immediate plan - I'm going to explain away the mysteries. Black smoke, the whispers, what happens when your body dies! We will explore intuition, mediumship and channeling -which not only were part of Hurley and Mile's experience but also Kate, Sawyer, Shannon, Sayid and, OMG!, DESMOND. We'll also delve into the mind boggling subject of 'TIME'! Ahhhh yeah! Multi-dimensional existence, reincarnation/reincarnational projections or the validity of Deja vu's, co-creation and the truth about so called 'Past' lives! Cuz LOST was about ALLLL of that!

There will be lots of time stamps along the way so you can re-experience these moments yourself. As you're reading, you'll occasionally come across something that looks like "(Season X Episode X @ XX:XX)". This means if you go to the lost footage (like, on Netflix) you can use their tool bar to choose the season and episode. Then using your mouse over the time bar (near the bottom of the screen where you click for play and pause) to select what minute you want. What minute to look for is the last portion of the time stamp. I've done this because I want you to be able to see exactly the moment I'm referencing. Sometimes it's just the look in someone's eye and I'll give you the time stamp so you can go there and put that picture and part of the story together with the messages being delivered on these pages.

Then, to undo the mystery about all these subjects we've got to gain understanding of the different 'states of consciousness' especially the 'unconscious' which allows the conscious connection to these other dimensions.

Besides the results of my own multi-dimensional recon, I figure, what better way to get information on a different dimension than to communicate with someone who is ... in that other dimension presently?! Logical, right?! Of course it is! In fact, how about a FEW of those people?! Absolutely! We'll do that, here.

I've been a student of metaphysics for more than 40 years. I am many things (Minister, Medium, Channel, Intuit, Reiki Master) in a nutshell, I am a 'Light Worker'. This term, Light Worker, is one I use to refer to anyone who works to move energy consciously in service to others. By moving energy, I mean ...just that. The at-will push, pull, drawing, mapping, blessing and clearing of energy. I draw from a wealth of personal experience and knowledge to create these pages. In the process of this project, I also turned to several physical mentors and Light Workers including renowned Channel Shawn Randall through whom 'Torah' is allowed to express and teach. Torah is not physical. He is a Spirit Guide. In fact, I studied under Torah for many years as he taught me how to be a Channel and how to navigate and interpret inter-dimensional information. (If you are not familiar with "Light Work" and "Channeling", know that I will explain them more shortly herein.) It was exciting for me to request an interview with him and then what an honor to sit in his space for the first time NOT only as a student but as a colleague in a mission to find the words to share the comforting blanket of truth about the eternity of life and how we create what we live.

In an interview that I will share here, Torah totally dropped a bomb on me and mentioned parallel lives within this same time frame, in this same earth dimension, as something that is real and absolutely happens. And then there are 'walk-ins' and in fact I had never even heard the term. Some moments in LOST can only be explained as Walk-ins. Like - Sayid got rescued from the island and then did a walk-in, into another incarnation where instead of starting as a baby, he started as he currently was. Never realizing he'd died (!) he just...walked into that dimension where Nadia was also in a 'walk-in' existence, same time frame as when she was killed after being interrogated by Sayid. They got married and enjoyed 3 years, until her murder. Sayid then does a walk-in back onto the island. Walk-ins. They are not fiction. It's exactly and precisely like time travel...only *different*!! I promise you a full explanation as we explore the lives of a few real life people who are living walk-in existences today, like, as I type, here in Southern California - 2015! Real people. Stick with me!

When I realized I was really, really doing this [book], I also called, emailed & texted (damn near simultaneously) my dear friend and incredibly gifted channel, medium, intuit & multi-dimensional healer Lori Board-Camacho. Lori 'channels' to bring her Guide 'Raina' in so that through Lori's body and voice, Raina has a platform to express, teach and heal. (This is not mediumship. This is channeling. We'll talk about the difference between channeling and mediumship, shortly. 'Raina' is also a multi-dimensional healer and teacher like Lori but multiplied by 1000. That is with Divine purpose. Like Torah, Raina is also a Spirit Guide; a non-physical being whose forte is guidance and teaching. Spirit Guides are personality beings -

just like you and me, but they are no longer living in a physical body or reality. They...commute, so to speak, to this (our) dimension from the spirit world to be of service to those still in the physical realm. A channels relationship with their guide is a very intimate and sacred one. The wisdom and nurturing, on all levels, that can be gained from Spirit Guides is something cherished by those blessed to be bonded in such relationships.

Like Shawn and Torah, for years Lori and Raina have helped thousands of people though private sessions and classes all over the world. I know that I also will at some point(s) channel one or more of my guides so that they can explain something if I'm not doing so well at verbalizing! I will make sure you know when you're getting deliberately channeled information. I also am in agreement with Guides who assist me on a regular basis in different areas of my life. I also have writing Guides who I have been aware of for decades and I venture to say 'lifetimes'. They often make suggestions along the way but in those cases, they are just friends lending a hand and there's no need for me to mention them. We are also, so in sync I often don't realize when they've lead me somewhere or given me something I'm writing. Its part of our agreement (we'll talk more about this) and I acknowledge I am often C.U.I.: Creating Under the Influence (of Spirit Beings and or one Source greater than, yet, one with me)!

So, there are people (using that word [people] for simplicity, *personalities* would be better) who are at such an elevated state of awareness that after doing a multitude of physical incarnations they have chosen to have the ability to exist multi dimensionally and communicate without having physical bodies, telephones or ....email! They live a full life and ...communicate! And they do so with the intention of being of assistance - of service for the greater good to those seeking knowledge on the meaning and navigation of this life and its lessons. So, my logic is -if you wanna know all there is to know about Tortola B.V.I. - go to Tortola. Right?! In these pages we 'cross' to find that nothing and no one is ever really LOST.

My goal is that through this exploration of the LOST story & its characters, you are brought comfort regarding ...the 'D' word (not divorce. The OTHER D word...) as well as the opportunity to ground in truth of yourself as an *eternal* Spirit Being having a very, very important and temporary human experience.

2
Intentions II

"Guys? .....Where are we??"

Season 1 Episode 2 @ 39:21 Charlie asked this ominous question. What IS this place?! Purgatory? Hm... I disagree with Damon (Lindelof) who reportedly said in that E-Online interview that, "It's not purgatory, this is real. We're not going to Sixth Sense you". Hm... Damon - you might nota meant to but you DID sixth sense us and - I'm not mad atcha!

    I offer for your consideration, the perspective that *purgatory* isn't something ya have to die to experience. Purgatory is anytime we're in need of healing. When we are experiencing the weight of an unresolved issue, we're in purgatory. Until we find and experience the resolve, until we get to our lessons and especially until we allow ourselves the mercy of compassionate SELF forgiveness, it is purgatory. And so while we're in this incarnation - we go in and out of purgatory and as we learn our lessons, we go in and out of heaven. So the quote, "It's not purgatory, this is real" twists my brain as an oxymoronically rhetorical moment! A conflicting sentence as purgatory is part of life...which is real. And even if there's a mega session of purgatory planned for right after we exit this particular incarnation - it's still real because...we're still alive! - But hey, I am totally cool with LOST creators having handled the press as they did. The bottom line is the larger picture. With the creation and airing of LOST such a tremendous gift was bestowed on the masses! It was time for a story like this to be told - EXACTLY the way they told it.

It is my intention in these pages to explain why I believe the LOST creators and writers were *influenced* in their creation process by seemingly invisible Guides and/or...a Source larger than, yet, one with them... I look forward to explaining how this is possible and, frankly, how it happens to all of us on a regular basis. It especially happens when we create masterpieces. LOST, passed off as science fiction, was actually a Metaphysical Masterpiece.

I do appreciate the creators of LOST for acknowledging plentiful room for interpretation. This book is the interpretation of a Meta-Physician.

While I've had a lot of experiences to share that are pertinent to these subjects, I don't expect you to just take MY word for any of this. So, I have spent months gathering from my sources information to present to you here. I present in these pages, all the information that has brought me peace... And as I do this writing I find my own process, awareness and *peace* deepening in ways I never dreamed or anticipated. A byproduct of an effort for the greater good.... There are no words for how blessed I am for this experience. -A journey that started from a new 'healthy' addiction.

For me, middle of the night TV was healthy because I found a form of R&R that my type-A personality could really get into. My escapes from workaholic overachiever behavior had me trudging gleefully through the crazy jungles of LOST with my dear lost friends, Kate, Sun, Jack, Hugo, Sayid, Sawyer - O M G! Love them ALL - even the ones I didn't mention yet.

To get to the end and understand that these wonderful, vibrant people had transitioned in the crash - was sad yes, AND it was also SO amazing. I was so relieved to see the reunion between Jack and his Dad (Season 6 Episode 17 @ 135:33). But I didn't get the magnitude of this moment the first time I watched it. Upon 2nd view I really got it and was completely undone (tears in the gut wrenching category).

So while it originally appeared Jack was flying back to L.A to memorialize his Dad, he was actually flying out to work on a very important project; Jack. His mission was to work on his inner issues and ultimately heal the severance between him and his father by first healing the broken part within himself. This inner work, benefited him in a parallel incarnation allowing him an easier path to healing the wedge between him (Jack) and his son (David).

In Jack's case, one of the classrooms where he could learn through experience and get the needed growth and healing was in that realm where he was most…LOST. This place, where he could fully immerse himself in much needed self-realization curriculum. We'll scroll the incarnations and some life lessons of several characters as we journey these pages.

There are people out there, who got to the end of LOST and were so upset by how it ended they threw it all away. -All the beautiful lessons. The ginormous underlying message!! Just tossed it! Like, 'WTF?! The whole thing was a waste of time'! None of it had any 'value' because…it was a story about DEAD people, damnit!! Lol!

They felt ripped off because for six seasons they were rooting for the underdogs, the rare survivor like the ones who made it off the Titanic. Like, what are the chances you can survive a plane crash like the one depicted in LOST? And if you did, yeah, what would happen? Of course! And so they finally get off the island (a couple-uh-few times!!??!!) and now you find out all of their physical hearts stopped beating when the plane crashed on the island originally… And for that matter…even though it looks like, sounds like, smells like, behaves like a regular ol' island… - it might not have even been an ISLAND they actually crashed on!?!

Said all that to say, it seems the line dividing who loved the ending and who didn't, is also the line dividing those who at least 50% believe life is eternal and those who don't or who have high doubts that it is and therefore have little value for any focus on a story about life after now.

For those who believe that when you're body dies - that's it - **The End**, you're absolutely right, this was a ridiculous way to spend 121 episodes. Damnit! :)

For the others who feel as I do, you might agree that LOST kind of gave the word 'dead' (and LIFE, for that matter) a new view & definition!

My effort here, ultimately, is to put into words the secrets of LOST. By 'secrets' I mean the subliminal as well as to bring as much clarity as I can to the broad daylight phenomena depicted in LOST. Those kinds of secrets. And as many secrets as I can all the way down to the selenite and obsidian stones Jack found by the skeletons in the cave (Season 1 Episode 6 @ 13:34).

This project also meant I'd have to watch LOST - AGAIN! At first I wasn't in harmony with this. Felt like a waste of time since I'd already seen it. But then I acknowledged to myself, I'm ALREADY re-watching it so NOW I have a *responsible* reason to!!! :) Relief from any guilt -NOW I had a *productive* excuse to escape with *the LOST people* for another couple of months!! YES!!!

Let me tell you, watching LOST for a 2nd time has been priceless. I missed some stuff while multi-tasking payroll and billing! Won't do THAT again! I will also make an effort to reach creators of LOST; JJ Abrams, Carlton Cuse and Damon Lindelof. Just …not yet! When I'm done writing this, I'll reach out to them. If they are available for an interview, I'll grow the book to share the conversations with you!

3
Victories & Destiny

I went back to school to get my Masters Degree at the University of Santa Monica (USM) in the fall of 2010. One day in a lecture, Dr. Ron Hulnick shared a great quote from a great philosopher who was in conversation about a tragedy. A plane carrying more than a few hundred souls crashed taking nearly all who were aboard. I remember the quote was something like, "do you have any idea how hard angels had to work to bring all those people together, at the same time, on the same plane?!"

...As if, the work of these angels, bringing these people to this ill-fated flight was ... a victory of some sort!

At first, I didn't understand this. Victory? (Eyebrows raised) The angels ...did GOOD?! Hm...

-Everything for a reason, all in right time and order. As hard as circumstances tried to keep Hugo Reyes a.k.a. 'Hurley' from making Oceanic flight 815, he damn near broke his neck to get on that plane (Season 1 Episode 25 @ 10:12)., burning an easy 2000 calories on the way! Something inside him told him he HAD to make that flight. Turned out, Hurley was lead angel of the LOST team. His part played a key role in their survival via love, compassion and community ... from beginning, to end. They would have been truly lost without him. He DID need to make that flight. What a truth he spoke on his newly created golf course for the one n only 'Island Open' (Season 1, Episode 9 @ 19:07) when he advised they basically *be in the now*. Never mind their issues and missed connector flights in L.A. - there's a bigger than life monster and polar bears on this crazy ass tropical island and they should seize this opportunity to forget about it! Let's have fun - RIGHT NOW! Otherwise they were just waiting for the next ephed up thing to happen. And in fact with focus only on the negatives they would attract more of the same, faster. He was brilliant.

Flashback

One day early in my first year at USM I found myself in a randomly selected small work group with two other students, one of them looked SO profoundly familiar to me. There was something about her... It was a warm, kindred spirit kind of sensation. I found myself thinking, "she's like, the Webleys". By that, I just meant the energy I felt reminded me of them. The Webley's are family friends and growing up I was close with two of their daughters Denise and Dina. Would have `been closer to Tovi, too but she was just a baby! Denise and Dina were closer to my age. I absolutely LOVED the time I spent with these girls. These guys were my buds. It was a guaranteed good time. And ... the friendship we had...the color of it, feeling, vibration, comfort of that energy...is what this woman reminded me of. -A fair complexion with black hair. -A calm demeanor and a genuine smile. Being before her had me wrapped tightly in a dejavu sensation that wouldn't let go. It struck me viscerally. I had no words only feelings but I felt enough that I had to say SOME thing.

"You feel SO familiar to me... Like REALLY, REALLY familiar", I said. At first I had her attention, "really?!" she smiled. "Yeah", I said, "like I KNOW you from somewhere." Suddenly, the joy of figuring it out seemed to dissolve within her and with great disappointment. The smile left her face. It was as if she'd UNFORTUNATELY figured it out. She started to speak, "It's probably because... never mind". She turned her head in a kind of *I give up* sort of gesture. In a flash, even with her fragmented sentence, I got a strong sense of what she wasn't saying. It was hard but I made a decision in that moment to respect her privacy and left it alone. But in that moment, I also noticed what seemed to be a decision on her part. I felt an energetic wall go up. I got a sense that she might be an actor or something and was making an erroneous assumption that this is how I knew her.

I'd done 20 years in radio as my first career out of college. The entire time I hated (with a passion) being on personal time in a public/social setting and what felt like superficial attention

I got from people who knew me as an air personality. Suddenly my ratings were at stake as I decide maybe this is not the night to dance on a table or tell one of my wild secrets! "... Bummer"!

So though I was disappointed, I kind of understood. I let it go... A blissful bubble of mystery and anticipation of a potential new friendship popped and I left her alone for the rest of our time on campus. I sometimes even went so far as to make sure our eyes didn't meet. I didn't want her to think that I was thinking whatever she was thinking I was thinking. - Whatever that was! And I needed to appear unaffected by what I perceived as her wall. But it was a bummer... Rejection! And please know, I never talked to her about this so these are MY perceptions. Very possibly my MIS-perceptions! MY projection. OkSoFineWhatever. Yeah... I was a little hurt!

Hit home....

Please know that prior to 2013, I wasn't a big TV watcher. In my radio career, when I moved from Broadcast Journalism to my original radio intention; being a DJ/Air Personality, I also swore off Television. I was also (involuntarily -or so it seemed) completely done with radio and my career in it by January 2000. No radio, no TV, no commercials, no news. I selected and played only my favorite music from my personal library.

I remember September 11, 2001 getting a phone call from my news monitor Mom, "did you hear what's happening?" After being briefed on the disaster unfolding I spent an easy 15 minutes pacing my living room floor, frantic and feeling for the first time I needed a television. "Oh my God... I need to see what's happening" I said to myself. FINALLY I remembered, "Oh shit! I OWN a TV!!!" Ha! Kinda funny! It was even already plugged in! That's how NON TV I was! And once I turned it on and saw enough (that took about a week) I turned it off. During the week I watched, I was using the time to create my prayer list. It was long. And beyond that, I didn't need TV anymore. I didn't need T.V. to help me grieve and I didn't need it to help me pray. I definitely didn't need TV if I wanted to remain positive enough to make a difference in the midst of the darkness we were breathing. So my TV went back into dust collecting off position hibernation.

Said ALLL THAT to say - my late-late nights changed dramatically when I discovered Netflix in the summer of 2013! I do not own stock in Netflix! This is not an endorsement campaign. I get absolutely NOTHING for telling you how they rocked my world by giving me the ability to watch what I want, as much as I want, WHEN I want for only a few bucks a month! Dude!

It all started when a series of people told me I needed to watch 'Orange is the New Black'. People would go on and on about this show. So, I got Netflix and yeah, season 1 of OTNB was OFF THE FRIGGIN HOOK! I absolutely LOVED it! That got me goin'. - Prior to this, I had no idea how outside the box television had gotten!

So very impressed, I had suddenly found something fun to do for a couple hours at the end of a 16 - 18 hr day! But the material would have to be REEEALLY good to get my precious time.

I quickly devoured 'Scandal', 'Weeds', 'Breaking Bad', 'Prison Break' and finally in the Spring of 2014 , looking for another great escape I saw LOST as an option and was like, "hm... wonder what THAT'S about?". It wasn't long before I was euphorically captivated. But LOST was a long one and I'm a busy girl. -Three businesses, nearly 150 employees and seemingly endless days. I did my best to gobble up as many episodes at a time as I could. Sometimes LOST would share my screen with payroll or the weekly staff schedule! I was so into it and had invested so much time that ending before the last episode was NOT an option. EVEN when I was ....kinda confused! I had to hang in there.

Near the end, season 6, with only about 5 episodes to go, I got a dreaded phone call. The call every adult kid dreads. My Mom was following an ambulance carrying my Dad. MY Dad! You don't know my Dad.... First of all he's bionic! Firm, fit, handsome, smart and SO *sweet*. One of the KINDEST people many could ever meet. I'm telling you... If you met my Dad you'd totally feel me here. He's so...amazing, and oh so perfectly loveable. I'm an only child and an absolute Daddy's girl! In fact he calls me, 'baby girl'. "How you doin' baby girl?" and I just melt inside, every time!

I'm one of the lucky ones with the most wonderful, compassionate, intelligent, understanding, funny, supportive, perfect - ya just wanna hug & laugh with him all the time kinda Dads! He was young when they had me. I met him when he was 22! So I've watched him (and my mom) grow from kids themselves, to the beautiful people they are now.

Yeah...

Like that.

A Thursday afternoon, June 26, 2014, to be exact, about 3:30pm the client line rang. I saw the caller I.D. but habit had me pick up with the regular, "Valet Of The Dolls, this is Gillian". My Mom in R.N. mode was straight to the point, "G, I'm on my cell. I'm trailing an ambulance carrying Dad. We were having lunch and he just went ...static. So I cleared the food so he wouldn't aspirate and I called 911. I shouldn't be on the phone. I'll call you from the emergency room." My mom is 82. 82 is the new 61! Her back is a mess (sciatica) but her mind is sharp as a friggin tack! I asked her which hospital. "Community" she said. "I'm on my way" I told her, hanging up the phone and reaching for my purse.

Yeah... THAT kinda dreaded phone call. I had no idea what she meant by 'static' ... I knew I'd find out sooner or later.

The next week would be very emotional for me and I couldn't get myself to write or process my feelings. I was simply...having them. Bunches of them. I cried every night, every morning and here n there throughout the day... while managing to run the businesses, especially

VOTD (Valet Of The Dolls) which is beyond a handful. I so needed to write. I needed to hear myself. The following is a journal entry I managed to finally get out almost two weeks later.

Journal 1

July 11, 2014 ending around 11:38pm

I haven't wanted to write. Haven't wanted to express what I've been feeling triggered by my Dads health crisis a couple weeks ago. My Mom called me while on her cell as she trailed an ambulance carrying him to Riverside Community's ER. It was about 3:30 in the afternoon. Valerie had cancelled for her afternoon shift so no other admin was here in the office. "Oh fucking well", I thought. "I'm out of here". And I took the opportunity to write a quick email to the Doll House team so they would understand what was up. For the first time in our 12 year history, the office was now empty before the close of business hours and …I didn't give a shit. Yeah -kind of angry…..they couldn't feel that but my quickie email was a call for everybody to be aware of the situation and step up to this job no longer being a test. This is not a drill. Be available, be productive and be able to do the work without me. I was partly frustrated with myself. I had a way of coddling my staff. That needed to stop. Immediately.

On the drive to Riverside…. I felt the gravity of the situation with my Dad… I *trusted* that I was going to get there on time… My Mom called me once again… We had to keep it short. "My cell is going to die and I don't have a car charger", I told her. Dad was still waiting in ER. She described, for a moment, what happened earlier. -What caused her to call 911. -Which was good because I needed her to break it down in 'normal people' language! My Mom uses medical terms regularly because of her background. Half of me thinks she's showing off! lol! The other half knows she really can't help it after all those years as an RN. I was like, 'yeah, what did you mean by 'static'?

She says they were eating lunch at the kitchen counter. All of a sudden she looked to her left at my Dad. His head was back, mouth open, eyes wide. He's got a mouth full of food but he's not chewing. Something was terribly wrong. She called his name. Nothing. She swings into RN mode, taking the food out of his mouth so he wouldn't choke. She brought him back somehow and called paramedics. By the time they got there he was fine and agitated that an ambulance had been called. Pride. I think we all kinda do that. I know I did when a similar thing had me in an ambulance about 5 years ago. But my Dads would be a little more scary…he's 78. He's a healthy, firm n fit, a 62 year old lookin' 78 but… he's 78. That number wanted to torture with me as I drove as if a number means anything. I guess at some point the number can make a difference but I've learned that some 78s are very, very young. For others 78 is 97! For my Dad 78 is 62.

Rev. Gillian V. Harris M.S.P.

Though I try, there truly are no adequate words to describe how deeply I love, adore, respect and admire my wonderful, wonderful Dad. I was resting in my trust in God. I was conscious as I drove of my open channel & oneness with Source. In this awareness, I found myself easily trusting that the rush hour traffic between Woodland Hills and Riverside (roughly 80 miles) wasn't an issue. And as I moved along with the mass of commuters, my guides seemed to be rushing to give me pictures and words. I opened for their download: I got that my Dad would make it through this; that doctors would have to 'do something'; that he would return to healthy. I then saw him sitting in their living room talking with a group of friends. Like a small party. He's holding a beverage and talking, past tense, about this current episode. I was comforted by all this information.

The drive had only been about 2 hours. Not bad at all. Knowing this hospital very well, I was quickly in the emergency room lobby where I was directed to cubicle 'G'. My Dad was laying there in a very 'I'm in control' pose, on his back - hands propped under his head on the gurney. Still in his street clothes as he'd refused the hospital gown! :) Like, *Oh no. That won't be necessary*! Pride (masking fear). My mom in all her cuteness sat in a chair on his left. I kissed them both, talked for a split second about traffic as I walked to the only other seat on the other side of his bed. As soon as my butt hit the chair, I shared the messages I'd gotten about this chapter eventually passing. That needed to be heard immediately. My parents listened attentively. "They said doctors would have to do some THING. But other than that, this chapter passes uneventfully.. ". I could tell Mom's medical brain was spinning in overdrive. She knew stuff...medical possibilities, probabilities. She, in fact, knew almost too much and was clear something serious was going on medically for him. This fainting thing was not a fluke.

When he passed out, he didn't really know he passed out! I'd soon get to see what she had experienced...only this time it would be multiplied by five.

I'd been there about an hour. They'd taken him for tests and brought him back. Nurses all loved my Dad and family pretty instantly. The three of us are easy like that! I met the ER doctor assigned to my Dad. And then a little later… my Dad started talking about the symptoms he'd experienced before. "I got really sweaty. In fact, I was drenched and my vision got blurred." About a minute later he said "kind of like my vision is getting right now". He got quiet and... slowly...his head went back, mouth open, eyes wide and he was out. "Leroy! Lee"! My Mom called out to him and went over to him. I looked at my Mom for direction. She read my mind and nodded which meant, "Get someone".

I flew into the hallway for assistance. I called for nurses. I remember trying to be quiet so as not to upset the other patients who were clearly going through their own dramas but I was hell bent on getting my point across. They were lackadaisical for a few seconds. - Seriously?! I'm thinkin', "no, you won't ignore me right now". So I did the ol' *reach out and touch* routine. Ya know if you just lightly place your hand on someone's arm or shoulder - they can't ignore you anymore! And when the first nurse turned around to find out who the hell is *touching* her - she met my eyes where I was wearing my heart, "Please!" I whispered intensely, "my father just fell unconscious and I'm not sure he's breathing". She put down her pen turned and followed me. Within just a few seconds there were 8 nurses around my Dad doing stuff…Three in the hallway in curiosity. They had an oxygen mask on him. They were talking to him. He was struggling to come to. I heard him gasping for breath…. It was probably fear and tears and adrenalin but I didn't think of that then. I only heard my Dad struggling and gasping for air, coughing and … OMG! I darted into the hallway again this time for an MD. I stood in the center of the hallway looking at all the hospital staff, "We need a doctor. -ANY doctor, PLEASE". Within a minute his assigned doctor was there. He immediately ordered several tests and walked away as if on a mission… I walked back into the room and stood in a corner where I was out of the way.

I didn't know what to do. My Dad was sooo struggling to come back. His vision was so blurred and he was so afraid. His eyes were so WIDE as he was trying to see. He turned his head to the left his eyes almost bulging to catch sight of me. "I'm here, Dad" I said. "It's gonna be ok". Oh my God. . . This part hurts to remember…. I could feel the fight in his being. And I felt sort of helpless. I know he was on his own journey… And I knew what was happening was between him and God. I just…really needed his journey to last longer over here with me… In THIS dimension.

From the corner where I was, I looked to my left for a moment. My Mom was out in the hall way to be out of the way…. Her hand over her mouth, tears in her eyes as she watched. I could see her analytical medical mind working as she stood there and let her successors work on her beloved husband. My Mom was a Head Nurse at this very same hospital for more than 30 years before retiring a couple decades ago.

I backed deeper into my corner and closed my eyes. All I could feel to do was consciously channel the energy of Love into my being and as fast and as potently as possible. I instantly felt the beam coming in through the top of my head and body and filling me up. I remember a bit of me took note – how surprisingly CALM I felt while doing this despite all that was happening in front of me. My arms down, fingers open, my hands directed toward the room and everyone in it as I directed the Love I was channeling at them sending a disproportionate amount toward my Dad. It's all I had to give and I gave it with everything in me...

Pretty soon, from under his oxygen mask, he was cracking stupid jokes, "you guys are making me see double!" and everybody laughed with him. Relief. Oh my GOD! It was so good to hear him! Deep, deep gratitude... Dad was now going with the flow. He removed his street clothes in exchange for the hospital gown! What had just happened scared him. Scared all of us...

While he was out (unconscious)... for a moment, he was REALLY gone! Like, his whole personality vacated his body - I don't know how else to say it. Like...he was GONE-GONE more than 'asleep gone'. He doesn't remember any of it, only all the commotion around him as he was coming back. The scariest moment for me was to see him completely leave his body like that. Eyes wide OPEN. Shit. In that moment I didn't know whether it was a stroke, or what?! Had I talked to my Dad for the last time? Then there was the moment as he was struggling to breathe. The *sound* of that struggle..... To hear him like that and know that he was probably terrified.... Then the third moment that wasn't so much scary but... I just can't seem to shake it...was when he looked toward me... trying so desperately to see me but couldn't. It's now been about three weeks. Whenever that picture pops up in my head, I still lose it...

Relishing time with my parents. Realizing a lot of things. 25 years ago my Dad had a medical scare. When I knew he was in a hospital in Berkeley – my Mom at his side but I was left a bit in the dark, in Los Angeles, I was angry. Not only about not being allowed to be there (cuz they knew it would freak me out) but because it seemed like God was thinkin' about taking my Dad. "Are you FUCKING KIDDING ME???" At the top of my lungs I SCREAMED at God. OMG I let him have it. I went absolutely ballistic. If there is any truth to blasphemy – I was all up in it that night. I basically told him (God) that he wasn't thinking this through. "WHAT ARE YOU DOING?" I demanded, "Do NOT - FUCKING - DO THIS!" (Then I'd throw something!) MAN – I was mad!! I yelled and cried and ranted and raged in my little Eagle Rock (Los Angeles) house for a good HOUR on my Dads behalf. I was in so much pain... I didn't care about neighbors hearing me... I didn't want to call anybody. This was between me and God. That night I'd genuinely lost my mind. I remember being amazed that even with all the energy I'd unleashed I wasn't tired. But I was tired of screaming so I laid down and managed to cry myself to sleep...

This time, two and a half decades later... I remember feeling very different. After the 2nd episode – the one I got to see while he was in ER, we knew that he was going to stay overnight. They needed stuff from the house so I volunteered to go. I was like, "yay!" I so wanted to be of service. I drove to the house and I remember being in the kitchen and I stopped for a minute to thank God SO much for the last 25 years. Once again, I apologized for the way I'd behaved 25 years earlier and I thanked him for giving us this wonderful time. 25 years ago… my parents were about to suffer a teenage revolt I forgot to have during my adolescent years. One I had instead waited until my early 30s to express! I'd come out of that chapter committing to re-bond with my parents and so it was. And once the healing was done I just adored them. We adore each other. They had me young so…we're friends, too! The time has been well spent. The three of us are crystal clear that we love each other. And so I stood in my parent's kitchen that night and thanked Him … "I simply ask that you be gentle with us on all this stuff.… "I asked the Great Source of all Life to please guide us with much grace through whatever we're facing and to help ME be what I need to be in the line of service to God and my family.

I'm back to walking and doing inclines. Started lifting weights again today. Whatever I'm needed to do I want to be able to do. If I need to lift someone, I want to be able to do this. I've never been more motivated. Of course, my Dad would NOT appreciate hearing my thoughts on this. He got his drivers' license suspended as a result of passing out. It'll be a minute – at best 60 days before a doctor says ok again. Or is it 90 days? Is it a certain amount of time and/or diagnosis?! IDK….

It's bad enough my Dad is a busy guy still running a business of his own but check it out, two weeks prior to this ambulance moment, my Dad was in a really bad car accident. Totally not his fault but it totaled his Lincoln Town Car. So – he got a new one a week later! Then a week after that – he passes out! Noooo!!!! There's a silver lining on this but my Dad isn't seeing it. It's so much better that he passed out over lunch, rather than behind the wheel of his new car!!! - So see! That's a GOOD thing!

There are lots of beautiful parts of the story, of course. I am SO touched by how my father is cared for in his neighborhood. The outpouring of love has been potent and apparently at their church it's even more so. He looks so much younger than he is… his strength and fitness are helping him fight this. I would love him to get through this and live another 15 or more, happy years in this incarnation! That's my wish. …But like I said, I am grateful for what we've had. My big thing now is to be okay with whatever happens next.

….Contemplating being alone here in this incarnation. When one of my parents goes – the other one is hot on the first ones trail. That leaves my ass here …. Shit!

And so on that front I have once again begun to contemplate 'consciousness' which is what we each are. Contemplating this…consciousness…and how it is free flowing and has nothing to do with one's human body. I'm getting used to communicating with the consciousness of people who are still in this incarnation. When I work in my garden I commune with my Dad because I want to get used to what he feels like when communicating with him that way (metaphysically).

Then I realized that I have this feeling like my mom, is going to live in this incarnation for EVER! I need to not get blindsided by that. And at the same time, if she's like her mom, she has another 19 years. (Grandmother transitioned about a year ago at 99!)

And so now… I find myself in a rush on the goal line as I feel 1) it's my responsibility and I want to be ready to provide certain things, like maybe shelter, or money at a certain point. 2) a rush to create my products and make my businesses more self-sufficient without so much of my energy - allowing me balance. —A healthy amount of regular time to spend with family without stress and constant goal accomplishment.

Just a few weeks ago, out of nowhere my Dad said to me, "Doesn't matter. I'm not going anywhere 'til I'm ready, anyway". I friggin LOVED that comment. But -it was a little out of context. Like, *where did THAT come from?!* I'm guessing he might have thought the same thing!! Now I understand it…. I take comfort in this declaration. He seems to have channeled it.

And so, two days after being admitted to the hospital, he was released. Doctors determined he was fine enough. They changed his BP meds. There MIGHT be some clogging of his arteries and a ton of tests have been scheduled. So we left the hospital - my parents went back to the house and I took off to the pharmacy for new meds for Dad.

With him cozy back at home, I felt I could get back to L.A. and catch up on the business. Once I got to the end of my night I realized I no longer had a knot in my solar plexus and I could enjoy watching an episode or two or 5 (lol!) of LOST! If I did 5, I would finish the 6th season. I sat down at my favorite computer monitor and went for it. Man was that craycray leading up to the final episode. I wondered and wondered where they were going and then Jack talked to his Dad. O M G!

I don't know if I can find the words for how I felt upon reaching the end. My mind SPUN with facts that I know about transition, incarnations. -What happens when a Spirit leaves the body - especially as the result of a violent accident. I think what touched me SO deeply was more validation of life after life just by the mere fact I was watching it. There was something sneaky about it, too! - Like, the makers knew it was a metaphysical piece and they figured out how to get non-believers swept up in it thinking it was just…*science fiction.*

So, there was Jack in sort of a victorious surrender...laying on the ground and closing his eyes in the jungle beside Vincent and my reflex was - to immediately click from the last episode to the very beginning of the first and I watched Jack wake up from the crossing in the first minutes of the Season 1. OMG the circle is complete.

I am whelmed with aw...

4
Forward To The Beginning

First thing we see (Season 1, Opening scene of Episode 1)...is the right eye of Jack as it springs open and he starts to come to in his new reality! We see what he sees, the sky the sea of leaves and tall stalks of bamboo moving in the wind. A beautiful view if not for the predicament. He moves his fingers... I sense in this moment he's not really conscious and then suddenly he GASPS. It is my contention that at the moment he gasps, his consciousness has caught up with his Soul's completion of crossing. Waking up to life's continuation but he's now on the so called 'other side'!

Jack looks around, he sees Vincent, which, to me was...weird. Good goin' writers cuz I was like, 'what the hell is a Lab doing here'? Then as he takes off, Vincent clumsily doggie jogs across Jacks head - which is kinda funny when you see it the 2nd time! lol! Jack starts to get up and notices his physical pain and injuries. He manages to get to his feet. Notice it's quiet. The only sound is the wind through the trees and his moans of discomfort. He reaches into his pocket and comes out with one of the mini booze bottles a cute flight attendant gave him. He held it and it was like it grounded him in helping him get centered in his consciousness in this new place as he was probably thinking "I'm alive". It also helped him realize, *holy shit... I just fell out of an AIRPLANE!*

And…this little bottle of booze was symbolic of the reason he was on the plane in the first place. Alcoholism. He judged his father for being an alcoholic. Now his dad had died a drunken death. Jack was on that Oceanic flight to bring his body back to the U.S. for a funeral. Their relationship was part of an emotional web connecting Jacks life to alcohol and pills as a way to cope, something for which he had judged in his father. How about THAT for a mirror!

Jack puts the bottle back in his pocket and, as he starts to run, I am immediately reminded of Patrick Swayze in 'Ghost'! His good guy character was stabbed by the bad guy but the victim's spirit was still fighting and took off in a sprint after the bad guy. Bad guy got away. Good guy comes back to his girlfriend (Demi Moore's character) and it wasn't until then that he realized…she couldn't see him cuz he's not in his body anymore and further…the body he WAS in, is now laying on the ground terminally incapacitated (in a parallel dimension…in that case he was now in a life space between lives - viewing where he used to be - bewildered - bummed)! Similar reactions happen after a violent death. Car accidents for instance - so fast and in the instant of impact a persons' body stops at the windshield but their Spirit will continue through. *Whooooops! Forgot my body!* Imagine the spirit being hurled passed that impact. Now looking down at the situation…the car, motorcycle, PLANE - at what used to be his/her body, they can suddenly be confused yet in brand new awareness that…they have stepped outside their most recent incarnation. Realizing that they are still alive, this must be a different 'dimension'. And different people take different routes once leaving here. At the point of exiting their previous physical body most are met by loved ones or guides. This, as it's been explained to me, helps them pass some dark or heavier vibration areas with ease. Without this guidance, due to our state at the time of crossing, we can be vulnerable to unhealthy energies and environments (..like crazy islands with wild assassin smoke monsters!)

Some people are ready to move on. Some are not. Some pop out of their bodies - stay out of their bodies - their bodies get buried during a funeral yet…they do not realize they've made this transition and or they are not in harmony with it! -Hence, a lot of my work, as a medium in House Healings (a.k.a 'clearings'). Several clients have been referred to me by realtors. They've just purchased their home and either they sense something (or someone), or they want to be sure there's no one sharing the space. Some Spirits (A.K.A. 'people') hover over their operating table while the heart monitor is flat-lining… go off into the universe and have experiences, then pop back into their bodies with NDE (near death experience) stories to tell their doctors and families. And some pop out of their body and go directly to 'The Light' with or without a loving entourage. I wonder if other dimensions are part of 'The Light' experience. I wonder if THIS dimension (the one that has me writing this book that you are currently reading) is part of 'The Light'. . . . One new thought interpretation of a popular Bible passage is "the Spirit of God is within and the Kingdom of Heaven is here now".

Rev. Gillian V. Harris M.S.P.

My haunted hut in the woods

I loved the consequence of stormy weather, here. A few feet from the terrace, what was normally a creek with beautiful babbling brooks would become a ferocious, potentially lethal - almost mechanically powerful river making its way to the ocean. Winter was the best here. My 'haunted house' in 'Monte Nido' which is a *mountain nest* community located in Malibu Canyon, California. My friend & neighbor Ellen had transitioned in this little guest house several years earlier.

For clarity; There were 3 dwellings on this property all owned by a wonderful and 'crafty' man named Alan. He is so talented at building, fixing…creating, he could have his own HGTV show! He creatively turned two dwellings into three. There was the main house (his). Below (what used to be a garage and yard space became) a 1000sq ft 1 bedroom unit and across the yard was a miniature 400 sq foot cabin guest house I'd call a 'studio'. The big rental was mine, the studio's was Ellen's and she shared it with Griffin, her loveable and protective Boxer/Lab.

Finding this location was magical in itself. At age ten, watching the news with my mom one day, we were glued to a story about houses falling off into the ocean in Malibu. With a knowingness that I was destined to live in the Malibu area, I said, "oh no! Mom, is there a Malibu CANYON?" "I'm sure there is" she assured me. "Good. Then I'll just live there cuz I don't want my house falling off into the ocean. That's awful!" I spoke in a very matter of fact tone about this and was grateful to have found a solution. I then proceeded to forget about this conversation until 25 years later at the end of a 3 month search for a new rental when I saw an ad in the 'Recycler' classifieds for this little spot in 'Malibu Canyon'. This was just a click before everybody had computers so, when ya wanted to buy/rent/sell something you counted on this little newspaper called 'The Recycler' which came out once a week on Thursdays. For 3 months of Thursdays I'd gotten a new one and scored it studiously. I wasn't having good luck. I knew I wanted a wilderness area and was focused on Topanga Canyon. I was now running out of time. I had, literally, about a week to find a place when suddenly this Malibu Canyon rental came up. I dialed immediately. There had been a couple other callers ahead of me but something between myself and the owner clicked. We talked on the phone for just over 45 minutes. An awesome conversation which ended with, "well, the place is yours if you decide you like it". I couldn't believe my ears! I told him I'd be by that afternoon to take a look!

The drive over, alone, told me I had found my next home. Rolling meadows to my left and right as I traveled south toward the ocean from the 101 freeway. Beautiful mountains directed me to paradise. This move would also fulfil my purpose of wanting to get as far from the city and it's chaos as I could. I needed pure space to do some serious personal healing away from… for simplicity let's just say… *unhealthy influences*. I knew part of living on this property was supporting my life course correction and in dedication to that I promised myself I would not share this address with my *friends*. It would be my haven, retreat, my healing space.

It was mid-September 1992. Bottle rockets and smoke were still fresh in the Los Angeles air from the *Rodney King Riot*. I parked my car on a rocky dirt driveway and thought "Ha! They'll NEVER find me HERE!"

I want to say it was quiet there…but it wasn't. No, Amaretta was talking to me the instant she saw me step out of my car. This big voiced horse greeted me with a hearty hello! Her corral and stable were on the other side of the driveway. From my rental, I'd open the front door, look across the driveway, past the cars and there she'd be! I was sold. Amaretta was one happy poodle of an equine! What a lover!! She was only 6 years old when I got there and she was a childhood dream finally come true for me. She belonged to Ellen, the retired model was grateful for my interest because she was older now and after three strokes (and a continued relationship with cigarettes) was more frail physically. So she gleefully taught me how to care for and bond with 'Am', as I called this blonde maned, chestnut bodied Arabian/Quarter horse. About a year or so later, while hanging out in her little cabin, my friend, Ellen, suffered her 4th stroke this incarnation and transitioned onward. The only one with her was Griffin, who was stuck in the house until her daughter came by to check on her Mom the next morning.

I remember that day… They brought a grief stricken Griffin to me to watch after while paramedics tended to Ellen's body. The dog was beside herself with worry…frustration… She didn't want to be with me. She wanted to be with Ellen. A couple weeks later, upon finding a card I'd written to thank Ellen for the experience I was having with Amaretta, her kids decided to gift the horse to me. Thank you, Ellen! And I wanna thank her kids, too. Amaretta was one of the most beautiful chapters of my life. –Expensive! Challenging! But beautiful!

Amaretta bit me once. And she kicked me once -I decided the cool horseshoe shaped bruise left on my left back thigh had branded me as a REAL Cowgirl! And that was just part of getting to know each other! She never threw me. Tried once but I won!! I only fell off that time I didn't put the saddle on right. Now THAT was funny as I got on and the whole saddle immediately rotated to her right side. She was a 'push button' horse, schooled by one of the finest horse trainers, ever, to respond to 'pressure'. She felt the pressure of my full body on her right side which told her to move to the left! I was like, "Whoooooooooaa there girlfriend!!!" She stopped and I hung in this position for as long as I could, trying to figure another way out. I was in a ridiculous predicament! (LMAO as I remember this!) The only way out would be to DROP – on to the asphalt street! I would land on my back and …it was gonna hurt! I really wasn't looking forward to it. And…it took a while to let it happen but ultimately I did it. I let go with a THUD! There I was on the ground lookin' up at Amaretta. She didn't move. Head turned, looking down at me, she was like "…you're pitiful, dude".
   Ahhh yeah. Memories!

About 13 years after moving in, my landlord's daughter, 2 children and new husband were expecting a new baby soon and space was quickly becoming even more of an issue as they'd been living in Ellen's little 400 Sq ft studio cabin. Solution: they'd take my rental instead. – Please understand, it's not like I said, "hey, you guys look squished over there. Here, take my rental instead!" No! I hadn't even noticed them. I mean, I knew they were there. I was the photographer at their wedding! I'd privately marveled at how they utilized the small space to fit everybody in there. I was impressed and … went on about my business! I was 100% focused on launching my company with every waking moment. There was no time to gaze out the window and wonder what other people were up to and whether they were cozy. So the knock on the door surprised me. It was my landlord one afternoon as he explained he was going to give my rental to his daughter! Luckily, I was given an option; either leave the property or ... move into Ellen's little place which would now be vacant.

Ultimately, this move needed to happen for my growth spiritually – but… I didn't know that then. I only knew this was going to be SO inconvenient. My couch didn't even fit over there! I'd just have to put almost all of my furniture in storage. Okay - yeah, I admit the silver lining was a smidge hard in coming – I was initially quite annoyed! I loved my landlord and I understood his position but boy was this ever a troublesome, ill-timed (or so I thought) development! And the idea of living anywhere but on this property did NOT resonate with me. I couldn't even IMAGINE being out there again in a….normal neighborhood with a bunch of other….humans and CAR TRAFFIC - Sirens. Helicopters! Noooo!! I loved living on this secluded woodsy property, in the environment of this rural neighborhood. I felt safe there. Being there was nurturing for me. I still needed to be right where I was. AND I had free horse lodging!! PLUS I'd just started a very expensive endeavor, my company, Valet Of The Dolls. I'd just finished spending every last dime of money borrowed from Grandmother and Dad for the venture. There was no spare 'first/last/deposit & moving van' money for a new place! The math was simple, really.

Valet Of The Dolls, is a private event valet parking service. A buncha people are comin' over and you don't want them to walk far to your house or venue? You call us and we send the appropriate sized team of valets to park your guest's cars. Besides being 99% female, we specialize in private events, i.e. weddings, mitzvahs, fundraisers, grand openings, performances, dinner parties, cocktail parties, birthday parties, wrap parties, after parties, party parties! About 600 of those a year! At this point though, the first year, we would do 119 parking operations. I knew to pull it off I needed to be right where I was. I didn't need to be traumatized in some new environment. I chose to stay. Under an umbrella of oak trees one Saturday afternoon, with the help of a small army of Dolls on my side, I and my landlord's daughter's family swapped living spaces!

Before putting the furniture in, burgundy carpet was quickly installed by the carpet people. Then another couple hours we spent painting the small area of walls that were not wood, a warm PINK! Running my new company from home and busy making lemonade out of the situation, I realized this was actually a PERFECT space for an office. I also knew the private event valet business very well, already. You tend to work Monday through Friday, really hard, all day so that every evening and every weekend is filled with party assignments. To that extent it is pretty non-stop. Someone needs to be by the phone until parties are done. That can be…nearly DAWN sometimes! I wasn't interested in coming out of a commercial building at those hours or spending nights in such structures. So, I got a wooden plaque and affixed it to the front door naming it, 'The Doll House'. This would be the secret headquarters of Valet

Of The Dolls. Our publicized address would be 6 miles away, down Malibu Canyon Rd to Pacific Coast Hwy in a little box! That's ANOTHER reason I opted not to get a commercial office. For what?! Who's comin' over?! Everything is internet and telephone. And if we need to meet the client, it's at the location we're going to work, not at our office. The Doll House was rockin' with personality, work and the backdrop of cool music which would range from Top 40s/Hip Hop to New Age Instrumental. I ran my company and continued to enjoy the gifts of nature as part of my living environment for the next 6 years.

Though I knew of Ellen's transition while in that little house, there was more than just one Spirit there. And it wasn't a 'scary' haunted house but there were several Spirits who lived ...in a dimension that shared this space. They had their own world of 'physical' goin' on, on top of mine! And according to Lori, none of these people were Ellen!

Lori Board-Camacho, the dear friend and healer who I mentioned earlier is the one who first made me aware of my ...invisible ....roommates! One day soon after I'd moved across the yard to this smaller unit she and her friend Clarissa (another medium & intuit) stopped by to check out my new little hut in the woods.

Shaped like a long trailer, it was all wood with a massive deck that over looked the creek. Clarissa and Lori were wowed when they walked in and started detailing what they were experiencing. Lori communicated with a female who was being held against her will by a male spirit in the bunch. I was like, "Oh my gosh! Why doesn't she just LEAVE? She'll be fine. Does she know that?" Lori said, "I know, I told her but she says she can't go". Bummer...
I wanted to be sure that he wasn't torturing her or anything and he wasn't. It was a choice the female was making to be captive, *stuck*. If I knew then, what I know now...If I was then where I am now, I would have attempted to coach her spirit to a place of stronger resolve or at least in realizing her self-worth challenge. I knew I was a medium at that point but I'd had absolutely no true practice at it. I was repeatedly called a "natural medium" many times, over several years by people already seasoned in that gift - years before I realized what was happening. By the time I lived in this little Spirit busy house, enough had certainly happened but I still didn't know how to consciously coordinate my ability. Simply put - stuff would happen and I'd be wide eyed n goofy as I wouldn't know what to DO! And I couldn't consciously MAKE anything happen - stuff just happened when it happened! This mini hut in the woods was rich with learning (and visits) for me. I miss the dark wood walls. Against them it was easy for me to see the white foggy forming of a Spirit.

The first time this happened is my favorite because I had a witness. In LOST when Kate saw her black horse for the 2nd time she had Sawyer to validate it (Season 2, Episode 9 @ 41:01). In fact, he saw it first, that 2nd time. Shannon saw Walt but got validated when Sayid saw Walt, too (Season 2 Episode 6 @ 40:15)! We're funny like that! So quick to think we must be losing it. 'That …can't be real!' I would not have thought I was losing it without a witness but… yes having a witness definitely brought me instant clarity. In fact, without my witness, I wouldn't have even KNOWN this being was behind me!

It was evening. My late kitty 'Bella Tyrone' was on my shoulder. You should know Bella was brought to me by Lori supposedly only for 2 weeks. Lori was transient at the time and I was just cat sitting. Now, this moment I'm about to share, happened about 2 years later. One of the few comforts of home in this miniature space primarily used as an office was my love bundle, Bella-Tyrone! I'd wanted a pet to name 'Tyrone'. Bella came to me as Bella so I added the Tyrone on to her name. She loved it! Her nick-name was Bella-Ty!
On this evening, I sat at my desk. Bella was on my shoulder. I had turned away from the computer. I had my back to it while I watched something on Television (which was on a bookcase behind my desk). To my left, I notice Bella's head is kind of …darting left & right, she's kinda squinting (if that's possible for cats!) like she's trying to get a visual fix on something. Curious, I spin my chair around and ….. WWWWWowwwww! There it was! A huge white ball of … life. Someone else's life! I stared at it. And…I'm pretty sure it/they/he/she was staring at ME! I understood this was a Spirit being and I hoped it would keep forming. I didn't so much as move because I didn't want to interrupt its process. I hope they understood that… I later had to forgive myself for this moment of naiveté when I learned how difficult it is for someone to present themselves on this side like that. I SHOULD have said something…. They formed for a reason. It was important enough to want to present themselves to me. They wanted to communicate and I didn't get it any more than Shannon got Walt's meaning when he appeared in her tent for a few seconds and mumbled water garble (Season 2, Episode 6 @ 6:30).

I've always wondered who that was who presented themselves to me & Bella-Ty that night….. Yes, I've always wondered if it was Ellen. OR was it my Granma Sue (Dads side), or was it one of the people Lori had mentioned a year or two earlier (invisible roommates)? Asking would have been good! -Concept!! - I didn't consider that at that time!!! I lived and learned from that close encounter! The lessons from that moment became a blessing for the future!

In this virgin-esque chapter, I counted on my feelings. I was calm, unafraid. In fact I was eager in the moment. I felt …'honored' to be sharing physical space with this soul! This was absolute confirmation for me that life outside of these bodies is absolute! Any doubts I had prior were now completely gone – poof – irrelevant and dissolved into nothingness!

It's from this point that I really began to focus on my metaphysical studies. Classes and even 'homework' as I studied psychic ability and eventually channeling. For a couple years, as mentioned earlier, I studied under 'Torah' who is channeled by the Shawn Randall. I was also gifted with years of guidance from Lori whose instruction was especially helpful in the early days of my decision to step into my natural gift of mediumship. That was nearly two decades ago and I now use the gift in service to others and just life (mine), in general.

You get what you expect

Many, many people who've had near death experiences recall beautiful places... Beautiful like the island Oceanic flight 815 crashed into. The greens and blues and vibrancy of flowers, life energy and nature sounds made an incredible backdrop for most of the LOST episodes. In seeing this, I couldn't help but think about the 'Law of Attraction' and then the school of thought that "in heaven you can create whatever you want". The movie 'What Dreams May Come' depicts this beautifully! However you see it, is how it is! And...what you believe you deserve... is what you tend to get.

Always wanted to have a mansion? - You can create one in the after-life. Want to do a walk-about on a crazy, beautiful tropical island?! Do you really dig your work or current life and not ready to move on? You can keep doing it in the after-life like Ana Lucia (Season 6 Episode 16 @ 39:07) when she expressed herself as a (bribe accepting) cop and helped Desmond, Kate and Sayid escape jail.

Many years ago, an aunt of mine was in a terrible car accident on the Santa Monica I-10 freeway in Los Angeles. Auntie Sheila was wearing her seatbelt but ended up in the backseat as the car flew and flipped over an embankment. In great pain from broken & bruised parts, she is freed from the vehicle by a passer-by. A man. White guy. He told her he was a paramedic. He was off duty. When help arrived, they took notes from this person who didn't leave his name and is identified as a 'passer-by'. He gave a run down on her medical condition to paramedics then vanished leaving her in their care.

She told me that in the ambulance she asked about this man but was told they didn't have his name but whoever he was - "they said he saved my life". My guess is that this angel is enjoying working in that capacity at this time. Medical rescue is something he mastered in an incarnation that he really loved, so instead of moving on, he hangs out in this dimension ready to help people and vanish! Help. Vanish. Help. Vanish.

Another moment of being stuck in a chosen chapter of your life was Rose and Bernard as they'd made a wonderful home on the island! (Season 5 Episode 10 @ 29:11). That is a perfect example of living what you're attached to because ...you love it and so you choose to stay in it even though it's not a physical dimension. It's possible that Jack was dwelling on a cherished incarnation when he went to the concert late and met Kate (Seasons 6 Episode 17 @ 1:10:47).

Kate is actually one of his soul mates in at least a couple incarnations and in this scene she ...helps him see. She guides him home (final minutes of last episode, 'The End').

Flow with me now and let's say reincarnation is real; - which life, then, is *the after- life*?! There is also the philosophy that THIS current incarnation (the one that has you experiencing my words right now) is heaven and is laid out exactly as we each are creating it for ourselves ('Law Of Attraction'). And one of the ultimate points to get to is a place of understanding, we are always safe, there is never anything to fear. Sun and Jin had this realization (season 6 Episode 17 @ 1:01:27). This is the goal, isn't it?! To be able to live from a place of knowingness that no matter what the drama - everything is perfectly fine and

"I Am safe ...because I AM." "I AM" meaning oneness with Source and all there is.

At this moment, our paths have crossed by way of this book - just like the characters of LOST crossed paths on flight 815 and then in the jungle. They each played an equal part in, literally, co-creating the experience they each individually lived over those 121 episodes.

5
Written Versus Outcome

A couple weeks into this book process I stopped telling people what I was working on. That's hard because I'm SO into the subject and ecstatic to be expressing it in writing but a friend had suggested I keep it to myself. She was right. The few people I told were all trying to be helpful but - oy! People were bringing me LOST box sets and trying to fill me with tidbits of information on the actors who played the LOST characters. I had to stop them. Slamming my hands over my ears, "LALALALALALALA - I CANT HEAR YOUUUUUU!" They look at me like I'm crazy! lol! But they also stopped talking in realizing to their surprise they are NOT helping! I'd briefly explain, "I can't go there. It'll greatly disturb my process". I needed Jin to stay Jin and Hurley to stay Hurley. Most of these wanna be helpers were people who had NOT seen all of LOST. They had no idea. No - I DON'T want to know who the guy is who plays Charlie, just yet and what other shows he's on. Kate, Jack, Michael - none of em. Not yet, damn it! The box set is unopened and sitting.... over there somewhere! And my lips are now zipped as I work to complete these pages uninterrupted by the well-meaning who don't yet know where I'm going with this.

So, I'm goin' along and everything is fine 'til I had dinner with Berson the other night. That's my boyfriend. He is the first serious relationship I've ever had with someone older than me! Lol! I just realized that! He's a Gemini, too. Gemini's are children forever! And though 65 he is SO young at heart, still has a full head of very thick brown hair that likes to reach down to his shoulders. In fact, to me, his very much resembles the face of the Eskimo on the back of Alaska Airlines planes! Lol!!! – Take the Eskimo guy, groom him a bit, put him in a leather jacket and some cowboy boots. That's my Berson! Almost 6 feet, trimmed beard, blue/grey eyes, Berson is a rebel raised in conservative Orange County. Attracted to the New Age/Ancient Wisdom life philosophy I live, I am also blessed to finally have a partner who is in harmony and support of all I do, including the time I spend with fleshless friends. - More on that soon!

    Together nearly 2 years now, he has been one of the easiest men to love. Might have something to do with the fact he treats me like a Queen, calls me his "Angel". When he's not consumed by one of his work projects, I am very, very spoiled by him. We're always working to swap the ratio so that he is consumed less and I am spoiled more! – It's a challenge!

I looked forward to going to dinner with him on this particular evening. But during the meal he buzz killed me with a question. "Have you read the pilot to LOST yet?" Aye yai yi! I had hoped this question would just...dissolve and go away but no! And no, I hadn't read the pilot! I had to say that to him AGAIN! With this feeling like the bzillionth time he's asked -- I was suddenly very uncomfortable - embarrassed - like the I was half assedly going about this project as I admitted, once again, "not yet". He looked stunned. And majorly disappointed because he got that 'I' didn't get it!

Though his career is rather scientific, Berson is also a hobby reader and film buff. Very analytical about it all, he knows what makes a good book or movie! And he knows ME. VERY clear on what I'm creating and why, he also knew I needed to read the pilot. He'd originally made the suggestion that I read it about a month earlier. In the face of my disinterest, he ... Hell, I really don't know WHAT he did but suddenly one day - BAM! - 'LOST: The Pilot' is in my inbox! Shut UP! I'm thinkin', "Damn it, honey!! But you know what? I know how to ignore an email". So, that's what I did! Ignored it!

The BF's also mentioned, like, half a dozen times that I need to talk to the creators of LOST. I haven't wanted to do that, either. My answer is always, "Ok, maybe when I'm done". I don't want to be influenced by what they have to say. I didn't want to read the pilot because I didn't want this book to be influenced by another writer any more than it already is as a result of seeing their finished T.V. production. But now we're at the 3rd or 4th or 5th friggin time that he'd ask me if I, "read the pilot yet?" and I'm feeling so LAME with the goofy "not yet". "You HAVE to", he said. His voice and face took on a serious pose, complete with the wrinkles between his eyebrows. I thought, "oh shit! Not sure I've experienced him this intense before". He now had my full wide eyed attention. I could tell that he could tell, that 'I' could tell, I was a little in the dark and needed a refresher on why this was so important.

All he had to do was remind me of my purpose. Reading the pilot would be an excellent way to compare the differences between what they *intended* and what *ultimately was created and aired*. - ESPECIALLY since part of MY contention is that, unbeknownst to them, the creators were 'influenced' by seemingly invisible sources while putting LOST together. "Hm" I thought out loud, "I guess that would be smart, wouldn't it?" Duh! And since it was such a metaphysical piece, did they give any indication in the pilot that this would be a theme in the series?

On another occasion, we'd been at the same restaurant when this whole book thing started. I was eagerly working on a different writing project when he brought up an email I'd written him one night after watching the final episode of LOST. "Why was that so profound after the situation with your Dad?" he asked. I vented with out of control abandon. He was like, "Wow! I'd read a book on that". "You would?!" I hadn't even THOUGHT about writing about it though as I heard myself talking… I definitely agreed! Like a bolt of electricity the notion hit me hard. The same way I felt when the name Valet Of The Dolls was born. BAM! There's something… an energetic yes that is felt systemically throughout not only my physical but ethereal body. I know a YES when I feel it. I felt it that night and it was *ON* from that moment! So…

Pilot-oscopy

I LOVED the written pilot! Kick ass!!!! I SO love these writers. OMG!

I was enchanted by every 'M F' in the narrative of the script! lol! It was just bubbling with *colorful* language to clarify the energy or intensity of a scene! In becoming a Minister, I didn't drop affinity for this kind of language as expression in certain moments. Sometimes there's just no better way to fully explain!!

IN SUMMARY first, then SPECIFICS

To answer MY main question - the script showed that there were differences between what was the original written intention and what ultimately ended up being the aired version. This may be normal to the creative process, too. Please know that I do NOT have a background in 'the film industry'. - Not THIS incarnation, anyway. I mean, I was in radio for 20 years. But that is SO different from movie/TVland. Ok - I DID do ONE movie (*The Journey of Jared Price*, 2000) and totally loved it but - that was an *accident* (is there such a thing?). I didn't go to an audition. I was 'discovered' by one of the producers, Robert Edgar, as we flew from Tortola BVI on a connecting flight from Florida to L.A..

Funny thing about that flight. -My traveling companion and I got tickets that were in separate areas of the plane. From the two seat options I picked 38D because it was my bra size I figured, "that's gotta be my seat!!" Robert and I found ourselves sitting next to each other and very quickly - not sure how it happened but - we were fully engaged in conversation about Spirits n Ghosts – He told me how his deceased Grandfather playfully makes noise and draws attention to himself at his moms house! - Intriguing stories - true stories - FUNNY stories. We were laughing SO uncontrollably. We intrigued and entertained the hell out of each other (and everyone within ear shot) for the entire five hour flight. I remember when the plane landed and we stood up there were about a dozen huge smiles looking at us as they finally got to see the faces of all that conversation and humor!

A week later, Robert called me while I was on-air. While songs were playing, I was one of those DJs who actually answered the phone, taking as many calls as I could. To my surprise THERE he was on the other end getting quickly to the point as he begged me to do a reading for a part in a movie. I'm like, 'Dude, you're *begging* me?! Are you kidding?! I'd LOVE to!!' 103.9/98.3 FM, KACE (Southern California's BEST R&B Oldies station) was about to go off the air. Forever! Long story but it was in the days of the great Clear Channel takeover. While this transformation of radio was happening, my history with it felt to be closing. Until that point, radio was all I knew I loved and I loved it with everything in me. Not knowing what was next, I was absolutely tickled to get this film opportunity! But this was it for film. I didn't pursue acting or any other work in the industry after this. Loved the entire process but I can't say this one time experience with my little 8 pages of lines makes me an expert in this kind of production!

Anyway.....

THE PILOT:

Most of the changes I sense were for the sake of flow and timing. But the beginning... the VERY, VERY BEGINNING was profoundly different. I will explain in a moment.

To answer Berson's main question; No, the pilot did not acknowledge or even give a hint that it was about life after life!!! That the characters had transitioned in the initial Oceanic Flight 815 crash. Yes, they duped us and probably the networks! lol! I friggin love it! Why eph up perfectly good wool eye covering?!

In terms of what was written and the final product; the most PROFOUND of the differences happens from the opening scene. As it is written, Jacks beginning moments in the jungle have background noise of the severed jet engines. He began to run BECAUSE of the urgency he felt as a result with the loud engine noise propelling him. In the script, he stopped to look at the white tennis shoe hanging on a bamboo shoot. But in the actual footage we saw, Jack was running so fast, he didn't even NOTICE the shoe! - What shoe?! Lol! And there were no loud engine noises until several seconds after he reached the sand. When Jack first got to the sand on the outer edge of the jungle and he's standin' there with that "WTF?" look on his face - it was still SILENT. To the right - beautiful beach & ...silence. In front of him - just ocean and ...silence. But in the script - it was noisy - he could hear all of the crash aftermath terror MUCH sooner. It's my contention that the creators and editors were lead to depict what might really be the case; in that moment of emotional desperation, *Jack (co-)created* what he needed to live out in line with his life curriculum. He co-created with others this experience that now would start to unfold in 3,2,1 - Deafening silence turns to crisis sounds; Swirling, mangled jet engines roaring, Shannon SCREAMING her fool head off in the background! (- I DID enjoy how they colorfully worded that in the Pilot! lol!)

There were lines in different places... I don't remember the guy with the tourniquet on his leg making it into the final footage. They definitely edited out the line between Jack and the flight attendant when she says (in the written pilot) she noticed him earlier when he'd apparently given up his first class seat to an older woman and Jack's response to that. (Good thing he gave up his seat but we were fine without that serendipitous detail!!).

There is definitely an awesome moment that I didn't think about when watching but it struck me profoundly when reading the pilot. It's when Jack, Kate and Charlie are going to look for the cockpit. As they hike along, Kate, as if having thought about it for a while, asks Charlie if they've met before. Despite Charlie's contention and the way Drive Shaft took over the conversation, I believe Kate was having a .....dejavu as a result of 'all time happening..... NOW'. - Sorry, jumped ahead. The chapter on 'Time' is coming. It's possible Kate was **remembering** events with Charlie - many of *which had not happened yet.* (Read that again!).

In the script, to remind Kate of Drive Shaft, Charlie didn't sing 'You Are Everybody' (or is it 'You ALL everybody'???)! In the written pilot, it was a different song! And after they find the cockpit... the part where Charlie is in the bathroom trying to find his stash where he tossed it before the crash; in the written pilot - Kate catches him over the toilet...but in the aired footage that we saw she doesn't find him again until he comes out of the bathroom to her question "what were you doing?" In the written pilot, he doesn't have an answer. In the aired pilot, Charlie STILL doesn't have an answer! lol! Just a slight difference, though.

After leaving the cockpit and losing the plane pilot to the Black Smoke Jungle Monster, they found a better way to discover the pilot's body than was written. In the written script, Kate looks down and sees the pilot's flight pin then *intuitively* looks up and sees the pilot's body in the tree. What ended up happening was SO much better. The pin was in the mud but the mud was by water and on the water was the reflection of the tree above which held the pilot left strewn by the jungle monster! Excellent change!

Scenes are moved around... The flashback of Charlie's point of view of the ending of flight 815 as it begins to crash comes up sooner than in the written script. Lots of little tweaks like that. -I continue to contend, the unfolding of this presentation of LOST was the result of creators working while riding the vibration wave of cooperative co-creation within this dimension and cross dimensionally.

The Marshall - the one who had Kate in handcuffs - he dies in the 2nd episode which is part 2 of the written pilot. But somehow in the aired version, the Marshall hangs in there longer and tortures everyone with a miserable death complicated even more when Sawyer tries to *help* by shooting him but shoots him in the wrong place – and with the last bullet (Season 1 Episode 3 @ 31:50)!

My guess is this trend happened throughout the writing and filming of LOST.

6
C.U.I.: Creating Under The Influence

Unlike a DUI, a CUI is actually a good/healthy thing and has nothing to do with drugs or alcohol. While C.U.I. CAN be intoxicating you are perfectly safe (and legal) to drive or operate machinery simultaneously while in the midst of a CUI episode!

It's my contention that not only were the creators and writers of LOST influenced by outside personalities like Guides (allies these writers may or may not be aware they have) but we are all also VERY influenced by our SELVES. I separated that on purpose; our 'selves' as in the different selves or us' (you's) in the simultaneous multiplicity of life experiences we are living. ... I know! Feel free to read that one again!

I may not be in the film industry but I'm an artist. I first expressed this phenomenon of C.U.I., professionally, in radio where I got familiar with creating a blueprint and watching it unfold magically into something better than I'd previously imagined. In production, creating commercial copy then doing both the voice over AND the sound production to complete the commercial, I would watch the evolution and marvel at an amazing final product. Often it was nothing like I originally intended. Sometimes I'd chase a vision that didn't seem to be mine. An angle that just popped into my brain space from ...somewhere (or someone) else and captured me with its brilliance. Acknowledging here that I, too, can sometimes birth shear genius! I am also clear when 'that' was not mine, i.e., given to me other dimensionally with intention and I run with it! Equally profound is when I do something in a way I've never done it before but on some deep level it feels familiar and ...it's a masterpiece.

When I'm up, I'm excited, positive, in joy - such a high vibration it's easy for me to get into a zone. THEE zone! Personally, I COUNT on getting in this 'zone' which is a space where I am my own force but I'm 'open' to the assistance of Spirit, Master Guides and others who may specialize in an area I'm working on. Sometimes I get in the zone consciously. Sometimes it isn't conscious but when the effects of this guidance are manifesting it is undeniable. On occasion I've heard people call them 'God Shots' - a moment of genius, these ...amazingly luminous ideas or pieces of information that one feels positive couldn't have come from within their own psyche. Like it was... channeled from somewhere.... Many, many times I would create my script and have a plan of how a commercial would feel & sound; beginning - middle - end. Then I'd go into production, get on the mic and watch it form. I bend my inflection in a new and unexpected way on a certain word and by that moment am inspired to take more unplanned yet perfect steps in manifesting the perfect product.

I now know that in the creation of pretty much ANYTHING it is to my advantage if I am open to guidance and influence. But in this open channel I am also cautious. I believe there are all kinds of 'guidance' routes available out there and not all of it is good or healthy! Conscious of this, anytime I go to work on a project, even this book, I start with a prayer and invocation. There are many ways to protect your influence space and most importantly foster highly productive relationships with the energies & personalities providing you positive influence!

There are many who will read this book and will continue forward in life totally ignoring this part about...THIER 'guides'. And that's fine. The agreements you made with these unseen friends still stands and, in fact, it was probably part of the plan that you would have this selective amnesia! This guidance and assistance you're getting is not guidance against your will. Not by a long shot. For those receiving this guidance, there is a level of our being that has agreed to this partnership as well as the extent of the partnership. This partnership is very conscious on the unconscious level! That's not a contradiction, I promise! We've co-created arrangements to have, sometimes, the same guide(s) working with us in ALL of our incarnations but in those lifetimes, on a conscious level, we are not aware of these connections.

Many people have relationships with their guides without consciously realizing they have guides, until they are in a dimension where this association is brought to light. What's beautiful about an authentic Spirit Guide is that they don't operate from an ego level. A Spirit Guide will never 'should' you. There is never 'judgment' or 'ultimatums'. So guidance of that nature is not that of a 'Spirit Guide'. That's one way to discern who you're communicating with. Spirit Guides, like archangels don't operate from an 'ego' place anymore. So, for instance, they don't necessarily need you to know their name! -Nor that they just gave you a great idea! If they're giving you great ideas, it's because they have high affinity for you and 'an agreement' with you! There is a standing relationship here, between you and your guide(s). We will talk about 'contracts' later in this book but in brief, the relationships you live no matter how blissful (or not) are situations lived out via a contract YOU agreed to at some point. The good news is, you can always end the contract. We will absolutely talk about that in this book of secrets.

Brilliance

"I don't know where I get these ideas from but whenever I get 'em from there, it's always amazing". I heard myself say that one day in the midst of creating a masterpiece. -It was a first time landscaping effort! I was coming up with radiant ideas for a *Meditation Garden*! "I don't know where I get em from but whenever I get em from THERE...." Lol! That's a way of saying I know exactly where I get the ideas from but...it's complicated!

Ultimately, pretty much anything I create is now done with this open channel which I protect with prayer and invocation. I absolutely delight in not knowing what's going to happen next or how something is going to turn out - fully trusting that I and the work are in perfect hands. I can 'feel' the success of the project before it's done. The energy and excitement of this magnum opus (which is actually a co-creation) propels me.

So I go into my projects with as complete a plan as possible all the while knowing, it is merely a skeleton which will be perfectly and sometimes 'magically' completed as I and ...the unseen energetically work in tandem bringing the project to masterful completion. How do I know when I'm in the zone of this connection and it's on? -When I'm 100% focused on what I'm doing and especially when *I lose track of time*. Then I know I'm there. In 'the zone'. 'The zone' is a meta-physical place from which brilliance and excellence is guaranteed. The Zone is the same place or state of being that Wayne Dwyer describes when he writes about manifesting your goals in his book 'The Power of Intention'. He describes this 'field' of intention of being the spiritual anatomy or psychological profile of the Creator (God). And he breaks down it's characteristics into what he calls seven 'faces'. Each face is a characteristic of Intention which, remember, is the Creator (God / Source) - which is greater than, yet, one with us. And then, since each of us is a unique expression of God, we have the same spiritual operating system. Our authentic selves are made up of the same faces as the creator. Amongst the seven faces is "creativity". It is our natural ability to create. We create all the time. If you say, "nothing I create ever turns out worth a damn", I'm willing to bet you have stats to prove it! You are creating with your belief!

On the other hand, if you are on a journey with your project and there is a part of you that is open to the magic of multi-dimensional co-creation, then you will experience master pieces on a regular basis. And here's the thing, your agreement to co-create with others outside of this dimension is not always a conscious decision made in THIS incarnation. It could be an agreement made in a different time and place but there was definitely an agreement. And sure, you can say, "Ok, DONT help me, this time. I wanna do this one alone!" - OMG, I, personally, NEVER say that but you certainly can!!! And in fact, one of the upcoming, already teased chapters on contracts is specifically about one of my favorite topics: How to kill a contract! Not the person, yo - the agreement. Destroy and nullify the agreement!

But when I talk about C U I - I'm talking about a blissfully perfect experience! In perfect CUI - nothings broken and the last thing you'd want to do is say "let me do this alone"! Hopefully, in cases like that, your agreement was "If I say let me do it alone - ignore me!"

The most important thing is that we can participate in global consciousness and healing especially when we understand that we don't have to talk to someone to communicate with them. We don't have to correspond via existing physical media and technology and we can still communicate clearly - even without words. Thought is not stuck inside the confines of our skulls. Thought moves freely as our spirits do. Whose thought we pick up and which thoughts resonate with and inspire us...is on a case per case basis.

Journal 2

9:30pm Thurs July 17, 2014

Okeedoke. Dad is clearly being tested and TESTY. We have SO much to be grateful for. His tests have all come back perfect. He's got the arteries of a 30 year old. Only problem has long been solved now, they needed to change his blood pressure meds. That's why he passed out. His heart rate was too low! He is hating life without his driver's license.

To ME - I get how frustrating it is but its temporary and - hello - I'm here! AND I want to help. MY help is NOT welcomed because... I GUESS it makes him feel uncomfortable. I think because he's always been the man-man king of the castle he's just not comfortable with needing help. He LOVES my driving when he has an OPTION. So, long story short, I feel rejected by my own friggin Dad - even though I GET IT. Damnit! How FRUSTRATING.

My Mom doesn't drive the freeway outside of Riverside so I called them. I said, "Dad, if you get the urge to do something out of town - something fun that involves a freeway PLEASE ask me. I would LOVE to." He said ok but I guess he didn't mean ok!

About a week later I learned from my Mom that Dad wants to go to Palm Springs! So I get all excited and I'm like, "awesome, just let me know the date and I'll coordinate". He overheard that conversation (it's called eaves dropping) and when she got off the phone he was annoyed, "I already asked Joe to take us to Palm Springs".

What I get is that my Dad and I are living the same projection. I'm kinda doing what he's afraid of. He' afraid of leaving this incarnation and I'm just as afraid. I seriously do not want him to go, no matter WHAT my experiences have been with the afterlife. I don't wanna have to go into trance to talk to my Dad. I love to hug him. I love to hold his hand! I love to punch him in the belly! Lol! He still maintains abs of steel with at least 100 crunches a night! And I'm seriously a Daddy's girl. He is just...my heart. He AND my mom.... They have both had a hard time understanding my passion to be there with them over the years but...I want to relish this time here. I don't want it to go by only to be too busy in my office to have enjoyed it.

I feel like I lost a lot of years in my late 20s to mid 30s. I need to work on forgiving myself and not seeing it that way. Back then I wasn't there for my family (OR myself!) and when I WAS there I didn't want to be there. I focused on and illumined everything about them that was different than me. It didn't help that I was fighting a cocaine addiction during a few of those years. I had great looking body! Hellllll yeah! BUT I was contaminated with drugs physically, emotionally, spiritually. Cocaine comes complete with a destructive energy field that will systematically work to destroy everything the user has. I prayed and fought hard to stay alive and to ultimately win my life back. Without even being aware of my challenge, my parents love was my strongest inspiration. Their love was the life line I used to pull myself out of the darkness. BY 1992 I was back in a healthy space - which felt like a serious miracle. The first thing I was grateful for was my family and I wanted to make up for lost time. Everything (including me) is so different now. I can finally breathe love.

Last year, Mom had a mini stroke, a 'T.I.A.' which immediately repaired itself (thank God). When that happened I moved my visits from once a week to twice a week. Thursday afternoon and Sundays are my favorite combo. We were on a roll!

NOW, I haven't seen my parents in a couple weeks and ....it's just awful....Especially NOW of all times!

Oh shit. . . Maybe this IS weird of me. I mean, this was MY issue not theirs. They didn't even know about the cocaine addiction and my damaging ways until recently! I mean...maybe my Dad is trying to make me ...get a life! I swear, 57 years old and I feel like I'm getting pushed out of the proverbial nest! I'm all sad n shit, sitting here alone on a Sunday.

Hm...

And all I can think of is to call the boyfriend?! SERIOUSLY!?! Is that all I've got? A boyfriend?!

I used to throw dinner parties and stuff. What happened to that? Used to have a horse, too! Don't even have a DOG, now... Daaaayum. And, where are my FRIENDS?!They got so tired of me saying, "sorry I gotta work" that they sort of stopped calling n now it's been years. I gotta figure out where they went!

>>>>>>HUGE SIGH<<<<<<<

—∞—

Shortly after this pitiful journal entry I remembered that I'd been invited to my cousins' wedding. Andrew and Brianne would get married in Hawaii August 30. In a statement of my independence from my parents and my commitment to my own self nurturing in the realm of joy and fun I declared out loud to my empty house, "You know what?! I'm going to Hawaii, yo!"

7

Killamystery: The Whispers, Mediumship & Channeling

Three in one! Such a deal!!!

No need to give you a time stamp of when the 'Whispers' happened. They are woven to disarticulate intermittently throughout the entire 6 seasons. Here and there. - And always spooky to those who hadn't experienced them before. The whispers never happened in a scene when Miles was around. Had he been around his reaction would have undoubtedly been different than the other LOST characters who were not familiar with this territory and its frequency. So, what they didn't know is that hearing the whispers was merely inter-dimensional or multi-dimensional communication.

I first became aware of 'the whispers' in a 'Channeling class'. Wanting to expand and further understand my abilities I was taking the course offered by Shawn Randall & 'Torah'. - Not 'The Torah', as in the first five books of the Hebrew scriptures (the Pentateuch). No. Torah as in, that's the man's name!!

Okay, now... I just now called him a 'man' out of simplicity and to make my point about Torah being a name. But I also called Torah a him when actually, he is a THEM. *A Spirit Being named 'Torah'.* And when he and other guides refer to themselves they say "we" in reference to what they are -a collective consciousness expressed by an absolutely individualized personality. Both Shawn and Torah teach the class. Shawn would do the first part - about an hour, and then she'd go into trance allowing Torah to take over the rest of the time. 'Upon reading this paragraph my mom expressed confusion, "are both Shawn and Torah real people?" Lol! "Yes!" I told her, "Shawn has physical body like you and me, Torah doesn't. Torah USES SHAWNS body to communicate in the physical". Shawn, channels Torah.

Torah has an accent. I'm not sure what it is... very proper, kind of British. I really need to ask but if he were to pick his own clothes, I imagine it'd be a dark tweed suit with a red vest and blending bowtie! And he might wear glasses! That's how he feels to me!

I remember one class in particular when the subject was about how to **go into trance** to channel and one student mentioned getting to a place where she "can hear whispers. It's like a bunch of voices all at once". Suddenly, around the room, there were a series of "me too" responses. One of those was me. I hadn't really made note of this area, like a part of me understands the function of my lungs without me concentrating on it. I can even go to sleep and they'll keep respiration going without my attention. I get this- 100%. I cannot explain to you how my lungs do this beyond saying they're getting a message from my brain - and God hooked it up so the cells of the body have their own seemingly independent intelligence. The body heals itself. It does all kinds of things all by itself! And - that's all I know! Beyond that... I've got nothin' for you and don't spend much time thinking about it.

The lung breathing thing is pretty profound but I'm cool with leaving it at that without having words to explain it. The area of dimension where the whispers are is like that for me, too. So in class when the whispers came up, I was like, "oh yeah me too!" Sure I'd noticed but hadn't really taken note. When you're outside the department store, it might be relatively quiet. You open the door and there's music, voices, cash registers digging. You've entered the 'shopping dimension' so of course it sounds different. But now, the folks in LOST didn't KNOW they'd entered another dimension! lolol! But that IS what happened. Richard TRIED to tell everybody (Season 6 Episode 9 @ 2:22) when a group including Jack was huddled around the camp fire Richard said he had a secret that he'd known for a reeeeeally long time, "You're DEAD! We're all DEAD....and this [island] isn't what you think it is". Okeedoke... So I guess what he was trying to say was *THIS is a different dimension than the one you were in at the airport in Sydney! This is where you went when your spirit popped out of your body via fatal plane crash. Hola!*

Being in **trance** is merely an altered state. In fact, close your eyes and- Bam! You're there! Of course that's not very DEEP but you have stopped a lot of external stimuli by closing your eyes which helps to quiet your mind. When I conduct weddings I often channel information from disincarnate relatives if the couple has asked for this AND if I can reach the deceased person. I don't have time in those moments to go into a deep trance but I will close my eyes to alter my state.

The less mental activity, the deeper your trance so the trick becomes to get internally quiet. And even to allow your mind to *fall back*. Ultimately, for dedicated Channels, our goal IS to go deep so that we can link to the higher vibration levels where Gate or Doorkeepers, Angels and Guides reside. On the way, we can hear 'the whispers' as we pass their field of space. But sometimes the commute (so to speak) to our destination is so rapid those whispers were barely a bleep. So there's that.

We (channels), meet and bond with 'unseen friends' and develop reliable & authentic relationships founded in trust as each needs the other in the process of disseminating information and bringing healing to individuals and often the masses.

Important: It is not a requirement that one be in trance before being able to channel in the performance of mediumship. Just like Hurley, there are many times when it just...happens as we become open eyed conduits for cross dimensional communication. These kinds of metaphysical abilities for ALL of us are natural but 1) depends on our level of development in this dimension and 2) whether using an ability like this would be productive to a persons' life curriculum. If a person is at a place where these tools can be used they may still need guidance. Just like our moms taught us to tie our shoe laces, guidance in using our natural metaphysical gifts - byproducts of what we are 'Spirit beings having a temporary human experience', is valuable in this dimension where we have a tendency to be hypnotized by all things solid and physical.

So, while there are those who need a little assistance in getting started with this, there are those ...like Miles (Season 5, Episode 13 @ Opening scene) who've got it naturally and at a very young age. Poor Miles! There are many out there with high sensitivities like this. While I consider myself a 'mini Miles', - Lori Board-Camacho is a Master Miles AND a Master Hurley! She is clairvoyant, clairsentient, clairaudient, claireverything. We oughta change her name to Claire (but not right now! For the purpose of this book that might be confusing here n there)!

As a mini Miles, I do most of my house clearing and house healing work via the reading of imprints. Energetic patterns, signatures left by thought and emotion. Lori can do what I can do multiplied by 100. As a figurative 'Master Hurley' she sees their bodies and communicates with disincarnate spirits. She sees them as they are experiencing themselves in their current dimension. I call it 20/20 cross-dimensional vision! Just like Hurley. Me n Miles WISH we had it like that! lol!

Nearly 20 years ago Lori had experiences she didn't understand and I'd say she was just as freaked out as Hurley was that day at the convenience store. Okay, she never played out her experiences as dramatically but - remember Season 4, Episode 1 @ 1:03? That's when Hurley is tryin' to buy some jerkey and a slushy and sees Charlie (who's dead) over there by the Ho-Ho's?! Yeah! Stuff like that!!! There are people who've got it like that! And through Lori's journey I have learned that work within brings peace to these experiences. Like Hurley (and Lori) mediums eventually grow used to their gift as they begin to understand it. And as they heal their own personal figurative demons they are then able to be of service to others.

I also want to say ROSE was ...an intuitive. An intuitive (able to read energetic imprints) and possibly a channel. Hell, she mighta been a medium, too. We don't know much about her communications while she sat on the sand. I know that in the beginning she FEARED for Bernard's safety. My sense is that when we see Rose rocking as she sits on the beach kissing Bernard's ring, tears streaming down her face, (Season 1, Episode1 @ 13:00) she was connected to her husband's current plight - which was iffy at that moment! OR she was in so much fear she was blocking the messages which can also cause tears to stream down one's face.

Either way, while she cried, poor Bernard was still in his airplane seat (Season 2, Episode7 @ 6:05) up in a tree, on the verge of an ugly demise if not for Ana Lucia who saved his life. This was at the very beginning of their stay on the island when they were separated because Bernard going to the lavatory put them in separate parts of the plane when it crashed. Once Bernard was safely down from the tree, Rose was at ease and 'somehow' confident of his wellbeing even though they were on different parts of the island. She either got the information that brought her comfort in direct communication with his soul or from God and/or her Guides or all of the above! Yeah, the info could have come from any and all places. I'm not sure she had words to explain why she was so clear on her husband's wellbeing but as we all saw, she was absolutely grounded in her knowingness.

I bring this up, not only for the memories but to express that there are several ways to express mediumship and channeling. And between the two skills there is a difference. Some channels insist they are not mediums and vice versa! But...at the same time, again, due to the definitions of the words, some channels are mediums and some mediums are channels! In simple terms: Mediums talk to normal people who are no longer in their bodies; Folks who just did an incarnation or folks who are still in the 'physical reincarnation circuit'. Mediums can talk to your late Grandmother, Brother, Friend… Channels … I want to say don't talk to anybody! Channels allow others to talk through them. But these OTHERS are specific. They are Guides & Angels & other higher vibration entities offering information that is of benefit to the masses. That's in simple terms.

And though I am a natural medium and a conscious channel, I want you to know I struggled a couple good days, over this section before deciding to channel my own Guide for clarity in explaining the difference between the two; mediums and channels. Rather than paraphrasing my Guide's words, I would rather share them with you verbatim.

You're about to meet 'Margaret', an energy essence, as we all are except that she is no longer focused in physical reality. My longest multi-dimensional relationship this incarnation, Margaret has been speaking through me for over six years now. She has a deep, rich voice. It's deeper than mine, sounds wrinkled (if that makes sense!) and fairly British. I went into trance to communicate with her and recorded the session.
Here is a transcription of her response to my questions about the whispers and mediumship versus channeling:

December 12, 2014 (7:35pm)
"...The whispers that you are hearing... is a layer of life just prior to where you are going. There are layers… These veils separate the dimensions but you already know that. This dimension [of whispers]- this 'lobby' as you call it - is indeed disincarnate beings - some socializing - many communicating with their loved ones - this dimension is that of those who are hovering, so to speak. They've not left the earths' plane yet. They are still here for one reason or another and there are many of them. And being out of their bodies... their senses are heightened, therefore they are aware of you and your ability to communicate with them and so they are attracted to you like a magnet. And so as you are enter into your trance and your journey to meet your

unseen friend or whomever it is you are calling in, there will be an area of fogginess or *the whispers* and then it's like tuning into a radio frequency. Your focus on where you are going gets you there.

"The whispers will be for a moment, like passing a neighborhood on a freeway and then they will not be as you reach your ethereal destination. So to answer your question, they [those whispering] are doing [saying] many things with their voices on the other side. Some are talking to you. Some are talking to each other. Some are talking to loved ones. -Loved ones who may or may not be able to read [discern] what their disincarnate beloved is saying. But yes there is lots of conversation. Our minds do not stop just because we have left our bodies. We are mind. In fact we are one mind, hence, the ability to connect at all but we can talk more about that another time.....

"Mediumship - as you already know it is the communication with those who just did or recently did a physical incarnation so we call them disincarnates, as, they have left the physical existence that we knew them in.

"And so you can be a medium silently. You can silently communicate with a disincarnate without opening your mouth, without writing anything down. That is mediumship. The minute you share the information by writing it down or the minute that you verbalize to someone else, what this person has shared with you, you are channeling. You are channeling the information. So a medium can be a figurative channel.

"There are those who are merely Channels who do not consider themselves Mediums at all! These people are channeling particularly high frequency, high vibration entities. These entities, Spirits, these *personalities* no longer do physical incarnations. They have...not that one is better than the other...but they have graduated in a sense beyond this. This is where I am. It isn't that I don't appreciate physical incarnations. I appreciate them very much. So much so, that in this stage I am here to assist others, those in their physical incarnations with how to - what it is about the purpose of life and how to find your authentic joy and bliss. And so as a channel what happens is...there's mediumship, as, the channel is a medium in the sense that she is allowing her body to be used as an instrument - a *medium* through which the Guide -not a disincarnate, not your uncle Joe, your aunt Mary, friend Susan, not your late husband, a...SPIRIT GUIDE... can communicate through. It would be a personality essence, a Guide like me. You've never met me in the physical. You and I have not done a physical incarnation together. But you may have other guides who come along who are no longer doing physical incarnations but you, Gillian, in a different lifetime experience have encountered them in a physical incarnation - could have been fleeting - could have been a deep bonding but some kind of relationship or encounter and so they are here for you now. You will encounter those guides who have known you from other lifetimes. I am not that person though. I am one who meets you now...as I am out of body while you are in. We meet this way which is just as special.

"And so the information that comes from your guide is generally information that is not only good for you but good for everyone. So the minute that you share this information the minute that you speak it -write it -you're a channel. Yes, you can also share it telepathically if the person you are sharing it with is accurate at reading what you are sending. Otherwise I would say that in order to really be a channel you must deliver the accurate information given to you by the guide. And to do this, the most accurate way, in the physical dimension, in the earth realm, would be to write it or to speak it. To confuse matters a bit further, there are also those who see the golden opportunity to channel their Spirit Guide and allow the GUIDE to then perform the mediumship. The Spirit Guide is using the channels body and voice to communicate to physical entities what is happening, what is being communicated from…the other side. That would be 'channeled mediumship'!

I hope this answers your question in regard to mediumship versus channeling and being a Medium who channels! "(Ending transcription here.)

The other interesting difference to note between mediumship, channeling and intuitive work is that all of them require concentration - except channeling. In intuitive work you have to concentrate. You're reading information that is traveling in the stream of consciousness that fills the illusionary space between us all. And each intuit is different. Many of us have been given different symbols to mean precise things. You're feeling emotional sensations and or seeing pictures and/or you're getting words, some in your head with sound, some on your mental screen like fragments from a script or even just a single word here and there. And sometimes the words are a razor sharp and physically audible as you hear them outside your body. You're awareness to your feelings are turned all the way on as you work to discern ' whether that emotion, picture, word is yours or is that a message from____'? Again, with practice, this discernment process becomes easier and can be reflex fast - instant knowingness.

Mediumship is actually work/ effort, too. Over time and practice your ability to go into trance (or not!), communicate and to 'discern' is heightened. With Channeling it's the opposite. Completely relaxing the body and quieting the mind are key to conscious channeling. The goal being to kind put your mind in your back pocket, so to speak, so that your body and brain space are somewhat vacant for your guide to come in and use as a tool express the messages.

Journal 3

11:30am Monday 7-21-14
A few minutes ago a question occurred to me; "where was LOST filmed?" I Googled it: Hawaii! Seriously!?!?! Shut UP! -My brain is buzzing right now cuz... I had NO idea it was filmed in Hawaii. Coulda been the Caribbean, the Dominican Republic. I seriously had no idea. And - I'm GOING to Hawaii! WHAT are the friggin chances?! So then I'm thinkin' "

I wonder how many islands am I gonna have to hop to get to where they filmed it?" I Google it: LOST was filmed on Oahu!

Andrew & Bri's WEDDING is on Oahu! Ok! - THAT is just.... SHUT UP!!

O M G!

There's no such thing as a coinkidink...

8
There Is No Life After Death

That heading is not a typo. It's the truth. Sorry if it seems confusing coming from me, of all people but, that is the way it is. -Deal with it.
There is no life after death. PERIOD.
Know why?! Because...
There IS NO DEATH!
Ha! Gotcha!
There is only life ...after life... after life...
(Yeah... Let that sink in.)
As I watch LOST, approaching season 4 for the 2nd time, knowing that they'd all actually died in the opening episode of Season 1, we're meeting all these *Others* on the island who were there BEFORE and at first ponder I realize... they must have...'died previously'. Like Richard or Charles Whidmore, Ben, Danielle & Eloise... And so for a moment, it became this odd challenge to figure out *when* THEY died. But seeking that answer is as ridiculous as seeking the answer from 'you', the reader of this book. When did YOU last die? Would it be the same date as your birthday in this incarnation? Or... 9 months prior to your birthday at conception?! Were you in the previous incarnation up to the moment you became an embryo in this one?! No. Maybe. Yes & Kinda.
In reading the interviews of the LOST creators Carlton and Damon - they didn't mean for LOST to be more than 3 seasons. They had to BEG for a deal to end it at the 6th season. So, they had to STRETCH the show to make it 6 seasons instead of 3. In doing that they displayed how life reincarnations can be experienced. I'm willing to put a significant amount of money in a bet that they did NOT realize they were doing this! In the coming pages look for the flower analogy! This explanation will be part of bringing clarity to all the wacky back n forth n sideways of time in LOST and show how those episodes accurately illustrate the point that - as I type, as you read this, we (you & me) are as 'dead' as dead gets!

As Maryanne Williamson explains in her book 'Illuminata', life doesn't end it transmutes, "Jesus didn't die when he died, neither do we".

Journal 4

Journal Monday July 28, 2014 (ending 11:32pm)
I booked my plane ticket today. Did it on-line. Hysterical when it got to picking a seat! LOLOL!! Oh no, I'm not affected by writing this book! Ha!!

OH Lord... The first good thing is I'm not flying Oceanic! I'm going Hawaiian Airlines. Any bad things I've ever heard about flights to Hawaii - especially stuff I read during my newscasts as a Broadcast Journalist back in the 80s and 90s, I am pushing from my brain right now.

...Pushing all those thoughts right OUT of my mind....

B'bye scary thoughts! . . . Yeah... there they go. Dissolve.....

Oh gosh - LIKE THE ONE (lol) where a piece of the plane blew off ...or was it a door?! - No, it was a huge piece of the ROOF! Right! OMG. I was on-the-air that day on 1110AM KRLA and had to do this story over n over n over again. April 28, 1988, a great big plane doin' a little island hopping, Aloha Airlines flight 243 flying from Hilo to **Oahu**. According to reports, while at cruising speed, it suffered "explosive decompression due to metal fatigue"! METAL FATIGUE!?! I read the sentence over again. I had kinda enjoyed taking comfort in the idea that metal could never get tired! Especially when it's carrying me!

Anyway, when the metal got too pooped to pop and a piece of the roof blew off, a flight attendant was sucked out of that hole... The plane DID manage to land and there were magically no other fatalities. But understand... it now had a large open SUN ROOF. Can you friggin imagine being in one of the seats on that plane under the OPEN SKY knowing full well there was a great big ocean below?! DUUUDE!

Maybe I should change my seats again.....

I gotta go back to the beginning of LOST and figure out what seat everybody was in. OMG, on the airline's plane seating web page, I kept moving around! I loved the idea of the leg room by the doors but then you have to meet requirements. I meet these requirements but... the list unnerved me starting with the first one: "Are you willing to assist on an evacuation"?! O M G we are about to fly over a GANG OF WATER! IDK If I can do an ocean evacuation?! I ended up picking my seats outside of the evacuation row! I choose 14 G on the way there and then 14F on the way back! Both are Isle seats! Lol... No characters were sitting in these seats!!! Normally, I'm a window flier... not this time! - I ....don't wanna SEE!

Its possible Clare was sitting in row 14...otherwise, it appears I have chosen a seat none of the surviving LOST characters picked. Lol!! G would be the aisle seat across from the Marshall! Hm... Maybe I shoulda taken the window where Kate was! :/ See what I mean?! I honestly have no idea whether I'm done with this part or whether some crazy idea will make me log on and change my seats again!!!

I was gonna take a flight that departed at 8am. But then I thought...what if that meant it didn't really hit the runway to fly until.....'8:15'?! So I leave at 10am! Ha! Flt #3. The choices were 1, 2 or 3! Lol. I think Hawaiian Air knows not to have any three digit flights!

I gotta create an excel sheet and chart my process on this.

Gotta find a room or rental property!!!

Gotta figure out transportation. Where the hell is Ke iki Beach and the North Shore?! - To the NORTH, I suppose... Googlemaps here I come...

9
Guys, *WHAT* are we?

Well, we're a couple of things. We're humans and we're spirit beings. Actually we're more spirit beings than humans. -Kinda like I'm a human first, American second. We're Spirit Beings first and foremost. At this moment, we're Spirit beings having a human experience.

In order to make the truth of multi-dimensional existence make sense... it needs to be plausible. It won't be plausible until we understand how it is that we could be part of ALL of it. -We are each SO much more than our human condition, on the surface, implies.

I want to start with ...'thought'. Have you ever thought about ....thought?! Like...where do they (thoughts) come from?! How about the word 'consciousness' – does it resonate with you? Not as in 'awake versus asleep' so much but consciousness in terms of the expression of a personality, Spirit...Being. Where does personality... or spirit... come from? We are all consciousness.

We, as consciousness, generate thoughts. The thoughts don't stay in our bodies. And as consciousness we don't stay in our bodies, either!

I'd like to do a little exercise with you to show you what (and WHERE) YOU really are.
Memorize these steps then do them:

1. Close your eyes and sit in a very still position
2. Become aware of your body. - Aware of gravity as you focus on the sensation of your weight against the chair or surface you're sitting on. Keeping your eyes closed, focus on this feeling underneath you.
3. Now, notice the point from which you are observing this. This observer... is who YOU really are. This point of consciousness is where you are. It MAY or may NOT be located in or around your brain. This observation point may not be anywhere near your head! You can move your point of consciousness, anywhere you want!

Personally, when I do this exercise, I find my Self observing from just below and behind my right shoulder. Where did you find YOUR self?!
This place, from where you find yourself observing your body and sensations is also the place from where you observe your feelings and even thoughts. This place from where you perceive all these things is where you are, this is your consciousness and it is not dependent upon your body and its parts. It is independent of your brain. It only needs your brain to work your body. Otherwise, it is able to do things independent of this organism and its physical sensations.

Modern Neuroscience would have you believe consciousness - the mind - the soul - the personality - the invisible energy stuff that makes you who you are, comes directly and exclusively from the brain. Period. If your brain is absent - modern neuroscience declares - you are absent as well. If your brain doesn't work - you're a gonners. Done. Finito. You are past tense!
OH wow - great moment at Season 3 Episode 12 @ 29:47 when Jack (and Clare's) dad Christian tries to suggest that Clare not keep her comatose mom plugged into life support for the wrong reasons. At this point, Clare had a flat tummy. He was trying to say, it's too late, she's not going to come conscious again in this incarnation. And so, as Clare got to 8 months pregnant, we see that her mom is STILL in a coma and on life support (Season 3 Episode 12 @ 35:54). Not sure whether Clare was already pregnant when the car accident happened but at the very, very least, her mom was in a coma for 8 months and then, what? -Woke up sometime after the crash of flight 815? It's either THAT or, she did a walk in? Because she sure was present in Jacks dimension for his dads memorial (Season 4 Episode 12 @ 35:05).

By a 'walk-in', I mean she had transitioned from this life and then, came back to this incarnation so that she could be there for her grandson, Aaron. I admit, I'm torn on this one!

Lol! As I type, I realize that on this particular situation, I will be much more clear on how Mrs. Clare's Mom showed up post coma after we delve into 'walk-ins' in a subsequent chapter. But yes, after reading up on others who have awakened from really long comas, I suppose she could have finally awakened from her injury induced sleep in the nick of time to meet her grandson and collect her daughter's airline settlement money! In LOST, in the incarnation where flight 815 didn't crash, Dr. Jack Shepard met a terminally brain injured Anthony Cooper (John Locke's Dad) and Jack advised that Locke step up to accepting that his father is already gone - like 'dead' (Season 6 Episode 14 @ 38:46). And I say, if his vehicle (brain) was now permanently broken and unusable in this lifetime...on the other side of those catatonic eyes he very well could have been gone (like, out n about) and doing gloriously fine as Dr Alexander was while his brain swam in a river of yellow infection being attacked by an incurable 'itis'!

Now I'm talking about Dr Eben Alexander. Loved reading his book, 'Proof of Heaven'. This acclaimed neurosurgeon believed as many of his A.M.A. colleagues (that science is all there is) until ... Well, that is until he was LOST in a Near Death Experience (NDE) that left him comatose for 7 days with a one of a kind medical condition for which there was/is no cure! Dude!! He was on his way OUT! Okay?! Brain RAVAGED with special brand of meningitis. In his book, he minces no words as he describes the "puss" his brain was swimming in. And while his body laid there barely more than a corpse, Dr Alexander - left the building! That's right. I said, his body was laying there (for Doctors to try to fix, for family members to pray over and give unwavering support) and meanwhile - he was 'consciously' out n about - places to go, people to see, things to do, huge stuff to learn. Stuff he couldn't have learned while in his physical body even when it was at maximum fitness.

It's very much like the condition made it so his brain could get out of the way!!! I agree with Dr. Alexander when he basically says our brains filter the vastness, the ginormity of life. I think the brain was created to do this so that our experience in this realm is not overwhelmed by experience in all the others combined with all that life truly is. And also I think, at this stage of our existence, in this dimension, we need the filter so we can concentrate and maximize each life lesson, one incarnation at a time. So, I see that the brains very function, connecting us to this physical experience through sight, touch, sound, taste and smell has us mesmerized with so much external stimuli we bypass much of the meta physical by simply being so inundated with the color and volume of the physical.

Dr. Alexander was not all that Spiritual minded prior to this coma thing! Wanted to be but.... Just couldn't connect to that outside the physical stuff... Christmas and Easter were the extent of his church attendance. Not that going to a church defines your spirituality but his point was that his staunch scientific view of life and the world, over time, undermined any hope he had of believing in ...something larger...or 'Divine' let the alone the idea that he is not so much human as he is a 'Spirit Being'! For many people, transitioning from this life (or in Dr. Alexander's case, being on the verge of transitioning) provides them their first true experience of 'Spiritual' awareness. And a multitude of NDE testimonials acknowledge 100% clarity in the realization that we are not so much humans as we are 'Spirit Beings' and life is massively eternal.

Earth is but a spec in the whole picture. There are other Spirit Beings having temporary experiences that we 'humans' might call 'alien'! But let's not go THERE right now. Keeping this book in Earth realm as the story of LOST was. And within this realm there are dimensions, just like beyond this realm there are dimensions. - Hold on to that...

So, there's the neurosurgeon, layin' there in ICU... on the 'verge' n whatnot, right?! His brain was not capable of functioning. But the doctors MIND was conscious - totally lucid as he journeyed and had intellectual (and other amazing) encounters... on the OTHER SIDE.

Another purely amazing NDE testimonial is shared in detail by Anita Moorjani in her book 'Dying to be Me'. Unlike Eben Alexander, when Anita's body was on the verge, she still had her human identity. Eben left his name and human identity on the hospital bed with his body. I personally had not heard of this before from an NDE survivor. I found it profound in an...'advanced' kind of way that he would leave his earth identity on the table and take off as his Authentic Self which is more than just a one incarnation character masterpiece. And then this is not to say that the other experiences are less than. Not at all. I think I would enjoy knowing I was Gillian while having an NDE- if I were to have one. But to make that journey as my authentic self - the core me, the one that is connected to all there is, would be absolutely...magnificent.

When Anita's body was within hours, then minutes and then was mysteriously overdue for shutting completely down from the cancer that had completely taken over, she left. Girlfriend went places. And as she did, Anita knew she was Anita. She witnessed conversations far away from where her body laid just one bleep from flat-lining. Then she went to other dimensions. She hung for a while with her father who had transitioned prior to this. I can't remember the quote verbatim but when she protested about going back (into her earth body and earth realm) he told her something like, *'now that you know what you know - go back and LIVE. And LIVE FEARLESSLY'*. Anita got the same knowingness Sun got. I mean, in LOST, Sun didn't have an NDE - she actually died after being shot in the stomach. When she awakened, the hospital setting was part of her transition as it is for MANY people who've transitioned from illness or injury. All time is happening now. Jin was there. Doesn't mean Jin died in the same moment she died, but he is there for her transition as her soul mate. I also venture to say this is the only way I can explain in short that he was in this hospital setting as part of his transition at the same time (season 6 Episode 17 @ 18:47). - I'm ahead of myself here and I apologize. I'm basically saying there was a clip missing in the footage! -The part where she flat lines as a result of the bullet wound.

ANYDAMNWAY - while hospitalized for that bullet to the stomach, when Sun and Jin remembered the island they were suddenly anchored in an absolute knowingness and upon that understanding, the simultaneous realization that despite it all - plane crashes, gunshots, submarine drowning, they're safe (Season 6 Episode 17 @ 1:01:17). I love how at peace both Jin and Sun are in that scene, "we'll see you there".

Hyacinth. Not only a beautiful flower but the name of one of my grandmothers. I actually called her 'Grandmother'. When she passed away I was disappointed not to be in her physical presence at the time. I knew Grandmother was within minutes of crossing because my Mom had called to tell me. Since there was no way for me to get from Woodland Hills to Moreno Valley (about 100 miles) in the next few minutes physically, I would have to do it in metaphysically. Thing is, I was so wound up with emotion I couldn't get out of my immediate space.

In a saddened daze coupled with a bit of a panic I went outside to the back yard. The reality of the chapter Grandmother was living had me in a fearful grip. So much for calmly going in to assist her crossing. I was a friggin MESS. I stood on the deck overlooking the meditation garden as tears rushed down my face. As if on automatic, I picked up the hose and started watering. My emotion wasn't so much sadness for Grandmother as it was panic over this entire process. What was happening to Grandmother was just a wakeup call that this is what happens. Transition. "Oh shit! Shit, shit, shit! This is really happening…" Fear and resistance swelled within me. The tears were a rapid current as the reality of NOW made me think of my own mom and the future. Feeling frantic in a state of helplessness I thought "Oh God. I'm REALLY NOT ready for this!"

Suddenly, it was like I was in a swirling vortex of emotion. I could faintly SEE the energy and its color moving around me in a circular motion. It made a cylinder of pink and white around me….. and it wrapped me up tight. I THINK this was intended as love and comfort for me but it only caused my emotion to swell even bigger. I couldn't breathe. My Grandmother had my attention. As distraught as I was, I wanted her to know that I was there to be of service, "I'm here with you, Grandmother". I prayed for her comfortable and blissful crossing. And even with that, the energy swirl was still kind of … squeezing me. On automatic, again, I dropped the hose, went back in the house and took off out the front door. Instead of turning left and walking down hill, I turned right and went straight up the mountain my house sits on. So emotionally spun, I didn't even feel the burn. I had energy coming from what must have been a secret reserve space! It wasn't like me to take on such a steady and strong, unwavering stride while going up such a steep grade, and for so long. The part of me that would normally be panting, sweating, muscles burning- was off – not in service - disconnected. I could only feel Grandmother. She was moving with me. A massive space of energy was hers, to my right. Her communication was loud and strong, "enjoy your life, Gillian!" I acknowledged her with a tearful reception. "Live it strong". She said. "Live it large. Live it like I did! And live it like I didn't". By the latter part, I knew she meant allow love in my life. A very gorgeous and successful business woman, my grandmother had plenty of great choices in men but never really married. She regretted not picking one. I felt that was a direct suggestion regarding my then brand new (6 months) romance with my beloved Berson. It was at that point that I opened my heart and let him in. I thanked her and promised I would totally do that, "I love you, Grandmother".

-My main point about this part (she said, typing with one hand while blowing her nose with the other) is my Grandmother, now immersed in the true story because she's outside her limiting brain space, was sharing with me the fact that heaven is here, now. Realize it and dig in! Now is a GREAT time to live and love fearlessly!

One thing that is interesting is that every NDE experience I've heard of varies in ways that are pertinent to the growth needed for the person experiencing it. But the commonality I am mainly pointing out now is their BRAINS didn't have to function for their perfectly coherent experiences which they are then able to come back and articulately describe! Proof (as humans sometimes need) that what they experienced is real often comes when they tell you what you did or said while you weren't even in the hospital where they were hooked up to IV's n whatnot! And in Anita's case, in what should have been her 'last minutes' in this incarnation, she was in several places watching the reaction of several people, at one time. How could that BE?! Trust when I say she was in no condition, physically, to get up and run around the hospital and parking lot, the chapel and wherever else she witnessed her loved ones! So ... how did she accurately relay to them what they'd said and done in those places?! Yeah.... -One-uh-those things that makes ya go...whoa! The mind is not limited to the wrinkled greymatter confines of the human brain!

The Spirit/Mind is the driver. The brain is the car. Of course, there's nothing more annoying than a car that breaks down! In this dimension, we need our cars to be durable and long lasting! I think about those who've suffered strokes. Their minds are fine but their brains are broken. Those who make full recoveries talk with some amazement about how lucid (though panicked) their minds were while they couldn't get their bodies to move the way they needed them to! How frustrating!!

Soon after graduating from USM in August 2012, I began an apprenticeship in 'Transition Midwifery'. This had me learning my way around nearly a dozen hospitals and rehabilitation facilities between Los Angeles and the Inland Empire (Southern California). My first opportunity to work in this field was with, my Aunt Jean who had gotten very sick and consciously decided to make a fairly speedy exit from her physical body which, at this point, she was just over. Jean was beautiful, blonde, a brilliant 5'10" diva with a thick British accent! She was actually my Aunt-in-law, married to my mom's brother, Bernie. She and I shared a passion for the metaphysical. We had often talked about stones and crystals. She even shocked me one day by revealing her very own tarot deck!

As she was beginning her journey out of this incarnation, I knew she would appreciate my assistance and companionship. I would make the drive from Los Angeles to the facility where she was in Corona several times over a 2 week period. I wished I had been able to spend more time. This was part of my learning. She so welcomed me and metaphysical tools. I used Reiki to assist her Spirit, to help ease her mind. She openly received my new age style of prayer as well as my cocktails! I left her a special concoction of selenite, angelite, nephrite, rose quartz and obsidian in a little silk pouch. She had no strength in her hands and asked me to lay the pouch beside her before I left that evening.

This would be a first time experience for me. I was anchored to Spirit and following the footsteps into what would be more than a year of apprenticeship in the world of 'multi-dimensional transition'. Some call it 'death' but... again, the point of this book is to express how there really is no such thing.

Aunt Jean was sharing a room with a lady, Ms. Jimenez. What an adorable woman. She was 87 and at this point she was super frail. But her freshly dyed red hair and turquoise nail polish stood out and kind of italicized her zest for life! I was blessed with the opportunity to be in the room, one day, while waiting for my aunt to wake from a nap. Ms. Jimenez noticed me when I walked in, said hello and quickly went back to her personal gathering with people who'd come to visit. These people... I couldn't see. Ms. Jimenez was having a reunion party with friends and relatives (already deceased) obviously coming to guide her across! "Oh Daddy! Daddy!" Many had shown up before him, none got such enthusiasm as him, I mean she almost screamed his name when her father showed up! Clearly, she had not seen him in many years! "Daddy - I could catch a plane! -I could be there tonight!" she said. I knew I was witnessing a sacred and very real/legitimate moment.

There's a term, it's called 'Terminal lucidity'. The phenomena has been tracked for hundreds of years but a figurative minute ago, in 2009 a German guy, Biologist Michael Nahm actually came up with the phrase. In that same year he did an article in the Journal of Near-Death Studies where he defines terminal lucidity: "The (re-) emergence of normal or unusually enhanced mental abilities in dull, unconscious, or mentally ill patients shortly before death, including considerable elevation of mood and spiritual affectation, or the ability to speak in a previously unusual spiritualized and elated manner." Though given a label, terminal lucidity is still a vague concept for science which is still having a tough time wrapping its head around it. And to that end, I am not sure they include the ability for terminally ill people to also, lucidly communicate with loved ones who've already crossed over. Like Ms. Jimenez did with her Dad! That would certainly be speaking in an "unusually spiritualized and elated manner" - dontcha think!?

While I couldn't see the people she was starring right at (they were UP in the corner of the ceiling by the curtain that separated her section of the room from Aunt Jeans. I felt to whip out my phone and text myself her dialogue. I did so as quickly as my thumbs would let me. I remember a nurse came in a few minutes later and Ms Jimenez commented that she knows she "might LOOK crazy but ...I don't care!" she said. And this is what I mean. She was totally lucid. The nurse asked if she wanted some water and she was like, "no no. Not right now". She wanted to get back to her family and friends. She was amped. Excited! This was a huge day with all these visits!! "You're not crazy Ms. Jimenez" I chimed in from my chair and then backed her up by calmly telling the nurse "it's been very busy. She's had a lot of wonderful people come by. Did you know she had 8 children?! She's bionic, ya know!" The room laughed... Aunt Jean continued to sleep. I didn't get to talk to her that day.

Something occurs to me as I write this part and it's the ending of LOST. Imagine that in one of his incarnations, Sawyer is laying on a hospital bed where maybe he's been dying of.... something. He's on the verge of crossing when suddenly he becomes terminally lucid. The people in his hospital room can't see what he sees but his mind has left the building and he is focused on a different incarnation where he is at a vending machine in a hospital and he encounters Juliet. And all of the conversation (Sawyers lines only) that we heard during that scene when he and Juliet reunite (Season 6 Episode 17 @ 1:08:08) is actually happening multi-dimensionally. It is an incarnation they have lived already. He and Juliet are revisiting it in a reunion in an in-between dimension. And what if, as they kiss in front of that vending machine, he lifts from his body in that hospital bed dimension and he and Juliet go to the church to meet the others in this in-between place? This is actually how I see it. This is why I got so excited and needed to write this book. The writers were indeed showing us what happens when you...transition!

Back to my Aunt Jeans hospital room, two days later I went back to visit and Ms. Jimenez wasn't there. She'd transitioned. Suddenly I understood what I was supposed to do with the dialogue I'd texted myself. There had been some names mentioned... She'd said some amazing and wonderful things about her family! Her kids. It seemed one of her daughters was already on the other side. She talked to her. Then there was another person she talked to and in that conversation she mentioned a woman by name and apologized for hurting her feelings. She then went on to talk about how beautiful this woman really is like she had a new view from where she was in this moment. There was no way I wasn't supposed to give this to the family!

So I wrote a letter to them and then transcribed the conversations she had that day which took up more than a couple pages. I called the hospital and of course they were hesitant to help me. I assured them all I wanted to do was pass on this information which is probably important to the family. I said, "tell you what. Let me fax this to you. You look at it. Read it and you decide whether the family should have it." A deal was made.

I opened the letter by identifying myself as an ordained minister and metaphysician but other than that gave them no way to find or contact me. I hoped that this would further encourage the hospital to pass the note on. After faxing, I gave it about 30 minutes then called the caseworker back just to get a feel for whether she'd follow through. "Oh! Hi Gillian! Yes, we're sending the letter to the family! Thank you!" I was touched! Grateful to be of service...
Aunt Jean now had a private room but.... so what?! She wanted out. She was super ready to abandon her body as it, she felt, had abandoned her! 83 yrs old and out of the blue she suddenly had every possible ailment including the failing of her only remaining kidney. Carpal tunnel had ravaged her hands and she could no longer use them. Either of them! -She was just over it. She was far too much of a Diva to live like this so she was kinda like **Double-air-finger-snap** "Check Please"!

Other than the sadness she felt in remembering the good parts and the friendships like her sisterhood with my Mom who she adored and was so grateful for, she was calm about her exit. She took comfort in being able to tell me about the 'dark space' she was seeing, the ' light beings' how it felt "warm. They know me". She described them as all black robed beings with light coming from where their faces would be. "Do you know THEM?" I asked. "I don't know..." Again, I appreciate Dr. Eben Alexander's contention that the human BRAIN actually works as a veil or shield as it filters and hampers our ability to see the Whole Life picture. But then - I think this blockage to multi- dimensional truth is by Divine design and necessary for the actualization of our lives in each incarnation. The brain seems to play into our incredible focus on the now and our attachment to our physical present tense. Without this, we might not commit so fully to the lives we live and the way we live them. While the brain is reducing our visions ability to merely this incarnation, THIS incarnation is chalk full of reasons to pay full attention! So, in a supportive manner, the system is designed to give us full focus of an individual lifetime. This full focus and hence, full ability to heal and grow in and through our individual life curriculums ultimately (in a trickle down/ripple effect) enhances the human race as a whole. So the brain gets a thumbs up, for sure! Just don't get duped into thinking the brain is the end all! It is merely a tool you use while in a human body. It isn't you.

Within a couple weeks of Aunt Jean's transition I was driving down the freeway one evening, off to Malibu to teach a precision driving course when I got information on one of our lead

Dolls, Lynn Helmn. Lynn was Valet Of The Dolls strongest Team Captain (TC) at the time. She could supervise the largest of parking operations. If it was so large, layered and complicated that I felt I needed to be there but couldn't, Lynn was the only one who's presence on site would bring me peace of mind.

I was exiting the north bound 101 @ Las Virgenes/Malibu Canyon Road hangin' a left - southbound toward the ocean when the disturbing information downloaded into my being. Right in the middle of the turn - BAM – INSTANT information. Like NEWSFLASH! It was a sudden knowingness that something was going to happen to Lynn - something HUGE - something concerning her health - wellbeing... I felt an absolute 'severance'. It hit me HARD. I got an 'oh shit type knot' in my solar plexus. I guess that translates to 'fear'! I got it so intensely, I thought what I was reading was, she was going to DIE. My next thought was, "oh NO! What are we gonna DO???" That would affect and devastate the entire Doll Force. And she's the Team Captain of the majority of the parties. I decided to heed the warning.
That evening I looked at the roster of valets and started to identify more potential TC's. It was time to give them experience and discover more of the strong ones. "I'm sure they're in here somewhere" I told myself, "I'm sure this is why I got that message. I just need to grow the TC roster, that's all". A little bit of denial…

About three days later I got a call from Lynn. I knew she'd been having migraines but… I thought they were just…migraines! Lots of people have migraines. What?! She'd had migraines all the years I'd known her. With her lovely British accent she explained that she'd suggested to her doctor that maybe this particular bout of migraines was because of an aneurysm. To that, her doctor was like, "no it's NOT an aneurysm". As if that was an extreme and silly idea. Lynn then explained that her "Mum and sister" died of aneurysms to which her doctor was THEN like, "Oh!" Tests & images were immediately ordered and taken revealing a GINORMOUS aneurysm so totally on the verge. Ok, I'm gonna tell you a truth! I did not look at the ultrasound image of Lynn's aneurysm thou she'd emailed it to the Doll House. People try to share images of their injuries and I just can't figure out WHY I should torture myself looking at them! Lol! So I DONT! But my Personal Assistant Lisa said, "it's HUGE! It's like a QUARTER of her whole brain!" That description provided enough 'image' for me! Later I would learn Lynn had what is medically termed a 'Giant' aneurysm. That's what they call them when they're more than 2.5 cm.

UCLA had cutting edge aneurysm procedures and treatments going on. A particular procedure that Lynn wanted to have done was happening there. So she swung into action to do whatever paperwork was necessary so her insurance and UCLA would be in harmony. With that part complete, the surgery was scheduled for almost 2 months away. Um… Yeah!

Rev. Gillian V. Harris M.S.P.

I seriously don't get that part! Nobody does! You've got a clear photo of a time bomb in this patients head and you're gonna wait til ...WHEN?!

Weeks prior to the surgery date, it happened. It was morning. Lynn was dressing for her 9 - 5 and her son William just happened to be home. I don't know what she experienced as the aneurysm exploded but she knew what was happening and yelled for Will to dial 911, which he did as he raced to find her passed out on the bathroom floor. The EMTs were quick to arrive and living in Culver City put her pretty close to UCLA @ Ambulance Warp Speed.

Getting past the original ridiculous scheduling which I wanna believe was just a 'glitch' - they ultimately got Lynn to the hospital in time. Surgery was almost immediate and successful. Now, doctors would purposely induce a comatose state so her brain could heal enough to not swell when she regained consciousness. I found that interesting. I was getting metaphoric pictures of consciousness depicted as a space shuttle making its way back into the earth's atmosphere - the heat and fire of re-entry. Intrigued by this, I texted my personal physician Dr. Marc Lavin (best doctor in the world, BTW) to make sure I was understanding the reason for the medically induced coma. He wrote me back: "Yes. Here is a summary I found: When you put a patient into a medically induced coma, doctors can control their alertness level, so they don't feel pain, stop any uncontrollable seizure activity, don't fight the breathing machine, and subsequently do not raise the pressure within their head. The goal is to put the body to sleep such that all parts of the body reduce their oxygen demand and prevent high metabolic rates that the body is unable to support."

My take on that is that all of that life force energy in the form of 'Spirit', reuniting with the body is intense on not only the brain but the entire physical being. When we hop into these bodies, it's no joke, yo! And like the space shuttle re-entering earth's atmosphere, the vehicle needs to be ready! – No metal fatigue!!! Consequently, many of the nearly 30 nights I spent with Lynn, she wasn't there.

While she might not have been in the room, she was aware. In alignment with my belief in the power of love and vigils and their effect upon the target, I would visit any time after 11pm and hang for 3 - 5 hours. It was quiet then and I knew I wouldn't be interrupted in my processes.

To reach Lynn I would meditate first. Only a few times was she close enough to be available to communicate with me. The first time her consciousness approached me from the foot of her bed. In her dimension she was still in her hospital gown. Feisty as ever, one hand on her hip she points at herself on the hospital bed and says, "Wouldja look at this?!" and shakes her head in her very Lynn (sarcastic) way! Funny girl! Even in a coma! It was cool to know she wasn't at all worried about her condition. She knew she was in the best of care. At other times

I couldn't reach her. I didn't know where she was. I caught a glimpse of a busy city a couple times. But I only got flashes. I knew she was busy! And -elsewhere.

Prior to the rupture Lynn had said she was interested in my energy work and Reiki after the surgery so I took that as permission to give her treatments while she was there.

ICU at UCLA is the most impressive intensive care I've seen yet. Several R.N.s assigned to each patient and the compassion in their way of being of service was wonderful. Every time I was there, they immediately filled me in with an update on her condition. I didn't have to wonder. There were more than a dozen monitors hooked up to Lynn. If I wanted to move energy in the room, I did it remotely from my chair against the wall. I felt physically clumsy around all of the gadgets and with energy work, I often sway and do other unpredictable stuff. So - I just stayed in my seat! Lol! -Careful with what I did/moved/applied, so as not to adversely affect the anesthesia (as Reiki can). My Light was aimed at her consciousness which was outside of her body, so I didn't affect her physical being and the coma drugs! My intention was to support her journey and the attainment of urgent life lessons where ever she was as her body healed. What she experienced now was playing into all her other incarnations. I wondered if her energy was needed from this incarnation to support another and this was maybe the only way to call in all the forces.... Just...thinkin...

I saw a black angel one night. (Uhoh...?) It flew from in, like from another room. An Orb on a Mission, yo! Rapidly, it went across the wall, over the clock and swooped down into Lynn. This was a flash of a moment. Had I blinked I would have missed it. Scared me for a sec, too, because the only time prior that I'd even heard of 'Black Angels' was when Lori's Mom was transitioning about a year earlier. Black Angels can appear to the human eye as large black orbs of fast moving energy (like a big fuzzy ball about 20 inches in diameter) that gracefully and with targeted precision and purpose, fly into a space and then into the energy body of the entity (person) needing healing and alignment. Lori saw three angels the night she encountered them. Two of them went to her mother, another went to Lori. Even for Lori, this was a bit unnerving, as, she'd never encountered these Angels before and it was her first time spending time with a transitioning person. AND the person was her mom! So there's that.

These Angels are especially for removing emotional debris, aligning energy in preparation and as result of severe trauma (emotional or physical) and/or transition. They helped Lori's mother cross, while assisting Lori with the emotion of that crossing. With Lynn they were assisting in the healing of the trauma (emotionally, spiritually, physically), as, ultimately, she was to continue this incarnation using the same body that was temporarily lying on a hospital bed.

So, let's get back to influence, specifically, CUI (Creating Under the Influence) where the inspiration is someone or an energy field that does not have a physical body in THIS incarnation at this time: It all makes more sense with the acceptance that we are fields of consciousness, Spirits and that the mind is part of that field. Your body and its physical parts are merely CIRCUMSTANTIAL EVIDENCE! IT is not who or what YOU are! We step in and out of these physical bodies per lifetime, like we step in out of a new outfit per day. In fact, during sleep time – that'd be every day- (Oh and nap times! If you're lucky enough) we hop in and out of these bodies with grace and ease! We hop out and go places and have ongoing relationships! –Oops! Sorry! Jumping ahead. The brain is merely a tool. Thoughts happen with or without it.

Thought travels: The phone rings and you already know who it is before picking it up. You may not have communicated with this person in months or years but the phone rang - you knew it was Marge. You answered the phone and by Jove -Marge was on the other end! "O M G I just KNEW it was you! Isn't that amazing!?!" My Mom always says that, "I JUST thought about you! Wow! Isn't that amazing!?!" Often, I'm like, "no Mom! It's NOT amazing! That's how it works!!" to which she follows with "That's Amazing!" LOL! OMG, my mom is so friggin adorable!

So, how does this happen? Just a clue that thought is independent of the physical bodies we wear. Thought is also... on the move once released. As we are Consciousness, we are also creators of the thought but that thought is not then stuck inside the thinkers head. Once you think the thought, it's out of the closet!

10
Cameos......By Consciousness

Season 2 Episode 9 @ 12:28: Consciousness of Kate's biological father channeled through unconscious Sawyer. Still hovering in the earth realm and most likely locked in due to his anger toward Kate, Wayne took advantage of Sawyers vulnerable state by jumping into his body and using it to express himself to Kate. Clearly he's still in reaction over what happened, "You killed me! Why did you kill me?" Freaked Kate out so bad she forgot she was supposed to push the damn button at 108 minutes - she left the hatch! (LOL)

Season 6 Episode 12 @ 31:00: Hugo channels communication to Richard from his wife who is not in this incarnation. She's moved on - immersed in another life time but her consciousness crossed into their dimension because she knew that Richard needed her and she knew the truth about Locke - that he's NOT Locke. He's now the Black Smoke Jungle Monster guy!

Season 4 Episode 6 @ 4:58: Consciousness of Harper (a blast from Juliet's past when she had an affair with Harpers husband back in the 70s) finds Juliet and forms physically so she can be seen in this dimension as she gives Juliet a helpful message. Jack witnesses this woman before she dissolves before their eyes.

Season 6 Episode 12 @ 3100: Consciousness of Michael responds to Hugo's call and answers questions about the Whispers. Michael also uses this time to apologize to Libby. Understanding that life goes on (lifetime to lifetime) and that Libby is not dead, he knows that Hugo will probably see her again. Michael is also STUCK on the island because of what he did. Meaning; he hasn't forgiven himself. Self-imposed purgatory continues for him.

Season 5 Episode 13 @ 2:01: Consciousness of Dead guy yelling at 8 year old Miles. The man's Spirit - consciousness has left his body because the body died. Now...still in the room but...not in his body, the 'dead guy' is freaking out because he's just crossed. He doesn't really care who hears him, he's just glad to see someone is listening, though be it, a freaked out little kid! Miles is tortured by this!

Season 4 Ep 14 @ 2634 Clare's consciousness goes to Kate while she's sleeping in walk-in dimension and demands that Kate not even consider bringing Aaron back to the Island. "Don't you DARE."

11

It's In The Wind....

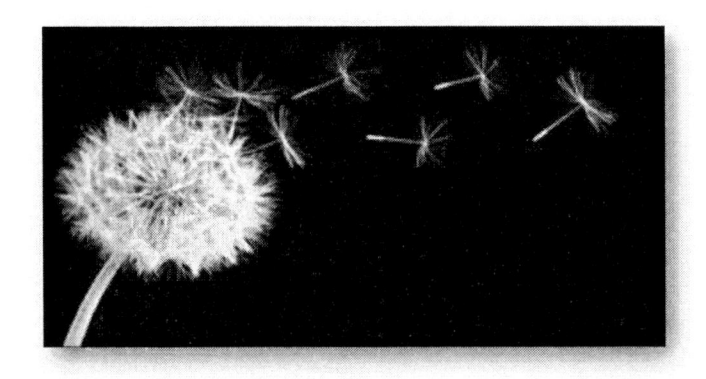

One day in the Doll House I was on the phone interviewing a prospective valet. The questions we ask are pretty standard; Do you know how to drive a manual transmission? If so, how well?! This is an athletic job are you cool with that? Within a few seconds I got a picture (sort of an evening, sun setting silhouette. The humans were like shadows, on a yacht or some sort of large boat, glistening water…) and I just went with it, "I'm getting …water I see a boat and people on it. What's that about?" I asked without missing a beat. Kind of taken aback and maybe realizing this vision I saw was none of my business she said, "oh, just a family outing we're planning this weekend". Realizing I was out of line, I was like, "Oh! Cool! So – we wear black pants, white shirt, running shoes…." I rolled my eyes at myself. OMG I couldn't believe I had done that!
OOPs!!

This was one of our busy hiring spree days. Dozens had responded to our ad. Later that afternoon, I got confused and among my phone calls I accidentally called the same candidate back. "Hey there wondering if you'd be available to start THIS weekend?" "No", she replied, "my families going to Catalina for my Moms birthday, remember?!" I was like, "Oh right! Catalina! That's why I saw the water! Got it!!! Ok, no problem, we can start you the following weekend!" She hung up the phone excited! I, on the other hand was like - whoa! I got that the Universe had me call her back for verification. That always feels good but... I was more intrigued with the fact I hadn't asked for any information on this person. Why was it given to me and most importantly, how can I get on that accurate intuit highway more often?! Like, at will rather than only at random?

Now, I'd had many an intuitive moment. Realizing I had these gifts, at this point in my life, I was consciously honing them. This situation left me feeling I needed an answer. How did this information make it from her mind to mine? I hadn't even met the woman. In channeling class I popped the question before Shawn went into trance. Told her what had occurred with the valet on the phone and asked how this moment of clear clairvoyance came to be. Where did the picture come from?! She explained something pretty simple; There is a "stream of consciousness" that is in constant movement. She used her hands showing me this consciousness is ...one with the air we breathe and it is everywhere, just like the air we breathe! How interesting, a synonym for 'spirit' is 'breath of life'. . . (and in meditation, channeling and mediumship, breathing techniques are important. The ability to connect with higher consciousness and Spirit is greatly in our breathing.)

This truth about consciousness and its way of being is the reason there really aren't any secrets! It's the reason people get busted being sneaky! All the information is out there. DUDE! -You think it's safe within the confines of your body but THAT is an ILLUSION!!! "Be careful what you think!" The consciousness highway is always open. OMG poor Juliet! After mentioning that the only way she could be successful is if her ex-husband were hit by a bus -BAM! (Season 3 Episode 7 @ 28:20) Though he was self-centered and unsupportive if there wasn't personal gain for himself, I don't think Juliet wished him dead. I believe her intuition lead her to make that statement. It was a bummer to watch her go through the guilt and grieving after his bus to body event.

We are ALL built with natural intuitive ability. Whether we have control in exercising it, is the question. I am so clear on this fact about consciousness that the minute I think of a business idea - especially the name - I buy the web site address first, then the trademark, almost simultaneously. After that, I can talk about it!

We are unique expressions of omnipotent perfection...

"And God created man in His own image, in the image of God He created him; male and female He created them." Genesis 1:27

My favorite part of the Bible is the first 2 chapters of the Old Testament; Genesis 1 & 2. That's when this party really got started! I admit...I like the first chapter better than the 2nd cuz in the 1st chapter God created man and woman at the same time, in the same thought. Bam! Man and woman. In the 2nd chapter (which was reportedly written 500 years after the 1st!) God creates man first. Man (Adam) is bored/overworked/under-stimulated - SO to stop his complaining God snatches one of his ribs (HA! That oughta shut him up for a minute) and uses it to create a woman. - Probably a skinny woman. I mean... one rib? Dang! And - he created the female like a friggin afterthought or something! As if woman was created merely to placate the male needs. There's another way to look at it, though. There's man, totally whining and so maybe God gets that...this guy is NOT gonna make it without a female, so he solves the problem by bringing in a woman. But then the woman's destined to deal with this whining guy! Okfinewhatever! - Other than THIS – Genesis is my favorite. I take seriously being made in God's image and I get that it has nothing to do with my beautiful body, my weave, acrylics, lash extensions :) n whatever else I've got goin' on physically!!! That likeness/image would be Spirit… Consciousness. It is in THAT way that we are created the same. And so I love reminding myself and others that we are all, individually 'unique expressions of God' - literally.

Our essence is spirit. When I really began to become one with this fact, I at first felt sort of …'alien'! "I am a Spirit being. …I am a…Spirit Being". I would say it over and over again before I really GOT IT…viscerally.

Part of being in this physical incarnation is being attached (physically) to this body which we use to function in this dimension. But our spirits can and do exist perfectly without these earth suits. And if in another dimension, our spirits can recreate the same (or different) earth suit to wear and use again. For that matter, WHETHER we need a physical body immersed in a physical dimension to live out curriculum is on a case per case, life time per lifetime basis!

In my training to become a Reiki practitioner I learned to view the body as energy rather than just flesh and bone. I studied energy centers, chakras and how the health and well-being of these energy centers are directly related to our physical, psychological & emotional health and wellbeing. These energy centers are part of our energy body which is like an echo of our physical body. Instead of the fleshy organs the physical body has (heart, lungs, spleen, tonsils etc.), the energy body has a plethora of meridians & 'energy centers'. More than 100 energy centers, actually! These energy hot spots are known as 'chakras'. There are 8 chakras that I focus on but the most popular are the first 7 which go from the base of the torso to the top of the head. The 8th Chakra hovers just above the head and is connected to our unconscious which governs our full life script – meaning not just this incarnation but … all of them! – The full blue print – how and why they connect to each other.

Here's one of the keys; while the human physical body can NOT exist without the energy body, the energy body does just fine without a physical body. The energy body is our natural state! And within this energy body is our consciousness. This consciousness is where our personality lies. A wonderful book that breaks this down is 'Anatomy of the Spirit' by Caroline Myss. I highly recommend it. As I often tell Reiki clients "If your spirit body was a car then I'd say it's time you realize you're driving a Lamborghini - NOT a Honda! You have buttons, horsepower n whatnot far beyond what you originally thought. You were most likely raised by people who also mistakenly thought they were driving Hondas. Every body is actually a Spirit charged Lambo!"

Shawn & torah part 1

Get it straight from the horse's mouth is what I kept hearing in the back of my mind as I got started with the pages of this book. I needed info directly from one (or two or three) who is (are) having the experience of cross dimensional existence. Cross dimensional = inter dimensional, okay?! You will hear both terms used as we move forward and even other ways of describing the ability to 'reside', so to speak, in one dimension but commune, with another (this one)!

I shot an email to one of my mentors mentioned earlier, Shawn Randall. I tried to be vague but clear at the same time. "I'm writing a book on multi-dimensional existence. .... May I please interview Torah?!" Shawn was quick with a yes and phone call for clarity.

We set a date for after my trip to Hawaii which she was excited to hear about. She told me about the sacred burial grounds at the Wailea Falls. These grounds are secret for obvious reasons. Knowing that I would journey with the highest respect, she told me how to get there and about this particular ...wall of little caves.

Shawn told me a story about having been there many years ago, back when she felt the energy to climb those walls. She climbed up to one of the caves and went in a couple feet where there were...some BONES! A small pile of them. She thought these must be animal bones. She felt the energy of them and thought it would be cool to take one of the bones to a local healer she knew in the area and have them energetically align the bone so it could be used in healings when she got back to L.A.. Her friend listened to Shawn's story with concern and then to back up her worry she took a look at the bone. "This is a human FEMOR!" she said. - I can't even imagine what that realization must have felt like for ANYone in the room. (And I can't help but think of Season 1 Episode 6 @ 12:59 when Jack and Kate discover the human skeletons in the cave.) Shawn was understandably freaked out and massively remorseful. Her friend told her about the caves and the burial grounds they provide. -How sacred these mountains, walls, caves and bones are and how the Spirits who guard these bones are probably pissed to high heaven! - That didn't scare Shawn, she was determined to right her wrong. So she declared "I'm taking this back".

The next day she returned with an offering which I would later learn was called a '*ho'ukupo*' which means gift. I guess the Spirits didn't know she had a gift for them. The entire way back to the caves she says she was "enthusiastically attacked by mosquitoes"! She climbed the wall again and found the cave where the bone had come from. She put it back. She climbed back down, went into trance and communication with the Spirits there. They were NOT easy about the situation. They ultimately did accept her apology for which she was tremendously grateful. "So beautiful" she said, "to sit there under a Banyan tree and talk with those ancient spirits -while scratching- to express my regret".

I get a strong sense that those mosquitoes were kind of a Black Smoke Jungle Monster thing! I even think the Spirits KNEW her intention was from the heart and that she was

71

coming to make amends but they wanted to give her a little hard time. Their way of saying we forgive you THIS TIME but... *don't do that shit again*!!!'

After telling me about this experience, she says "if you want some interaction with native Spirits of Hawaii, you have to go to this place!"

Shawn was eager for my trip ironically to this same island. "This is going to be a life changing experience. I'm so happy for you, Gillian!" "Wow", I thought..."how did she know that?!" I too, sensed this trip to Hawaii was going to somehow transform me in a way I couldn't yet foresee.

Journal 5

Wed 8-13-14 3:30pm...

Breathing..... I'm simply going to ignore any issues I feel brewing. Like the amount of energy Meredith seems to need from me. She seems to have come back because she likes us WORKING together. That's a JOY thing for her. Problem is, things have changed. I now have two other businesses including Bless & Clear where I'm clearing houses n marrying people left n right. I also have my parents who are older now. And they're lovely and fun! I want to be with them as much as possible. VOTD is an endless kind of business. I agreed to bring her back so that I can be LESS immersed in it, not more!

We've got another big event coming up in Malibu. 250 cars and so the party planner's got to get a permit and in order to get the permit, he's gonna need a parking lot. The city was being difficult. It can't be a 'commercially zoned' lot. Has to be a 'private' lot. We had to figure out the difference.

I was driving to Riverside today - a sacred day off and looking forward to being with my folks. Meredith calls. She's alone in the office and needed some clarity about this Malibu parking operation. I gave her my thoughts and which lot to advise William (the planner) to request and why. I was very thorough but she replied, "do you want me give you the number so YOU can talk to William?" "NO!" I shot back. I was stunned and a bit bothered, "I really DONT." "Ok" she said, "just checking".

Seriously?! I was starting to notice this.... A lack of confidence at handling certain complicated things... Where did THAT come from? Did she have that before? After disconnecting from the call I start talking to myself in the car. Goin' off, "Gosh - I just told you EVERYthing! And THIS is MY (RARE) DAY OFF!!!!! AAAAAND I'm paying you more money than I've EVER paid ANYbody per hour! Did you really just ask me that?!"

I managed to let it go. I got to Riverside and had a good time with my folks. I guess I'm just learning how to set boundaries...

>>>>>>>>>>Huge sigh<<<<<<<<<<<<<<<<<<

Breathing.....
Ignoring this.....
I'm going to Hawaii...

Journal 6

Saturday 8/23/14

OMG so much has happened. Me n my last minute behavior! I love working the law of attraction down to the wire! I scribbled a list of what I wanted in present tense and pictured myself having it as I wrote it: "I am blissful and renting a cozy private house. I have privacy and I'm comfortable and safe. And the price is in my budget, I'm paying less than $250-ish per night. I am close to a jungle and beach like the LOST people! I love the space and it feels like home. I can feel everything – so many sensations and creating is easy. This or something better for the greater good of all concerned".

Glad I did that! O M G! I needed the empowerment of that process as I'd definitely gotten to the 11th hour and learned that pretty much everything in the North Shore was rented this particular week! Energy work, particularly aligning my energy to create at will (Law of Attraction) was helpful. I found one! I found a cute beach house to rent through the 'Ke iki Bungalows' in the North Shore of Oahu. This, even though the Ke Iki Bungalows is sold out! Did I mention, EVERYTHING is sold out?! Lolol!!! (VERY nervous laugh!)

I was on it today! With a fever. Looking for vacation rentals I had gone on the VRBO web site last night and found a bunch of em. By this morning...a bunch of the bunch I'd found were RENTED already!!! HOW DOES THAT HAPPEN?! O M G! And then I had one of those situations where I accidentally called the same place twice. This time, the manager recognized my voice and I told him, "I think my cousins wedding party has rented everything in the North Shore!" He said, "is your cousin Brianna -" I cut him off with a, "Shut UP! - I thought I was exaggerating. O M G! Bri is gonna to be my cousin in-law!!"

With this information he felt motivated to work it out. He thought for a minute then said..."I think I have something for you". He rented me the apartment under the resort owners' house! He figured the owners' not in town that week so... -teehee! I just saw the photos - Star treatment! I am already in heaven! This is exactly what I wanted! - A house. And it's better than I envisioned cuz its RIGHT on the friggin beach! WOW!!! I will spend all my nights there, NONE in Honolulu. I'm from L.A. for heaven's sake. I don't need crowds, lights, cars, clothes, posh spas n whatever else. BOOOORING. Once my plane lands I want to get the heck out of the busy-ness as quickly as possible. *To the Jungle, James!*

On my way to securing this rental I talked to a lady at a Turtle Bay resort. We talked several times. I kept hoping to find something closer to Kieki Beach so delayed on saying yes to them. Then ultimately I called to tell them I'd magically gotten a room at the Kieki

Bungalows. -Hard call to make because they had been SO nice to me. On the phone, she's like, "bummer" and I'm like, "I know but I couldn't help it because it's right where the wedding is gonna be so I can get tipsy and stagger home safely!" :). Then I ask, "did you see LOST?" She's like, "yeah!" I went further, asking if she'd seen *the whole thing down to the last episode* "YES!" she said with definite enthusiasm but her voice was like a whisper as if she was acknowledging another from the secret LOST society! We understood each other! She continued, "You need to do the LOST tour". I gasped aloud! "Oh My God! Shut up! Are you kidding me?" "No there's a LOST tour and it's GREAT you HAVE to take it". I had NO idea! But of course I'm not friggin surprised! But then again I WAS surprised! And relieved. I'm not alone!! Ha! I'm not the only one who is SO incredibly taken with this series! I thanked her profusely and went on line to connect with the LOST Tour! Or I should say 'a' lost tour! There are many! I chose K O S Tours which I found at HummertoursHawaii.com!

Meanwhile, one of our alumni Dolls Joli Forbes reminded me that another alumni Doll, Michelle Moore, has been living in Hawaii for the last several years. I wasn't sure which island she was on so I figured I'd reach out and see if we could connect. We talked today. Turns out she's on a different island. "The Big Island" of Hawaii. Now that I've studied my map, I know what that means and ... I don't wanna island hop since EVERY thing I need and want is on Oahu.

Michelle said she might be able to come to my island instead. That'd be cool and in the meantime, I asked if she knew anyone I could hire to pick me up at the airport and tour me around. I gave her an abbreviated description of my LOST effort and she responded by saying she had yet another person she'd like to connect me with who was in the series! I was like "Shut UP! That'd be awesome!"

A little later Michelle called me back with names and numbers. I talked to both gentlemen. Paul will meet me at the airport Thursday the 28th afternoon, give me a tour and get me to the North Shore. I will meet with Rey after the LOST tour on Friday the 29th and interview him about his experience on the show! Yay!

Hairs done! Got my turquoise and blonde streaks! Got m'nails done violet! Lash extensions – check! Batting them now as I tell you I'm SET!

Computer guy Dave was over today and we have triple checked internet connections - cell phone - lap top - tablet - connections to the office - recording devices - speakers. Lock n load, baby! All needed apps are uploaded and ready to function. I wanted to be ready to channel, interview or supply myself the perfect music for meditation or just writing. I learned how to use my new water & shatter resistant digital camera! Once he was gone, I went about gathering my metaphysical tools which included unloading a few bags if goodies I'd just gotten on a shopping spree at my two favorite tool shops; The Native Spirit Lodge in Woodland Hills and the Aura Shop in Santa Monica. I poured everything out on my healing room floor. I was guided to which stones, which herbs, coal cubes, which singing bowl... chalice's used for incense crystals. The mini plastic baggies of incense look kinda like a drug. Hm... I wondered if this would be an issue getting through airport security! I was mischievously tickled by the possibility as I packed several mini baggies of Myrrh, Frankincense, Cedar, Gum Benzoin and Gum Damar which TOOOOTally looks like either rock cocaine or crystal meth! Lolol! I've got pictures in my head of educating some security person on how to use aroma to adjust their vibration and the benefits of this physically, emotionally, spiritually. I look forward to the bored look on their K-9's faces when they take a whiff of this!

I'm not even sure I'm gonna use everything or how - I just need to have options at my fingertips. I allowed Spirit to guide me through my healing room gathering up energy goodies. Stones of several variety and then a few silk bags in case I wanted to create and gift someone a 'cocktail'. I call it a cocktail because each stone has its own energetic properties and benefits. To consciously combine stones is what I call making an energetic concoction. I love a good cocktail any time of the day! And it is LEGAL to be under the influence of this kind of cocktail - while driving!! :) Aromas are the same, you can cocktail different herbs n whatnot and create a specialized tool!

I'm way more excited today than I was yesterday. In fact it feels like my excitement is growing by the hour. I realize it's just Hawaii... People do this ALLL the time from California but I haven't had a vacation in TWELVE YEARS. Now it's just about the company schedule... The Labor Day week and weekend is light. That's perfect for vacation time for me. But the following week is sold out - meaning; we have too many parties and so far, not enough valets. So the work right now is to close that gap so that when I come back there is no crazy drama!

12

Guys?...What Time Is It?!

Incarnations & sliding doors....
Guidance & consciousness.....

Oooooooooh yeah! I almost don't know where to begin to unravel TIME! In the unraveling, it's my intention to make the 'time elements' of LOST more understandable... plausible...and simple(r). O M G... So there I was - a ritual bag of blue corn chips, deeply immersed in another LOST episode. Everything was cool. I'm LOVING the vibration of the show, the challenges. I'm with them in the efforts. But then... there's a little flashback action in season 3. And then by the time we get to Season 4, my eyebrows were bunched! It took me a minute to figure out whether we're going backwards, forwards or ...sideways. And in truth - I didn't figure it totally out until I watched all 6 seasons for the 2nd time!

Back to C.U.I. for a moment. As mentioned before, LOST originally just a castaway skeleton was also only supposed to be a few seasons long. A few meaning - three! And so it was written; beginning, middle, end. But then they stretched it due to popular demand and a persuasive network, to six seasons. According to reports to stretch it, they started injecting the flashes; forwards, backwards and when they ran out of those - they went sideways! At first I was like, "Whoa - that's weird! And Awesome" and then I realized - "Oh! Sideways is parallel". Well, of COURSE!

With focus on time and 'when were they?' I remembered that all time is happening at once. I wracked my brain to remember where I'd first learned that. Another one of my teachers and influences this lifetime is 'Seth' who was channeled by the late Jane Roberts. Back in the 70s I *attempted* to read one of his first books. It was too much for me then in my young 20s but I gave it a valiant effort and got almost half way through it. I wish I could remember which one it was. I so apologize but I remember the theory of all time happening ...NOW. That stuck with me. And I believe my sub and unconscious minds are much smarter than my conscious one and they are always paying attention!

Seth's teachings work to give validity to the soul and its eternal nature. In picking up his books now, I find the information much simpler! Isn't that interesting?! I just wasn't ready all those years ago. -Evidence to part of the purpose of the 'clock' and how it unfolds and works in this dimension. It makes me think of the moment when Eloise was trying to tell Desmond HE wasn't ready for certain information (Season 3 Episode 8 @ 20:25).

Seth is one of many who attest to TIME NOT being 'chronological'. Like a series of moments. Like if ya pass away in 2015 your next incarnation could be in 2016. That...is not the way it goes!!! It's not a series of minutes like dots connected one AFTER another. In fact, there IS no 'after'! These lifetimes we live are part of the complicated scenarios/ life situations that WE scripted previously to play out now. Yup. We ... created what we're living including the clock perception. So while playing out these lifetimes we believe the clock to be pertinent and real. Believing that was also part of the plan! And the clock is important. -The almighty clock and all its' stress and wrinkle creating deadlines. The clock creates 'stakes'. This is part of the plan WE actually outlined for ourselves! We also, in the planning, pick when, where and under what conditions we want to live out a lifetime of clocked circumstances. But/and there are dimensions where there is life with NO clock perception! Or a *different* clock perception!

So, if lifetimes are not actually one right after another and time doesn't really exist, then, all lifetimes are happening at once. -Simultaneously. Or in *'simultaneum'* as I like to say which I realize is not a dictionary recognized word! *Carpe d'simultaneum!!* :) Ok, sorry!
My all-time favorite metaphor for 'reincarnation' is a flower! Each flower is a person. Each petal on the flower is one of the incarnations we are living. All petals on the flower are alive, NOW.

Understanding then, that all time (past, present, future) is happening in this one moment brings a great deal of simplification to all the time movement in LOST. At the same time, this conversation is not to invalidate time. Again, it is an actual tool that serves a Divine purpose. At the very least, time makes things exciting! The element of 'time' sure made that helicopter crisis much more riveting (Season 4 Episode 14 @ 21:28)! The island had dissa-friggin-peared like the last glimpse of a stone tossed into a pond and they were running out of gas with no place to land. Ahhh yeah! The ol' "running out of time" trick! That scene/situation would have been totally boring without the element of time and the perception of lack thereof! What we experience of the clock is only true in earth dimension and has great purpose here but in the grander scheme of things, time is not real. And in the case of our incarnations, the whole flower is working together for a common cause. You!

You may have heard at some time that in the process of reincarnation, we work certain issues until they are resolved. Then we move on to new issues in new lifetimes all the while evolving as beings. LOST was a great example of people living multiple lifetimes while working on the same issues. -Lifetimes that were very similar with slightly different circumstances, an effort to approach the conundrum from all angles. - We do that. I also have learned that we do lifetimes born under different astrological signs & psychological conditionings so as to approach from new perspectives.

For me personally, I know that in THIS lifetime from which I write, I have lived with glee all the things I judged as absolutely wrong and downright scandalous in a different incarnation where I was a staunch prude! And I know that as a result of my experience and evolution as a spirit in this incarnation, my being-ness has an opportunity to lighten up in that particularly prudish other. Maybe not knowing exactly why but freeing myself (on that other petal) of judgment and its unhealthy consequences going forward.

This is where I ask you to take that flower analogy again and pick a flower for YOURSELF. Feel free to go for the daisy or some other petal plentiful blossom. I've decided to stick with the Garden Pansy. I count 5 petals on this flower. Keeping it simple for less brain explosion! (And I get that there are flowers with less petals, like Cali lilies technically have NO petals -but that REALLY does NOT work for this analogy! Everybody gets many, many petals!)

To make that flower a flower, they (the petals) are all happening (alive) now! Let's be clear, the entire flower is you. Each petal is one of your lifetimes. In the center of the flower where you find the pollen, is your soul. All time is happening ... now. Each petal is alive NOW as is each incarnation in motion, right now. What's happening on one petal affects all the other petals. Each petal is aware of its connection to its soul. The learning and growth are systemic. The soul is connected to the stem which is the connection to the Source of all life. Enlightenment, evolution of any one petal has a positive effect on the life of other petals. Conversely, darkness in one incarnation can affect other incarnations especially other, already 'dim' incarnations. The brighter your light, the less affected you are by darkness. That's the good news; light dissolves dark. Darkness can't even be seen in the presence of light. Ever notice that?! So, the positive experiences and learning in one incarnation play into the evolution and even surprise victories you're experiencing in another. All petals in action, simultaneously! All time is happening now.

From the center, our Soul, they (your incarnations) bloom & then, they thrive! And there is communication…relationship between that flower and the earth, symbolic of our Source. All flowers are connected to Source. The experience of one flower plays into the experience of other flowers as a community. . . Okay, now - let's not get to plucked and wilting flowers yet! Lol! Let's stay with the vision of a bloom full of life!

LOST only showed us two or three petals per character. And some of the incarnations were exactly the same until a fork in the road of events or... the 'sliding door' as I like to call it. 'Sliding Doors' (1998) is also the title of a great movie about this same subject, by the way! Change one event and watch the new outcome unfold.

Watching LOST twice, helped me tremendously to un-tick the tock. They weren't just moving backwards and forwards within one incarnation, they were sometimes moving to different incarnations all together!! What an awesome opportunity to experience this kind of reality through the LOST story. Please know that not only are all incarnations happening congruently with all petals alive simultaneously but…there's also life BETWEEN the petals, as well. Non-physical states of…learning, preparation and decision.

And most of our incarnations are dealing with the same issues. The sooner we heal an issue in any one of our incarnations the enlightenment is multi-dimensional so that all of our selves benefit. Just like my prudish other petal benefits from the free spirited petal from which I write this book.

Follow me for a moment; I'm talking about reincarnation. I'm talking about 'time' being an illusion. It's a tool. It provides us a beginning, middle, end. Fade in - fade out. How much time do we have?! As if it matters! - Well, yeah, cuz in this dimension it does matter! A lot!

I remember going to see a Spirit Counselor once. Michael Hayes is known as 'the counselor's counselor'! Professionals from all over the world make the trip to see him at his office in the Palisades above Malibu California. He's amazing, incredibly intuitive and clairvoyant. While he could see some of my other incarnations and their themes he wouldn't share much of that information with me. He said if he did I would focus there (instead of HERE). Did I mention he costs about $6 a minute??? I had a lot of other questions and REALLY wanted to be done in half an hour so…I let it go!

Rev. Gillian V. Harris M.S.P.

Back in 1986, after reading 'Dancing in the Light' by Shirley MacLaine I was inspired to travel to Galesteo New Mexico for my first experience with *past life recall* work (which we now know should be called 'other life recall') at a really cool place called the Light Institute. I know from that experience where I explored three separate incarnations (I saw myself in lives as a Japanese woman, a Swedish mountain climber guy and an African Tribe Leader), that in this kind of exploration we will only get information from segments of those other life petals that are relevant to the incarnation we're living HERE, NOW. A few decades later I now also get two more points 1) I trust the process of systemic learning for the greater good of my whole self. 2) The best thing I can do on behalf of my selves everywhere is focus on THIS incarnation and my purpose in it RIGHT HERE, right NOW.

Taking in all our lifetimes at once is not necessarily productive. Further, while in this human experience, simultaneously taking in other lifetimes can be disorienting and psychologically disturbing if not downright dangerous if there is no psychological or spiritual anchor. Luckily I had an anchor and solution when I was a kid. And I remember the moment. I'd just had another episode. I walked into the house and as I headed down the hall toward my bedroom I prayed "God please stop that from happening. Amen". With 100%, unwavering faith in the power of prayer, I let it go with the Amen. The episodes of leaving this incarnation to 'visit' another and then returning all dumbfounded n whatnot stopped in that moment. Thank goodness. I wasn't ready for these cross dimensional travels! I didn't get it and it was really weirding me out. I don't really need to search much deeper for words to more clearly describe this. LOST did that for me. LOOK at what poor Desmond is going through Season 3 episode @ 8 11:21. DUDE! That was INSANE!!!!!!

There's a reason for the 'veil', the separation. There's a reason we don't, on a regular basis, bounce back and forth between dimensions and lifetime petals. It would be counter-productive! That is, unless, the bounce back is for the purpose of healing. Like the little kid James Leininger who made the news as a little boy when he started remembering/re-living another incarnation where he is an Air Force Pilot. As I type this book, these links still work: http://www.flixxy.com/world-war-ii-fighter-pilot-reincarnation.htm tells the story when James was a little boy and the amazing facts that solidified that he had done at least one other incarnation with the name, James. He was remembering his agonizing last moments of life as a downed Air Force pilot, James Houston, who died in a fiery crash. As a toddler little James Leininger was able to name the ship, the Natoma. When looking at a picture of the crew, he could name the individuals by their faces! He was able to tell them that his plane went down in the water off Chichijima. His parents asked, "Who shot down your plane?" They said he looked at them like they were dumber than dumb and exclaimed "THE JAPANESE", like DUH! – Um… What Toddler knows this kind of stuff?! He was being awakened in the middle of the night by nightmares of still being trapped in the cockpit of the burning plane and not being able to get out.

Ultimately, young James MET his sister from that other incarnation. Technically, it was James Houston's sister. She was in her 80s now. But little James Leininger said things and remembered things that only her brother would know and remember. She called it "too amazing to describe". Her brother who had been killed as an Air Force pilot was standing before her as a little boy in a new incarnation, RIGHT before her very eyes! This younger James pointed out to everyone the spot where his plane went down. This location was verified. And on a boat in the waters that had taken his life in World War II, he now got to make peace… through an emotional purging that seemed to heal him and set him free. His peace, never disturbed by the memory again. After you watch the first video, watch this one: https://www.youtube.com/watch?v=I9u2EpK35PY . This is also a great piece because it's a story of him more recently as a young adult. It seemed that much of the healing came in realizing that he didn't die in that plane, after all. Life continues. And the bigger picture is that the Universe used his story to share with the world the fact that incarnations may end but WE do not. His parents Andrea and Bruce Leininger wrote a book about it 'Soul Survivor'. I haven't read it yet, but it's on my list! :)

Back to C.U.I (Creating Under the Influence) and my contention that the writers of LOST got help from multi-dimensional connections and sources; there's the possibility (probability) that at least part of the influence that changed the scripted plan was drawn from the writers own connection with their unconscious. This would be the part of their selves that is aware of their ENTIRE flower and ALL its petals- as well as the life happening without a body, BETWEEN and around the petals. It is not only aware of these lifetimes but the unconscious is clear of our whole life blueprint and its purpose(s). - How and why the pieces come together. The unconscious gets how each of the petals fit, how they accent each other to make the perfect flower.

Ok, so there's THAT. But there are also other multi-dimensional or cross-dimensional connections … more of the 'unseen' that comes into our field and (at our sub or unconscious invitation) guides us. A lot of this communication can happen in the dream state when we are most relaxed and open to these experiences and learning. Much of what we get in dream time is directly related to our other incarnations we ARE experiencing on other life petals. What we see we are given to learn from. And in fact if you're curious about what incarnation you might live 'next' your dreams can be a great place to look.

I remember being in a dream once - I was standing in a living room by a stone fire place. A man was sitting on the couch. There were others there but the main thing is I woke with vivid memory of this dream, the darkness of the situation and the man on the couch who I recognized as a really good friend from this incarnation. But in the dream I didn't recognize or know him! And I didn't know the other two men in the room either. They were all being really nice to me because of the guy on the couch. Because of him, they trusted me. That's good because I got the feeling they were 'bad guys'. Yeah... A little scandal on another petal!

I can rarely remember my dreams, how 'bout you?! Usually, I'm brushing my teeth when I have a vague memory but by then, it's too late to grasp all the details. I have a suspicion that the brain does something to filter the logic out of our dreams! While in it, we can grasp bottom lines and knowingness! But once awake, we miss what was so profound and are left with fragments that make no sense!

Knowing the importance of dreams and with commitment to fully embrace the learning, I sleep with a note pad by my bed. The challenge is to grab the pen and write - despite my fatigue in that newly awakening moment! It also helps to set a clear intention a bedtime. Bedtime intentions are powerful. If you pray or meditate before bed also ask or intend that you be taught and enlightened during your dream time. Add a request that you are able to retain the information upon waking. "That or something better ...for the greater good" so you don't block any blessings! For me, my prayer is gratitude (like, in advance) for being taught and for helping me to retain what I need to long enough to jot it down! My effort to remember my dreams goes a lot better when I consciously go through the motion to communicate with Spirit to set my bedtime intentions! The good news is, we don't have to 'consciously' remember what that dream was about to have learned from the experience it provided and be inspired into action by it! And so, what we live in our dreams can actually build/create the life we experience when we're awake.

In our dreams we are deeply immersed in our other lifetimes. We also have friends and associates with whom we commune and bond with during sleep time, on the regular! These relationships are often helpful at the time of our transitions. We also have what I'll call 'off the petal' non-physical experiences with guides during 'non-incarnation' periods. And often our experiences there bleed over to affect life in a physical incarnation. It's kinda like subliminal influence...- You're getting guidance but not from a written manuscript or audio tape. It's Meta (outside of) Physical. - When I say subliminal I don't mean anything negative - like sneaky commercial advertising. I simply mean that the information is being received on a level that is - unconscious - hidden by the veil - concealed by the illusion of separateness between this dimension and ...another.

13

Petal Hopping

"When one has been born and has died many times, expecting extinction with each death, and when the experience is followed by the realization that existence still continues, then a sense of the divine comedy enters in."
Seth
(Jane Roberts, 'Seth Speaks')

Seth teaches that reincarnation isn't really a series of progressions as 'time' would lead you to see it. "Instead", he writes, "the various lives grow out of what your inner self is". He's talking present tense. The growth we experience today enhances our other incarnations. Seth teaches that our incarnations are "a material development, as your consciousness opens up and expresses itself in as many ways as possible. It is not restricted to one three-dimensional lifetime, nor is it restricted to three-dimensional existence alone". That last part makes me think of the Jungle Monster.....who definitely had ways of expressing himself out of body - bending trees n stuff.... And in non TV examples (!) it reminds me of people who have formed and dissolved in front of me repeatedly over the years! Those people...and even the ones who can communicate with me without showing my physical eyes ANY thing!

So, on top of getting in harmony with seeing life as 'eternal' and seeing that we are *eternal* Spirit beings having a brief human experience, we kind of need to let go of identifying ourselves with these human bodies. I mean, they're cool n everything but truth is, if we identify with them, we miss the point of what we are. We are not our bodies. We simply use them to play out our time in Life School located in this dimension.

"Not until we are lost do we begin to understand ourselves"
Henry David Thoreau

Petal to petal....

In completely separate but parallel petals Charlie's lifetimes are shown to us with a 'sliding door'. The plane NOT crashing is the shift in the two incarnations. We see that Charlie was bound to deal with his addiction issue regardless of whether the plane went down. Either he'd do it ...'holistically' on the island with Locke as his guidance counselor (Season 2 Episode12 @ 35:51) or he'd do it through the U.S. Criminal Justice system (Season 6 Episode 1 @ 40:16) which didn't solve it for him like Locke did in the crash incarnation. Notice in the non-crash scenario, Charlie is STILL messed up all the way to where Hurley goes to pick him up for 'the concert' (Season 6 episode 17 @ 9:27)

Get ready for quite a ride. What I'm about to unravel here is probably the most exciting part of the LOST series. The portrayal of lifetimes and ESPECIALLY the moments that were used by the characters later to revisit as part of terminal lucidity! What?! Yes! And THEN there are parts that can only be explained as 'walk-ins'. Angels do it all the time. Some of these angels and others, take total physical human form when they walk into a dimension, an incarnation that is already at play. To be clear, they walk in as children or adults not newborns. In fact, in the incarnation where they walked in - they may have never been a baby... Follow me here as we do a little petal hopping and know that shortly thereafter, we'll talk with Lori Board Camacho about 'Walk-ins'...

The petals of John Locke

I saw two lifetimes portrayed for John Locke. 1) Oceanic crashes. 2) Oceanic doesn't crash. Both of these are individual lifetimes.

Incarnation one:

Orphaned at birth by a rebellious teenage mom (Season 4 Ep 11 @ 00:18 & Season 4 Episode 11 @ 9:39). He has a tough childhood in foster care (Season 4 Episode 11 @ 12:34) and as he grows older, people peg him with an identity of a nerd/geek/math wizard (Season 4 Episode 11 @ 22:45). As a book he was being judged by its cover. He hated that because he knew he was a sportsman at heart.

Locke grows up to live alone in a one room apartment (Season1 Episode 4 @ 26:34). He's a salesman at a box company (Season 1 Episode 4 @ 9:22). His Dad scams him into giving up a kidney (Season 1 Episode 19 @ 28:00). His subsequent victimization and then obsession with his Dad causes his girlfriend Helen to break up with him (Season 2 Episode 17 @ 33:31). Then - his Dad shoves him out a high-rise window (Season 3, Episode 13 @ 36:01) and now he's a paraplegic thanks to Jacob saving him (Season 5 Episode 17 @ 21:32) or his body would have died after hitting the ground (as his Dad intended). But Jacob needed Locke to be alive so he could take that plane flight and crash on the island. So - Locke lives and takes his boy scout know how to a whole other level as he prepares, from his wheel chair, for a walk about.

I took a look at Wikipedia and was so intrigued to see Locke's personality defined in the definition of a walkabout! I gathered from their description that walkabouts can be a rite of passage for young people who live in the wilderness for a period of as long as 6 months. But others do walkabouts, too. As the balding Locke desired, with every step of the walkabout would be a deepening journey inward. Wikipedia says, "…in this practice they would trace the paths their ancestors took and imitate, in a fashion, their heroic deeds". Locke prepared and mastered some of these heroic deeds with a collection of 400 shiny knives that caused many a LOST soul's jaw to drop right there on the sand! (Season 1 Episode 4 @ 7:35) Wikipedia continues, with text regarding the perspective of what it defines as white employers who's workers would want to depart without notice (and reappear just as suddenly) as something inherent in this walk-a-bout, practice as "mundane" - like they didn't respect or value it. And that workers who needed this time "did not accept employers control over such matters (especially since permission was generally hard to get)." That was Locke. That dufeless boss of his would have never supported Locke's true intentions. He clearly had been subconsciously preparing for the walk about long before ending up in a wheelchair. He knew everything there was to know down to how to make a whistle out of jungle twigs (Season1 Episode 3 @ 26:20) and what to do when you've found yourself standing on a beehive (Season 1 Episode 6 @ 8:15).

Sent to Australia for a box industry conference, he decided this is it. He purchased his pass for a walkabout to take once he got there (Season1, Episode 4 @ 20:20). Before getting on the plane for Australia, he shared the news with his pay per minute 1-900 friend fictitiously named after his ex GF "Helen" -that he's going to Australia to do a walkabout (Season1 Episode 4 @ 26:34). She rejects his invitation to come along (season 1 Episode 4 @ 27:16) reminding him he's just a "customer". He's very hurt. He goes alone. He's rejected by the walk-about tour people (Season 1, Episode 4 @ 39.27). Luckily (!?), on his way back to L.A., Flight 815 crashes (Season 1 Episode 4 Opening Scene and @ 40:40). Locke now proceeds to do the Mac Daddy of all walkabouts!

Coached by the Black Smoke Jungle Monster who is parading as Christian at the time (Season 5 Episode 5 @ 34:43), Locke eventually leaves the island through a portal created by turning the dial in the center of the island (season 5, Episode7 @ 14:32) and goes on a mission to bring the Oceanic 6 back to the island (season 5 Episode 7 @ 12:05). Pretty much everybody tells him "no" (Kate- Season 5, Episode 7 @ 25:22 / Sayid - Season 5, Episode 7 @ 17:02). Then he learns that Helen (the real one) had transitioned while he was on the island (Season 5 Episode 7 @ 27:40). Bad trip, yo!

He'd been told he needed to die in order to get the Oceanic 6 back to the island. He didn't realize the Black Smoke Jungle Monster had eyes on using his body and character to dupe the others. Locke needs to vacate the body (die) in order for Mr. Black Smoke to use it! Not knowing this detail and having failed at convincing the others to return to the island, he decides to commit suicide (Season 5 Episode7 @ 3:33) but in the nick of time Ben stops him (Season 5 Episode 7 @ 3545). A few minutes later, Ben murders him! (Season 5, Episode 7 @ 40:41). Wait, what?!

Incarnation two - a sliding door of incarnation one:
(The Sliding door/shift of events starts with Locke NOT being an orphan and his
Dad is a good guy! Father and son have a healthy, loving relationship):
Locke is in a happier existence. He's a paraplegic but it was caused by a self- inflicted accident rather than attempted homicide on his life! He works for the same box company with the same knucklehead boss (Season 1 Episode 4 @ 20:01). He goes to industry conference in Australia

but ditches it to instead live out his new but deep passion to do a Walkabout. He gets rejected by the walkabout people (Season 1 Episode 4 @ 39:26) because he forgot to mention, he can't walk...let alone walkabout. The plane back to L.A. does NOT crash. Airline misplaces Locke's suitcase of 400 knives! He meets Jack (Season 6, Episode 2 @ 35:50) in Lost Luggage. He comes home to his fiancé Helen (Season 6 Episode 4 @ 2:21). They live in a big house (Season 6 Episode 4 @ 1:18). Locke gets fired for not actually attending the conference while in Australia (Season 6 Episode 4 @ 6:03).

On the way out of the building in a temper tantrum over parking spaces, he meets Hurley (Season 6 Episode 4 @ 14:56). Through Hurley he meets Rose (Season 6 Episode 4 @ 21:33). Through Rose, Locke becomes a substitute teacher and meets Ben (Season 6 Episode 4 @ 37:34)! He also meets the guy who blew up (as in C4, as in KaBOOM!) in one of the funniest LOST moments ever (Season 1, Episode 24 @ 8:19)! Why did that make me laugh so hard??! LOL again!

We learn that in this incarnation, Locke was paralyzed in a plane crash but this time HE was the pilot (season 6 Episode 14 @ 37:42). His father was a passenger. His father is left a vegetable in this accident (Season 6 Episode 14 @ 13:49). (Before you decide that was a karmic giggle you gotta figure out which incarnation happened first! -Oh yeah, there is no first! They both happened simultaneously! Hm...) Helen and a slew of coincidences convince him to let Jack perform spinal surgery (Season 6 Episode 19 @ 28:42).

Sliding door three (Because Lock is transitioning from an incarnation)

The scene of John Locke working as a substitute teacher after being fired by the knucklehead boss at the box company is not only something he lived but it is something he is revisiting as he transitioned from one life to another. This had been another incarnation where Locke's life was focused on not being able to use his legs. After leaving his body and crossing over, Locke enters a dimension that is like a....holding area. It's space between the life petals. Many, at this time are focused on the life they were living prior to their 'death'. Locke is doing the same. He is focused on the incarnation where, out of desperation, he was working as a substitute teach and he was stuck there. Desmond nudged him along by hitting him with his car! He said he was trying to help Locke "let go". BAM! (Season 6 Episode 12 @ 40:22) Desmond drove right into Locke's wheelchair, putting him in the hospital and under the care of Jack (who we learn later, is also crossing in this scene). Locke stayed stuck for a while but then decided to allow Jack to do surgery to regain use of his legs. This is an in-between life that MAY be reflective of what he experienced in an incarnation (where surgery brought back use of his legs) or it is a life setting in this in-between dimension, where Locke is having an opportunity to do this healing symbolic of his 'letting go' before moving on so he doesn't have to do this wheelchair life existence again.

Locke comes out of surgery (Season 6 Episode 17 @ 57:37) and after seeing the flashbacks to a different dimension - on the island, he not only remembers life in the jungle with Jack

Rev. Gillian V. Harris M.S.P.

but he knows where he is. He knows where he is and he knows that Jack is in this post life with him. He tries to get out of bed realizing its time to "go" and asks Jack if he'll come with him! Jack, also in an in-between dimension, doesn't know it and thinks Locke is delusional! In the incarnation on the island, Jack didn't have a son. Locke didn't know that Jack had other incarnations including one with a wonderful son named David.

Quick tangent:
LET'S TALK DEJA VU:

I just saw a definition which basically tells us everything we all, already know. A Déjà vu is a moment when things feel like a rerun! They feel previously visited, previously seen or done. "I've been here before". Here's the thing, this particular definition said basically that a Déjà vu is a moment when you've got the strong feeling an event or something you're going through at the current moment, has actually happened in the past. You have this strong knowingness - "regardless of whether it has actually happened". I say com PLETE ly ignore the "regardless of whether" part! That's denial! That's not wanting to explain because it's....complicated! Déjà vu's are deja vu's because they DID happen. Maybe in the future or in a parallel lifetime and we knew intuitively or we experienced it during dream time (which also could be a reflection of a parallel life).

If you have a Déjà vu moment, trust that it HAS happened and that's why you're remembering it. That's WHY you're having such a strong memory sensation! The other thing to remember is that it might have happened on a completely different life petal... OR it could be the current life petal but is a blast from the future! A bleed over, as, all time is happening now.

The petals of James Le Fleur
A.K.A. Sawyer

Sawyer is an awesome example of using more than one lifetime to resolve the same issue. Lucky for James, he reached his resolution while on the island.

One lifetime he's a conman, just like the man who conned his dad (Season 2 Episode 13 @ 5:05). Conman Sawyer is the one who ended up on the island on crashed flight 815. He is expressing the pain of his parent's fate by becoming a bad guy just like the guy who drove his dad to the murder suicide (Season 1 Episode 16 @ 1:11). It was called the Long Con when he gets someone to think it's THEIR idea to do something - like give him money! He does the con on his girlfriend. (Season 2 Episode 13 @ 33:34) He goes to Australia and shoots the wrong guy (Season 1 Episode 16 @ 36:09) then the plane back crashes on the island. He even does the con on the island (Season 2 Episode 13 - the whole thing!) but for the greater good, of course! :) He hooks up with Kate but messes it up in his fear of commitment. Kate leaves. Years move forward, back, forward, back a little less and along the way Sawyer finds inner resolve regarding his biggest demon which was hurt from watching his Dad kill his Mom and then himself (Season 5 Episode 17 @ 4:09). Part of his inner peace meant he could now love and be loved and so he expresses that in a beautiful relationship with his Soul mate Juliet (Season 5 Episode 8 @ 36:12).

Next Incarnation is a Sliding Door of the first: In another lifetime, the shift is that Sawyer expresses his intention to right the wrong done his family by becoming a cop. He boards Oceanic flight 815 as a cop. The presentation of these lifetimes in LOST gave the illusion that the plane not crashing changed Sawyers rap sheet from long to clear with an LAPD badge attached but that wasn't it. Those were two different incarnations.

In both of these incarnations, Sawyer is working on the same issue; finding resolve and inner peace in the face of the horrible wrongs done his parents by a con man. In both lifetimes, he goes to Australia and shoots the wrong guy. He shoots another victim, just like his Dad (Season 1 Episode 16 @ 36:09). In this other incarnation he flies back to L.A. and the plane doesn't crash (Season 6 Episode 1 @ 13:25). His partner is Miles (Season 5 Episode 8 @ 21:10). He helps Kate in the airport elevator, knowing she's in hand cuffs (Season 6 Episode 2 @ 9:38) probably because of the same kind of multi-dimensional information sharing that happened when Sayid didn't shoot Jin who was tied up in that storage room (Season 6 Episode 6 @ 31:31). Then Kate has another car chase gone bad as she crashes into Sawyers police car and he arrests her (Season 6 Episode 8 @ 39:58). At the hospital on a case or something, he happens by a vending machine (Season 6 Episode 17 @ 1:07:45). Touch over a candy bar triggers flashbacks - (Season 6 Episode 17 @ 1:09:13) as he is reunited with Juliet.

Rev. Gillian V. Harris M.S.P.

Petal to petal
(Terminal) lucidity...

Jack dropped the bomb (Season 5 Episode 17 @ 29:02) that Juliet ultimately got to detonate (Season 5 Episode 17 @ 41:31) but that only affected Flight 815 not crashing on a parallel life petal. For their current incarnation, the bomb finally exploding was merely an *incident* that didn't *fix* their current plight as the conditions that brought Oceanic flight 815 down had already happened. For the parallel existence in which a different incarnation was being played out, the explosion created new circumstances so that the "electromagnetic anomaly" did not occur again to bring the Oceanic plane tumbling from the skies into the jungle on that parallel lifetime. So in THAT case, the bomb explosion worked but it didn't CHANGE what had already happened in the incarnation they were already experiencing.

The important part is, while they were still in their conundrum with Juliet just moments from dying in James' arms, the action there in that present tense sent out consequences - some of them beautiful, for the other incarnations they were living. Juliet had just had a bit of a romantic temper tantrum as she doubted James' love for her (Season 5 Episode 17 @ 10:18)! Minutes later he's giving his everything to save her life and there is no question of their undying love for each other (Season 5 Episode 17 @ 31:45). Everything we do here, right now, affects future moments. -Even future moments in other incarnations. Other incarnations happening simultaneously in other dimensions means future moments...aren't really in the future, are they?!

That task (getting the bomb to explode for the reasons they wanted it to) was part of their life curriculum. Jack trying to fix one more thing and sweet Juliet again swept up in victimizing circumstance one more time.

Down in the well, under the rubble, Juliet ran out of breath trying to tell Sawyer *it worked* (Season 6 Episode 2 @ 10:45), meaning, the plane didn't crash. But notice how life continued on the island. To Sawyer, Jack, Kat, Hurley and the others still there - the plane had still crashed!! Juliet noticed this too and while in Sawyers arms explained that her intention was he never came to this wretched place. But there they were, still in this situation - another day in paradise! What had already happened had already happened and was... always happening!

But then... a little later, as she is half in her body and half out, with her last breath Juliet was revealing dialogue from a life she was fully living - a separate incarnation. Clarity: she was channeling from that other incarnation. She had one foot on the other side where she was living on another petal and she was channeling what was real from that incarnation into her present one. -Two incarnations were present tense for her, in that moment! She was saying her lines from the other incarnation "maybe we should do coffee", but doing so while in this present incarnation (Season 6, Episode 1 @ 3526). Where (the dimension) Juliet was coming from,

Jack and Kate didn't know each other and Juliet and Sawyer met at a hospital vending machine (Season 6 Episode 17 @ 1:07:45) -life was totally different. And there it is again - terminal lucidity! In the midst of crossing, Juliet clearly saw the truth. At a glance what we saw indicated she was leaving Sawyer because her body was dying. But as we continue to watch we see that she never actually left him. She joined him in another incarnation at a hospital vending machine! Their separation was an illusion as all separations are…

Petals of kate
INCARNATION 1:
The breakup between her mother and the military man she thought was her father was devastating for Kate. (Season 2 Episode 9 @ 32:27) Not knowing that he had begged to be allowed to take her with him, she felt abandoned. And then, her mom consciously chooses this alcoholic, violent, disrespectful, unruly man as a partner to love unconditionally. Upon learning this mean, drunken man was her biological father Kate tucked him into bed one night then blew up his house!

Caught by the law (Season 1 Episode 3 @ 31:44), Kate boards Flight 815 and crashes on the LOST Island. She heals her inner pain with her biological father (Season 2 Episode 9 @ 36:04). Crosses dimensions (walk in) back to previous incarnation with baby Aaron (Season 4 Ep14 @ 27:59). Deals with the court on her charges (Season 4 Ep 4 @ 4:21) fraud, arson, assault on federal officer and assault with deadly weapon, grand larceny, grand theft auto and murder in the 1st degree. (Phew!) She actualizes relationship with Jack (Season 4 Ep 10 @ 1:51). Jack starts flipping out (Season 4, Ep 10 @ 29:29 + 33:25) so Kate breaks up with him. She gives Aaron to his grandmother (Clare's mom) (Season 5 Ep 11 @ 34:45). She goes back to the island (Season 5 Ep 6 @ 28:14).

She gets rescued (Season 6 Episode 17 @ 1:22:29) again…leaving Jack behind, never to see him again in that particular incarnation.

INCARNATION 2 is a sliding door of incarnation 1;
Everything is the same in this incarnation for Kate, except Flight 815 doesn't crash. The guy who winks at her on the plane is not conman Sawyer, he's a cop going by his same first name, different last; James Ford. She gets away from the Marshall who suffered a pretty bad head wound (Season 6 Episode 2 @ 749). Seems he was bound to get bonked on the head (Season 1, Episode 2 @ 33:03) regardless of flight 815's well-being. I thought that injury in the ladies bathroom would take him out but minutes later (Season 6 Episode 2 @ 27:03) he was chasing Kate's cab! Regardless of the crash, Kate is bound to be friends with Clare (Season 6 episode 3 @ 37:17). She ends up in a car chase and gets caught by Sawyer (James Ford) (Season 6 Episode 8 @ 28:14). Goes to jail.

Rev. Gillian V. Harris M.S.P.

What happens when your body dies:

Now - we don't really know what happened after this in THAT incarnation, for Kate. But ultimately...sometime after that...maybe decades later she transitioned. Kate had a way of being athletic no matter what her life situation. From the city to the jungle she was very cardiovascular-ly fit. Let's say she's 93 years old and she's ending an incarnation. In her transition she is fixated on the very exciting running/getting away chapter of one of her lives, possibly in a different incarnation than the one she is finishing. Let's be clear - getting captured by Sawyer DID happen but not necessarily in the incarnation from whence she's seeing and experiencing it. None the less, she's laying there, in hospice care. Her vitals are low. Breathing is shallow and suddenly she says "You don't look like a cop" (Season 6 episode 16 @ 37:37). The nurse in her room shrugs it off. At this point, she is then channeling through her physical 93 year old body what she IS LIVING on a different life petal. Soon, she will slip from her physical body at 93, and become present in a familiar moment. For Kate, this was a jail cell! So there she was, laying on a cot (season 6 episode 16 @ 14:15). She's now is an 'in-between life' or dimension.

And in comes her Gate Keeper Desmond! Here to help guide her safely across. Sayid is in a similar situation, coincidentally crossing at the same time as Kate (because there IS no time!). In THIS dimension Kate and Sayid - who don't know they know each other, are joined by the consciousness of a few friends; Hurley, Desmond and Ana Lucia for the beginning of the journey across the veil (Season 6 Episode 16 @ 39:10). Desmond and Hurley are working hard as guides to assist everyone safely across without distraction. As you can see, this particular in-between dimension is full of potential distractions. Ana Lucia is loving the distractions! She has not completed her crossing. She took part in helping Kate and Sayid across in exchange for a fat sum of cash (season 6 episode 16 @ 39:03) :) ! Ya know how they say "you can't take it with you?" Well, Hurley took his millions with him! And he gave some to Ana Lucia!!! Notice that Kate doesn't know Desmond, Sayid or Ana Lucia. Ana Lucia only seems to know Desmond, with whom she's made deal for Hurley's money! Desmond and Hurley are the only ones who really get the whole thing! Notice how at peace and happy they are! Notice how anxious they are to share the joy!

My Aunt Jean wasn't sure who those beings were she was seeing, the ones who were there to guide her across. I'm sure they eventually revealed themselves to her in blissful memory and realization! Regardless of this, there is a knowingness that you can trust. Kate and Desmond weren't all that close on the island but my guess is in another incarnation, they had been. You never know what the scenario may have been. And so, she ultimately trusted him - taking a ride with a strange man who handed her a very short black cocktail dress! (Season 6 Episode 16 @ 40:24)! Along the way, Kate grew to understand where she was. With this new knowledge... she would meet her friend/soul mate Jack. It almost seems she was waiting for him on the grounds of the concert...

Petals of dr. Jack shepard

INCARNATION 1 - He has tough childhood with alcoholic father, Christian (Season 1 Episode 5 @ 10:51). He grew up to be an alcoholic, pill poppin' surgeon, (Season 4 Episode 10 @ 31:05) like his Dad. I mean…he'd experienced Flight 815 and had been to the island and back but, under the right conditions, he and his dad mirrored each other (Season 2 Episode 11 @ 18:18). Jack is married to Sarah (Season 2 Episode 11 @ 10:23). Sarah divorces him (Season 2 Episode 11 @ 38:24). Jack outs his Dad to the medical board, in the death of a patient (Season 1 Episode 11 @ 31:12). No longer licensed to practice medicine, Christian goes to Australia and drinks himself to death (Season 2 Episode 20 @ 20:15). Jack goes to Australia to claim the body (Season 1 Episode 5 @ 31:18). On the way back Flight 815 crashes on the island (Season 1 Episode 1 @ 23:09). Jack is rescued from the island (Season 4 Episode 13 @ 30:14). Fully engages romantic relationship with Kate (Season 4 Ep 10 @ 23:35). Does the memorial for his Dad and meets Clare's miraculous coma-marathon mom. (Season 4 Ep 12 @ 34:43). The fact this woman is standing remains phenomena to me! But let's move on with Jack! Soon, Island memories wig him out, "we shouldn't have lied". He drinks and uses (Season 3 Ep 22 @28:30). This is where he seriously becomes an alcoholic, pill poppin' surgeon just like his dad. Charges of substance abuse gets Jack banned from the hospital (like his Dad) (Season 5 Episode 4 @ 12:33). He boards a multitude of planes hoping one will crash like flight 815 did (Season 3 Episode 22 @ 1:26). He tests fate, not wearing a seat belt! The planes don't crash. His fiancé, Kate, breaks up with him over his using and flipped out way of being (Season 4 Episode 10 @ 3650). Through a turn of events he goes back to the island (Season 5 Episode 6 @ 00:37). He's still there and deeply wrapped up in the misidentification that he is the fixer. He needs to fix the troubles there on the island (Season 6 Episode 16 @ 34:52). He's saving everyone. And in this incarnation he is chock full of perfect circumstances within which he can give his everything to the cause (Season 6 Episode 17 @ 1:21:35). As he lays on his back in the jungle next to Vincent, he sees the Aljira plane fly overhead carrying his friends and a soul mate, Kate, safely off the island (Season 6 Episode 17 @ 1:43:46). He smiles inside and out as he knows his mission is accomplished. He saved them. He DOES have what it takes. He can close his eyes now . . . and cross again… (Season 6 Episode 17 @ 1:42:41).

INCARNATION 2 is a SLIDING DOOR of incarnation 1 - The sliding door/shift is he's married to Juliet this time and they have a son and divorce (Season 6, Episode 17 @ 28:10). He is still the adult survivor of a challenging childhood with alcoholic father, Christian (Season 1 Episode 5 @ 10:50). He still grows up to be a surgeon, like his Dad. Christian goes to Australia to see his secret daughter, Clare (Season 3 Episode 12 @ 2359). Clare's mother is on life support and comatose after a terrible car accident in which Clare was driving while raging at her mom. So she is guilt ridden because the last words her mom heard her say were wicked! As a doctor Christian feels certain that her mothers' physical incarnation is over (Season 3 Episode

12 @ 29:47). He tries to advise Clare. She rejects him. He dies in Australia, his body found in an alley with a very high blood alcohol level which probably lead to his cardiac arrest (Season 1 Episode 5 @ 31:05).

Jack goes to Australia to claim the body. Jack returns to do the memorial for his dad. Christian's body is misplaced in this incarnation, as well (Season 6 episode 2 @ 13:46). We don't see THIS memorial but we know the airline eventually finds the coffin so it can happen.

There is a severance in the relationship between Jack and son David that needs to be healed (Season 6 Episode 5 @ 5:25). David shuts Jack out because he's afraid to fail in front of him (Season 6 Episode 5 @ 36:46). That is a mirror of Jacks relationship with his father. BUT Jack is not his father and heals the severance with his son!

SLIDING DOOR #2 (Saved the best for last)

Calling this yet another sliding door because it's actually a new dimension. Follow me here. The shift is that it's in **some** incarnation (kinda doesn't matter which one) Jack is in the process of crossing over from that physical lifetime. The experience of him going to the concert late where he meets Kate is actually happening but in a different DIMENSION.

NOT a different incarnation. This is one of those life moments/spaces BETWEEN the petals. I'm talking about two things happening at once for Jack. In the physical (let's say, on a hospital bed), Jacks experience of this other dimension (in a suit arriving late to concert) is probably being expressed in an episode of terminal lucidity that those around him physically, don't understand. Or not. It's possible he's not saying anything aloud. He may only be experiencing it (inside) without sound being expressed through his physical being. But he's definitely living it.

For the sake of this analogy, let's say he is speaking the lines we hear in this scene. In this physical dimension where Jack might be, say 98 years old and on his last physical breath, he may seem delusional as everyone thinks he's hallucinating. Family and friends are huddled tearfully for his crossing. And as they watch his withered, frail body on that bed, he's ACTUALLY traveled to another space in time -back to his physique when he was in his prime: (Season 6 Episode 17 @ 2820). In this 'in between' he does what he is most familiar with - what he loved most about his life. It was the end of another long day of medically and surgically fixing people (like John Locke!). He focused in on the day when after work he went to the concert. His son was performing and unfortunately, by the time Jack got there it was all over. This time, one of his soul mates, Kate, steps into his field of space to assist him in a gentle crossing (Season 6 Episode 17 @ 1:10:47). At this point, as they talk on the lawn and Jack can't figure out where he knows Kate from. Re watch that scene from 1:10:47 to 1:12:49 and realize that while Jack was living that experience in THAT dimension, in the physical where he's 98 years old and his heart is still beating, he's actually saying the words we hear him saying to Kate! - So MANY people experience this type of lucidity in their terminal stages and the conversation can sound just like this. Imagine as you watch.

I bring this up because friends, family and even medical staff witness this and make the mistake sometimes of interrupting it or getting inside it - trying to 'correct' it! Lol! AS IF! OMG, they have no idea what's going on for the transitioning person!! On that hospital bed when he says "do I ...KNOW you from somewhere?" He's not talking to the loved ones gathered at his side, necessarily! Don't get offended! Lol! And no, he's not 'hallucinating' even if it appears he/she's looking right at you who's known and loved him your whole life! In this case, as Jack is saying, "What is happening to me?" he wasn't talking to the people in the room AND he was as lucid as his sharpest wide eyed surgical moment.

So, in spirit realm, he's in Kate's care now. In physical realm, nurses or care givers are calling next of kin who are not yet there saying stuff like, "his breathing has become shallow and labored we think you should get here as fast as you can..." Those gathered in his room are keeping a very quiet respectful vigil. MEANWHILE, Jack is young, handsome and in a suit. He's kinda bewildered but Kate is doing her part as friends and family do, to see him part of the way across. In doing this, she takes him to the church. Physically, Jack is still in his almost lifeless body until they pull into the church parking lot. I believe Jack lifted out of his 98 year old physical body on the ride over. A nurse or doctor is pronouncing "time of death" and logging the data on a chart. The sorrow is unleashed fully for his friends and family around him. MEANWHILE - Jack has just parked the car in the church parking lot. Kate asks him if he knows where they are (Season 6 Episode 17 @ 1:31:28). She doesn't mean what church, she means what dimension! Jack is still disoriented (this is normal) and refers to a moment he remembers about the church as it's the place he was going to memorialize his Dad. In other words...he doesn't know yet, where he really is. So she gets out of the SUV (setting an example) and tells him to come on in when he's ..."ready to leave". Now, that had to sound weird as hell seein' as how he didn't know he'd already lifted off a life petal. *When you're ready to LEAVE, come on in!* What?! Is there a heliport on the patio or something?! Space shuttle on the roof?! Where we going from in there?! Lol! But, thank goodness, one's unconscious can guide and so in his first seconds of crossing, he opens that back door of the chapel where there is the casket. It's empty because his Dad is alive because dead isn't dead. Know what I mean?! This is happening in a flash. He has just stepped across. In the physical, his family is trying to make their way to the parking lot of the hospital. A couple of them are already finding busy work to numb the pain - dividing the tasks in planning a Celebration of Life for him. So much to do; cemetery, flowers, caterer for the memorial.... And simultaneously in (another) real life, Jack is touching his Dads casket, remembering life on the island (Season 6 Episode 17 @ 1:34:12) and is about to reunite with his father (Season 6 Episode 17 @ 1:35:12).

Rev. Gillian V. Harris M.S.P.

Prayer in these early moments of someone's crossing is SO helpful for the person as they are STILL in the process of the transition. Pray and know that God has hooked it up so that we are always safe. Pray for them and their guide(s) as they make this journey.

In this case with Jack, his beloved father, Christian was right there to give Jack clarity on where he was and to hold him as he accepted that truth of his ...location...for the first time.

The next part to me is priceless. Take it from the hug at (Season 6 Episode 17 @ 1:37:08) when Jack asks if his father is real! So often I've heard that when we leave an incarnation the experience we had reflects back like a dream. So, of course, he would have this question about whether anything he lived was real. Christian set it straight. Everything was/is real. AND where they are right NOW is REAL! Hello! That is key! Where they are in the between petal state is real as well, this is just outside of the incarnation they were just living, it's still real.

This scene with Jack and his Dad at the church... Man. Ok, for those who still have your parents here, imagine them NOT being here anymore. For those who've already experienced this, you're already there. Now then, with all the TIME of missing them, loving them, grieving their absence.... you finally see and TOUCH them again! That is such a tender, raw, gut wrenchingly beautiful reality. The 2nd time I watched I wasn't being so analytical about the whole plot so I completely got it and lost it as I related fully to that eventuality in my own story.

In this scene with Jack and his father in the chapel, we don't know how old Jack really was at the time of his crossing. Those who've crossed tell us that we tend to go to our physical image that is most in our prime. Our aesthetically best lookin' years! OR we pick the image we used when we felt best about ourselves - when we were most productive and that may not have had anything to do with age or physical fitness! -So keep imagining, in the physical, Jack is 98. That means he hasn't seen his Dad in a REALLY long time. Maybe 40 or so years! Can you friggin imagine?! And as I write this paragraph, I'm flashing back on Ms. Jimenez and the reunions she had just a day or so prior to crossing. Her reaction to seeing her Dad was through the roof!!

In my experience in transition midwifery, I have learned the importance of quiet in the last days and hours. This hush is on behalf of the individual who is crossing. While you may feel like saying a lot of things, praying aloud, etc, what they will ultimately need more than anything is ...quiet. If they are conscious and confident enough, they may even tell you so! Yes, I've seen that happen! I tried to warn the talkative one! -Now is NOT the time for nervous chatter. If you didn't know this, ya do now! I should also mention, there are those who love the sound of familiar voices as a sound track and they may tell you so! But as the time gets closer... the less external stimuli, the better. And I believe the REASON this hush is so important is because of how much is going on, on the other side which they are participating in as they melt away from their bodies and THIS incarnation.

I also want to say that though I enjoy saying people "pop" out of their bodies, I have learned that it is more of a floating, than a POP! And because of the grace and ease this movement is for the spirit (where your consciousness is located) it can often seem as if ... nothing happened. People often don't realize for quite a while that they've transitioned.

14

Soul Mates & Spirit Family

Petal to petal

I used to think soul mates were only romantic partners. That is not exclusively true!!! Soul mates are urgent in our childhood. I recently was blessed with the reunion of my childhood friends Jackie, Debbie and June. We probably have other incarnations together and we perfectly planned to spend our childhoods together this time. These were my BFFs from the age of 7 thru high school! We each came from 3 families on a 7 house cul-de-sac in Canyon Crest (Riverside, Ca.). Tender years! We shared and supported each other with everything from our hearts desires, goals and inspirations to the emotions and challenges of a bad day or life chapter. Defeats and accomplishments! We shared our fears and insights! We journeyed together. These are soul mates and they are part of my Spirit Family. We've known each other over and over again as we've played different roles in each other's incarnations.

In my childhood (this lifetime), from the back yard of Debbie and June's house we would go "over the fence" as we grew to affectionately call it. This was a beautiful world of wonderful wilderness. This area is all houses NOW but THEN, it was miles and miles of trees to climb, trails to newly blaze. We ALWAYS had a BLAST *over the fence*. It was our version of a walk-about minus hunting food and sleeping over! Lol!

Plutonic relationships that were/are light beams in our lives, those are soul mates! Unions preplanned. -Relationship agreements within a Spirit Family. And then...there is romance.

I have encountered people who, after a long relationship, feel they've wasted their time. Impossible, I say. Everything and everyone for a reason. I marveled at how Kate was able to entertain feelings for both James and Jack with relatively little drama! I mean, there was a LITTLE! Like the moment when Jack defended Juliet against the interrogation of Sayid (Season 3 Episode 16 @ 5:21). Or when Kate re-arrived on the island and it was the 1970s and Sawyer was living with Juliet (Season 5 Episode 9 @ 40:46)!

In the lifetime on the island, as we all know, Kate and Sawyer vibed each other and had a bit of a relationship – sex in a cage (Season 3 Episode 6 @ 22:27)! I say a 'bit' because Sawyer, at this point, CLEARLY wasn't really ready (Season 4 Episode 4 @ 34:22) when she mentions possible pregnancy and he has the wrong friggin answer! Part of HIS time on the island was growing comfortable with that part of himself- the part that was loveable and could love. He realized this authentic part of himself in his relationship with Juliet.

Juliet freaked out on Sawyer at one point. She was nervous about the return of Kate. This makes me think of women who suddenly go there, seemingly over nothing. This jealousy was just a symptom of her insecurity. Insecurity that had nothing to do with Sawyer OR Kate! – Regardless of the caged sex they had that day. In fact, it was insecurity that was part of Juliet long before she even met Sawyer. Sawyer was in her life so this moment would happen and she would work it out, learn and grow through it! In this case, Juliet was dealing with her own self-worth issues. She actually had nothing to worry about, as, Sawyer was clear on his love for her. He proves that minutes later when she's magnetically chained and sucked down a well.

Later, on a different life petal we see that Juliet and Jack were married. So, when they knew each other on the island, the reason for the quick affinity was their experience with each other from another time. Important to note, they were NOT supposed to be in a romantic relationship this time (Island dimension) which is why it didn't work out. But they both certainly checked to make sure! J

Jack, lucky devil, was married then divorced from Sara (the miracle back surgery patient) and then post-island he was in a relationship with Kate. And on a different life petal he was married to Juliet. None of those lasted as Jack was always sidetracked by the rest of his life - the workaholic self-worth thing.

Sayid. Handsome, handsome, O M G SO HOT, Sayid. (I just went for a glass of COLD alkaline water to regain my focus!) There were three incarnations with Nadia. -The one where he was the interrogator (season 1 Episode 9 @ 13:21) and she died after he helped her escape. He left the island and did a 'walk in' into a parallel dimension/incarnation where he got to marry and be with Nadia for three years ending in her murder (Season 5 Episode 16 @ 21:33). There was also a parallel incarnation where he was the brother-in-law to Nadia.

So, in the first incarnation with Nadia, she is killed and Sayid ends up on the island where he meets and loves Shannon. My guess is that he and Shannon had loved on other life petals. Maybe we'll see that in a LOST reboot. Or NOT! Just to see Sayid again (ANY where!), period, would be amazing!

In this current incarnation - the one that has me typing away at The Secrets of LOST, I have known at least three significant romantic soul mates. Mark, Steve, Justin and now finally my current relationship. Mark (met in college), Steve (met in Santa Barbara at my first full time radio job), (in my 20s) & Justin (in my 30s - met in radio world) were all the right people, wrong time relationships. Steve and I were like Jack and Juliet on the island. We were so close I couldn't figure out why we weren't romantic. Truth is, at that point, I just didn't understand that we were soul mates and that doesn't necessarily mean romance every time. Justin was right person, right time -stressful conditions. Like, so stressful his name isn't really Justin! Lol but there was scandal so... Will save the "conditions" for a different book (!) where I may change his name yet again! But the important part to me is how the relationship with Justin lead me down a path of significant growth. I can't even imagine having done this incarnation without him. And through it all, I've learned so much about life and myself. Justin and I are still dear, dear friends. He's someone I trust without a second thought. This is without question, only one of many life petals we've experienced together. And then, when I was FINALLY ready I met Berson. He may be 'the one' this incarnation. Maybe. Either way, this is absolutely NOT a first incarnation for us. And though I begged the Universe to bring him to me way sooner this incarnation, I get that when we met again was perfect and with purpose. We're different in ways that challenge the HELL out of our relationship but I don't mind this challenge…this exercise. I don't mind now that I understand the feelings that come up for me, especially if they are uncomfortable, are golden opportunities for me to grow and heal. It's another opportunity to do everything with love. And who said you can't find romance after 50?! Whomever said that is SO misinformed! I love his blue/grey eyes, crazy thick brown hair, his brilliant mind and loving heart. Berson is my Bernard ...and I'm his Rose (Season 2 Episode 19 @ 5:35)!

-Soul mates. These are spiritual relationships. These people are in your 'spiritual family'. That means they are also multi-dimensional agreements/reincarnation relationships, as, you know these people from other places!!! The parts you play with each other are pre-prepared ahead of time. These are the relationships that can turbo-charge the greatest potential in everyone immersed in that intention. They're like an energetic "shot in the arm", that figurative "ray of sunshine" in your life. Now, when you think about it THAT way you realize you have more soul mates than you originally thought! Many relationships that fade in, shine light, then fade away... Like a high school yearbook, after a while you may not, in this incarnation, remember how certain relationships lifted and carried you for a time. And that's okay! These true love connections really happened!!! Your history of loving; friends, family members, associates and even... PETS is very long and spans all life petals!

Momentary buzz kill: As a tweak, I must throw in - not everyone who marries is coupled with their soul mate :(. We've all seen THAT.

You will know your soul mate by how comfortable and aligned you feel with them. You'll share desires and dreams. You'll lift and enhance each other. Sometimes we meet a soul mate and we're clear this is a soul mate but the actualization of this relationship has been set up for a different life petal - by YOU! Ahhhh yeah! You're gonna have to trust you did that for good reason and deal with it! In dealing with it (and moving the heck on), there is tremendous opportunity for growth!

How you deal with the problem...is the problem! The issues that come up, the pain that you might feel are arrows on stepping stones SPECIFICALLY designed to guide you to the areas within where healing is the order of the day! And with this, magically, your outer experience changes! Unfortunately, it's a process (not an event) but doing the work is what the school of life is about and why there's ...'time' to work on it. The transformation achieved in doing the work illumines the fact that what you previously thought was a problem, was actually a blessing! That's what happened with Sawyer and Kate. He grew from there and when Juliet came along, he was ready.

Journal 7

Monday August 11, 2014

I am SO hyped about Zoe and Elaine's wedding! What a beautiful and sweet couple! I just got off the phone from our 2nd & final consultation. I went over the ceremony with them, gave them options of vows n stuff like that! It was friggin AWESOME! I LOVE this part of what I'm doing now, growing Bless & Clear ™.

At the end, I told them I was going to be going to Hawaii and of course, I'm like, "have ya seen LOST?" Ha! I've GOT to stop doing that!!! Elaine hadn't seen it but Zoe had seen SOME of it. So... she got real quiet! Lolol!

I'll do their wedding October 4th. PIECE-UH-CAKE! WHAT?! - "Zoe", I said, "I'll be back!!!"

So in reaction to her 'quiet concern' I find myself giggling within. Her fear doesn't make me say, "SEE! I SHOULDN'T GO!" Instead, I feel the opposite. I'm humored! With a smile in my heart I know I will be fine! Of COURSE there's suspense... just due to the subject matter and the nature of LOST... Like, how it all started n whatnot! I'm wrackin' my brain, have I met and touched ...a Jacob?! Teehee!! All jokes aside, if anything gives me angst it's my knowledge of the fact that THOUGHT CREATES! I have to NOT think about LOST while I'm flying. Hm. Wonder how I'll work THAT out!

15

Guidance From ...The Others!

By 'The Others" I really mean, those on the *other SIDE who are ...NOT LOST!*

"If you believe firmly that your consciousness is locked up somewhere inside your skull and is powerless to escape it, if you feel that your consciousness ends at the boundary of your body, then you sell yourself short and you will think that I am a delusion. I am no more a delusion than you are".

'Seth' (channeled by Jane Roberts in 'Seth Speaks')

Just like the quantum physics behind the Law of Attraction, we learn from Spirit Guides that consciousness creates form. Not the reverse - as would be implied by modern neuroscience - that consciousness comes from... the brain! Instead, there is a portion of each of us that knows our powers are far greater than our ordinary selves would lead us to believe. As Marianne Williamson says, "our deepest fear is not that we are inadequate. Our deepest fear is that we are powerful beyond measure". And so, many go through their incarnations in a state of amnesia having forgotten 'what' they really are! This part of you...the 'what' of you...is reading these words, simultaneous to YOU reading them. (I know... read that last sentence again if ya need to!!!)

Again, we are Spirit Beings currently using human bodies but we are, also in reality, independent of these bodies. One of the features of our authentic selves (Spirit) is that we can project our thoughts outward... -Outward and into physical form. This is what the 'Law of Attraction' is basically about - developing the skill to *consciously* create!

In the study of how to manifest at will, you learn that it starts with what you believe. Your belief leads to thoughts. Your thoughts generate feelings. Feelings radiate out as energy. This energy CREATES. Sum of the equation is basically: Thought creates ...stuff. Then, we get so incredibly focused on the realities created, the issues, challenges...the pain, sweat and tears that we can forget we are the ones who created the circumstances in the first place and so consumed with it all we FORGET we can go within to create different circumstances.

I have occasionally found myself facing monumental challenges. I coach myself, "If I know me, when I planned this (prior to this incarnation), I probably also planned on a victory so let me just buckle down n figure this out". Knowing that I, no doubt, had a beautiful outcome in the script, I journey forward with that positive end result in mind.

This feature (creating by way of simply...thinking and feeling as a result of 'believing') comes complete with high responsibility as our outer experience is, then, a direct reflection of our inner reality. The good, the bad, the ugly. So rather than only taking a pat on the back for your positive life circumstances and then blaming a higher power for what you perceive as the negative life circumstances, think...again! The Devil and devilish things are a projection of one's inner psyche. Yes, the Black Smoke Jungle Monster was a collective projection of the folks who were LOST (Season 1 Episode 1 @ 20:00), as it was also for Jacob when he first created it in a pre-incarnation agreement his nameless brother. - An error in judgment caused by premature and hurtful conclusion (Season 6 Episode 5 @ 38.01). When that smoke came out of the cave for the first time, Jacob had to be thinking something along the lines of, "oh shit! Did I do THAT!?" It (Black Smoke Jungle Monster) was the personality and consciousness of his body-less brother who had transitioned (died) and was now hovering angrily in earth plane while expressing himself with bad behavior! But his presence in that place at the same time as the Oceanic 815 peeps was no accident, as we'll learn later when we talk about this kind of 'phenomenon' and who attracts it!

Each of us is involved in a much larger life production than the incarnation that has you reading this book. We did the analogy of the flower (my favorite) but let's do the one where life is a working television set! There are lots of channels. Each channel is one of your incarnations. All channels are streaming action, live, now! (There is no technical difficulty. None of the channels say 'Please Stand By'!) One channel might be called life in the 18th century A.D. or A.D. 3700 or 200 BC! Or 1932. In fact you might even have two separate channels called 1985 in which you're working the same curriculum but under different circumstances (sliding doors).

With Spirit, we co-create these channels and star in each one. The sets or backdrops are our environment. The environment surrounds our personalities in each incarnation condition. Thing is, most folks, unlike DESMOND, are so very focused in a single dimensional circumstance that we are not aware of the others in which we are playing leading roles!! And because of this - IF one believes in reincarnation - they are most apt to believe each lifetime comes one after the previous. The idea of all of them happening at once is weird...downright UN-believable. This is one of the reasons I LOVED LOST. Though they were still giving us 'clock' and telling us Desmond was bouncing from one year to another *'Yo Penny, I'm gonna leave you alone for EIGHT years n' then on Christmas Eve - PLEASE answer the phone'* (Season 4 Episode 5 @ 35:21).

He came up with this plan in a dimension where it was already 8 yrs ahead and Christmas Eve. So, he pops back over to his 'current' other dimension (8 yrs after the one he just visited a few seconds ago) and (talk about instant gratification) calls Penny in what was one of the absolute most romantic LOST moments ever (Season 4 Episode 5 @ 39:28)....

Where was I?!

Oh yeah! Poor Desmond! Dimension hopping looks absolutely insane, yo! Leme tell ya, when Desmond wrote the number Daniel told him to call on his hand in one dimension then came conscious in the OTHER dimension looked at his hand and the number wasn't there - ! - (Season 4 Episode 5 @ 16:10) DUDE! - I don't know what I would have done. I would NOT have been able to remember all that stuff about setting some device to 2.342 and then make sure it's gyrating – oh no wait *oscillating* at 11 hertz and if that doesn't work tell him ya know Eloise! O M G! I would have been like, ..uh, there's a THING....a er uh, GADGET *that you have, set to 2 point somethin-somethin and make sure its swingin' back forth. Then be sure to call Louise!* With all that adrenalin pumping - no way I would have remembered the right stuff. When ya write something on your hand you count on it being there when ya look at it again!!!

This oscillating between life times... doesn't tend to happen to normal people because we're not equipped to handle it at this level. For me, as a kid, prayer was all I needed to stop the conscious swinging from life petal to life petal. -But there is something called 'walk-ins'. I originally thought it was called 'walk-ons'. In learning that this actually DOES happen, I also learned the term is 'walk in' not walk on! Sorry – I just teased that again...! Stand by, yo! First we need more foundation.

In his book 'Seth Speaks', Seth uses Jane Robert's body and voice to explain life as he has lived it. He begins by describing himself as an energy personality essence - which is exactly what we are as well. Only thing is, Seth is no longer focused in physical reality - as we are at this moment. Like Margaret, who you met earlier in these pages, Seth is older than us in terms of 'time' as you and I think we know it. And according to these Guides, time, as we know it, is also...an illusion. -A delusional tool that works for this dimension (and others like it). And I've been advised by several from the other side, that once we leave this existence, memory of this lifetime, will be fragmented and ...like a *dream*. Despite the source and simultaneously because of the source, Seth and other Spirit Guides, their perspectives and ways of expressing are absolutely worthy of being heard and engaged.

While I use a 'flower' or TV set, Seth refers to each incarnation as a 'play'. And he refers to each of us as a multi-dimensional personality - each of us well endowed! :) Hm... - Let me explain use of the 'e' word! - Endowed, *energetically*! Endowed with the Spirit qualities of our Creator. Talk about 'empowerment'! It's larger than we generally know without significant enlightenment. So endowed is each multi-dimensional personality (you and me) that we can have these experiences, multiple lifetimes in all kinds of various settings, scenarios, predicaments n whatnot and still retain our identity in each setting. Like, on other petals - there's no doubt A LOT going on for me but here I am, centered in THIS dimension, sitting quietly in my little house with my acrylics tapping away as I write a little book! :)

Again, we are positively affected by the various plays and what happens in them... Enlightenment HERE enhances enlightenment there (all other dimensions). All for one & one for all & the 'all' and 'one' are you! There is instant communication and an instant, feedback structure within our multi-dimensional system. Kinda like when you cut your finger, there are intelligent components in your body that immediately swing into healing action without you even thinking about it. If anything, a couple days later you look at the cut and go, "wow, it's almost gone!" Magical, isn't it?! That's the kind of system I'm talking about that connects all the petals on a single flower.

Here's another angle on the same theme: In a parallel incarnation - Clare knew her baby would be named Aaron (Season 4 Ep 14 @ 2634) and that knowledge bled over into this incarnation. The sensation she might have felt in that moment, was dejavu-ish.

Funny story! Valet Of The Dolls worked a party a couple weeks ago in downtown L.A. on a Thursday night. We'd made arrangements with a nearby business to use their parking lot for the cars. We'd paid them and given them the insurance certificate two days prior. The gate to the lot was supposed to be open at 4pm. Well, it wasn't! Standing there looking at this figurative hurdle, one of the Dolls reached out and touched the padlock. Holding it in their hand they turned the knob in a combination to the right, then to the left, and to the right and - it dropped open! What?! Yes! ONE TRY – Bam!!

Ok, now, this was beautiful but it also kind of presented a problem for a moment when the people inside the building (located in the parking lot) called our office. They were unaware that we were using the lot. One hand not knowing what the other was doing! I called the property owner and I told him, "the valets are in the lot now, but the people there don't seem to know about this arrangement. Can you call them?!" I didn't mention HOW we got in past the gate! Lol! O M G!

Meanwhile, the valet who did this, one of only 5 males (out of a roster of 150) working for us texted me after apparently making a call to a friend to share his amazement, "a mathematician friend just told me the odds of me randomly opening that combination lock is 10,000 - 1". I wrote him back, "maybe you should accept that it was more than just statistics. Maybe you are more intuitive than you give yourself credit for. Either that or LiveScan (the background check we use) missed something!" He acknowledged being very intuitive "I KNEW that combination."

Me: Toldju!

Him: Yes you did.

LOL!

I love my staff. Seriously. When all is said and done - I'm the luckiest boss in the world. But back to the parking lot/padlock moment, is it possible he had that combination working on another life petal and unconsciously drew from it?! Hell, I would even go so far as to suggest that padlock may have even been 'teleported' from another incarnation where he uses it!!!

Another good example of inter dimensional unconscious knowledge is -in the parallel when Jin is tied to a chair and Sayid doesn't shoot him! (Season 6 Episode 6 @ 31:22) Why WOULDN'T Sayid have shot Jin? He was shootin' everydamnbody else!!! Sayid even perfectly positioned a box cutter, placing it in Jin's hand and wished him good luck at freeing himself! In this multi-dimensional system, envision an endlessly massive field of flowers connected by roots in one earth as a symbol of Source, which we are. There is feedback between all flowers (souls) and not only from this incarnation but from the other incarnations where they also thrive, and they knew via their unconscious that they were comrades on a crazy island! - It's that THING that makes us instantly drawn to certain people and yes, instantly repelled by others. And I say, in those moments when we find ourselves repelled by someone, "I don't know why, I just don't like her" - it's probable that one should take advantage of this as an opportunity to bring healing to the energy between you and that person. What's happening on this side will affect what you're experiencing with her elsewhere.

16

LAX

This vacation, originally set for 4 days had been elongated when I changed my flights! Yeah! + Hm = was that a good thing or... a bad thing?! Now instead of leaving on Friday the 29th, I would leave on Thursday 28th. Instead of returning on Monday the 1st, I'd return on Tuesday the 2nd!   Yay! Five full days! One of my seats changed, too! Now 33G on the way to Hawaii (basically the back of the plane but... that portion did okay, right?!), 14G on the return.

With hair, nails, lashes, computers n whatnot handled by the 27th, I was free to work into the wee hours of the 28th to make sure all was handled in the office into the next two weeks. This was good. I needed to be tired on the plane!

I promised myself I wouldn't even have a drink which I usually do. One or two appletini's would perfectly buzz & calm me (and at least make the scary more humorous) but no. Not this trip. Want to feel everything, lucidly. After a nap, I was up early and checked emails at 6am. I saw a few urgent things to handle. Quote requests and a few revisions to do thanks to stressed out event planners who don't know how to sleep!

I worked fast but at about 7am I got into communication with one of my favorite event planners, Eric Roth of 'Oh Eric Productions', about another great big complicated operation. I absolutely ADORE Eric. He is one of many dozens of planners and caterers who call us regularly. Eric has used us since the beginning. Somewhere around 2004-ish, I believe. And like all the others, I've never physically met him in this incarnation. It's extremely rare that a client meets me. In fact on our web site, I refer to myself as 'Charlie' and the Dolls are my Angels! I don't do this to be mysterious so much as there simply isn't time for me to meet them. I'm busy making it happen!

Since Eric was awake, I figured what the hey, I'm calling him. That would give me the opportunity to open with, "Oh Eric!! G'morning!" I told him I'd gotten his email to us in the nick because I was leaving for Hawaii in a minute! "I mean, my team is here but this is a whopper and they would have wanted my guidance so, here I am!" I told him what needed to happen for this location receiving that number of cars. I left the prescription (how many valets, shuttles, price and other elements) for Meredith to create an estimate for him.

Rev. Gillian V. Harris M.S.P.

A few more things happened, figurative fires beginning to spark and I could tell we were in what I like to call, 'a swarm'. It was already a busy day but I couldn't/wouldn't participate in it. This job is tough to pull yourself away from. It's so very like an air traffic control tower and I'm like, one more plane, just one more plane. Ok, wait - plane after next - that's my last one!..." Hours later I could still be sitting there. Ahhh yeah, very much like pushing the damn button in the hatch every 108 minutes. This time - IF I did that- I would miss my REAL plane. Couldn't let it take me like that today.

My driver and his Town Car had already been waiting in front of the house for a good 20 minutes and I needed to do my ritual: I needed to go over EVERY thing in my head. Do I have everything? Did I leave good enough directions for everyone? Every detail from the house, to the company, to my trip and suitcases had to be thought over systematically and intuitively, one more time. And I needed to pray, damn it! Not going ANY where without that! THIS would NOT be the trip to forget to pray first! - Yeah, let's get clear - just because I know what I know...doesn't mean I'm anxious to wrap up my life in this incarnation. I am NOT ready. Gotta pray.

By the time I was done with all THAT it was about 8am. I was a little behind schedule. We still had L.A. rush hour ahead of us. Long story short - we got to the airport in the knick of friggin time and, I guess because it's a holiday weekend, EVERYbody else was there, too. AND seems they were ALL lined up at Hawaiin Airlines!

Airborne
(The following is from my journal written on the plane, while in the air.)
8/28/15 ~ 10:30am

I almost missed this flight! UNbelievable! I mean, I'm cutting in front of people in the security line, "Sorry", " 'Scuse me...I'm sorry" I continued squishing past people with all my luggage at one point saying to someone as I'm cutting in front of them "this feels really weird but my plane is leaving and I really need to be on it - I'm SO sorry...'scuse me!" O M G! Finally got up to the security belt. Had to send my purse through twice. (I know! That's what I get!!) Put my tennies back on. No time to re-tie the shoe laces and here I go - laces flappin rhythmically against the floor with my steps as I power walk through the terminal to reach gate 28. Twenty Eight. I was stuck for a minute on that, like "oh shit. Wasn't 28 one of the hatch numbers? OMG!...Oh no, wait. That was 23. Ok, I'm cool." Too out of shape to run and I couldn't find someone to bribe out of their wheel chair so I'm hoofin' it as fast as I can turbo walk - knowing ultimately, this is good exercise for me!

Suddenly I hear my NAME on the loud speaker. NO FRIGGIN WAY! This has NEVER happened to me before. I & three others were being told "this is last call"! I couldn't help but feel oh SO very, very Hugo Reyes right about then! "Are you Gillian Harris?!" Yelled a joyful lady smiling at the gate! OMG – process of elimination. I was the LAST person to board!?! MY normal M.O. woulda been to hug this person but I'm thinkin' 'No! I CAN'T! Hugo did that!' (Season 1, Episode 25 @ 15:25). I nodded and kept steppin' "You made it girl!" she cheered. "Oh My GOD!" I laughed, "Thank you"! It took everything in me not to mention out loud how 'Hugo' I felt but I have promised myself not to talk about LOST during this flight! And I also gotta try not to think about it. ... Like I am right NOW! Shit.

(I close the notebook and....)

(...I continue a bit later)
-Turbulence!
Mild, yet I find myself going within to remind myself this is what flying through air is like. Rose said Bernard always says "Planes like to be in the air" (Season 1 Episode 1 @ 22:23) so... It's normal. It's all good. All is well. I got this! :)

(...couple hours later)
We've eaten, I've tried to nap. Noticing turbulence, oh no wait - that's a TODDLER - RUNNING!! - NO! It's both toddler and parent. Is this kid causing the turbulence I feel?! Its parent just jogged past me! NOT COOL! This should be against the friggin law to run in an airplane IDC (I don't care) how young you are! If I hear that little kid running back this way again...I'm stickin' my foot out! Yup! He's goin' down, yo!
    -Ok, yes. I'm a little edgy. Shit.

(A little while later)
The woman sitting next to me.... looks like Sun (Sun-Hwa Kwon from LOST) but of course it's not her. Just...LOOKS like her!!!
    Hm...
    Food was awful, did I mention that? I went into auto pilot with the rest of the passengers and ate it. AS IF we're all hungry at the same time! AS IF we expected airline food to suddenly be nyummy!! Insanity. OM G! Then I had to go to the bathroom. Captain had just put on the fasten seat belt sign, and wouldntcha know it – that's when I REALLY gotta go. I brave it. I get up and fight what feels like an extra pull of gravity to make it to the lavatory. Such a small

space. I looked at myself in the mirror. I thought of Charlie in his bathroom moment. I got close to the mirror...and smiled at myself (Season 1 Episode @ 3:13)!! Lol!

Then I noticed that Charlie was lucky the Oceanic bathroom toilet had the stopper at the bottom of the bowl! He'd reached for the handle to flush but didn't get to because of the sudden turbulence (Season 1 Episode 2 @ 3:26). If he'd dropped that heroine bag down THIS Hawaiin Airlines toilet it would have gone ...down, down, down to...where ever stuff like that goes cuz there was no stopper. It was just a big dark hole!!!! Hm... I wonder if the one on this plane is actually broken! Ha!

(A little while later)
- Turbulence -
"...The spirit of God is here with me making my way successful and — No wait... The spirit of God is here with US making our way successful and easy..." Adjusting my 'go to prayer/mantra' when I think I might need God to save my friggin life! I've changed the words for right now! Praying on behalf of the whole plane. Wanting the METAL to maintain its STAMINA and ENDURANCE! Oh yeah... talkin' to God on this plane much more than I normally do. Well 'cept for that time to Tortola, BVI...Ok now THAT was REALLY scary. Ok, SHUT UP, Gillian.

(A few minutes later)
I keep taking pictures of the monitor in front of me showing the planes progress from L.A. to Hawaii. 1 hr. 29 minutes to Honolulu. I must have slept 2 hours easy. SO grateful. I feel so much better! :)

Upon waking I felt hot. I knew from the bathroom moment my hair-do had gone terribly awry! I brushed it and took out my cute little hand held battery operated menopause fan! I closed my eyes and acknowledged to myself how comforted my nerves were by the familiar sensation of this little gadget... My friend :).

Touchdown!!

Once we landed I took out my cell phone. I texted my Personal Assistant Lisa Bogenschutz who I either refer to as Lisa, Agent Bogenschutz, Agent B. or LUCY! Regarding the latter name 'Lucy', to her, I'm Ethel! Yeah, work with somebody for more than 5 years and it gets crazy! "Luce! I'm here! Wooooooooohoooo! Please call my Mom and let her know I've landed and that I will call her later!" She wrote me right back, "K Have fun Eth!"

I was in for more cardio and looked forward to it! I made my way to baggage and called Paul to see if he was close, "I'm already here. I'll meet you at the curb. I have a burgundy Benz". Such a sweet gentleman, about 70 and full of life. He drove me the long way to the North Shore. Instead of taking the highway (H2) up the middle - northbound reaching North Shore in about an hour, we went south to the H1 and then connected with the 72/ Kalanianaloe Hwy which took us around the edge of the island to the east and then northward until finally we were in North Shore a few hours later.

On the way up I was being drenched by a sensation...difficult to find the words it was a vibration. I wondered if it was just...excitement but... this was different than anything I remember feeling when I used to vacation before. I'd even been to Hawaii before! I know I'm so excited about THIS trip it may sound like I'd never been before but I have. Maui in 1999. Stayed at the Grand Wailea Resort - but for reasons which will probably end up in a different book! - That was ...an unhealthy trip!

This particular vacation 2014 felt like none other! I understand now that 'I' was the catalyst for this intensified experience. It was stemming from the way I live my life now after so much growth and awakening. So much more sensitive to vibrations and imprints in the stream of consciousness, I was instantly aware of how my energy was up and my channel was open. I could feel everything Spiritual about this place. I could feel it in the air I was breathing. It was rich, it was pure. The beauty alone was so intense. -So radiant. There was a charge from it all and I was being doused in it.

Paul was great company. How awesome of him to do this for me without even knowing me and wouldn't think of taking my money. Partly, he did it as a favor to Michelle, his longtime friend. He mentioned that she wanted to start a branch of Valet Of The Dolls on the island. I told him she'd filled me in on that idea and that I totally supported her. I really didn't want this vacation to be about VOTD but it was an area of easy conversation with Paul so I entertained it.

We got to talking about parking laws on the island. One of the rules, I found particularly interesting. On certain residential streets, it was ok to park on someone's lawn (the part that meets the street) but not okay to have your tires on the pavement!!! In L.A., thou shalt not roll thine tires onto someone else's lawn! EVER! Are you kidding?! OMG! Different strokes!

"Show me a normal neighborhood with sidewalks, nice houses. -Inclines that people don't wanna walk up while wearing heels" I requested. Off we went and what an eye opener! Neighborhoods like Hurley's supposed L.A. post lottery win mansion (Season 4 Episode 12 @ 23:28) which was actually filmed there in Oahu. Granted, I didn't know WHAT to expect but there's some spectacular real estate in Hawaii. But of course! Why WOULDN'T there be?!

After showing me a slew of wealthy neighborhoods I felt for balance. "Show me a not wealthy neighborhood. Show me a poor neighborhood and a middle class neighborhood", I said. Soon we were driving past a very poor neighborhood where people had created makeshift clothes lines on their balconies for drying in the tropical wind because either they didn't have access to a dryer or were saving on cost of electricity. Paul told me about the prices of the dwellings in these 'poor' neighborhoods! It's EXPENSIVE to live in Hawaii, yo! -It's even expensive to be POOR in Hawaii!!!

Close to North Shore now, we see a food truck. These are EVERY where on the island. This one was gourmet burgers. I insisted this be my treat. They had a turkey burger for me. As we sat on the wall unwrapping our meals, it started to rain! We ran for shelter under the awning of the food truck. I deleted the top bun and pigged out on the rest as I hadn't in a while. What a wonderful experience already. I couldn't wait to get to my rental at the Ke Iki Bungalows.

We rang the buzzer and someone opened the gate at the resort entrance. Paul drove into the grounds and I hopped out to begin looking for the 'office', like, where ya check in! Before I knew it, I was gettin' my cardio on, as I tried unit after unit only to learn each one was NOT the office but instead, another rental. Really nice 1 and 2 bdrm apartments. Beautiful flooring, furnishings and decor but ...it's hot, humid. I'm gettin' kinda tuckered. The carbs from the bottom bun of that burger weren't helping. I check my EGS (Emotional Guidance System) and notice some L.A. agitation was waking up within my newly vacationing body. "Nope. Release that now", I ordered myself. Chose instead to take a deep breath and remember...I AM on vacation. I quickly reasoned with myself, "WHAT is the rush? – Notice nobody else is in a rush!" Paul wasn't in a rush. He seemed to be in harmony with this island time behavior. I dared myself to go with the flow. What would happen if I just... relish the NOW?!

Walking the grounds I've noticed preparations beginning for the wedding. At least I know I'm in the right place! Turning around to go back toward the gate and some units I saw near the entrance, I suddenly see a tall, blonde, very relaxed and happy spirit. Shorts, T-shirt, sandals and a sun visor. -Looks like he's finishing a sandwich and doesn't have a care in the world. I take note of his demeanor as an example of an awesome way of being. I am wowed by every spec of it! THIS is what he does for WORK!? !! Simultaneously, I know this is Greg Gerstenberger, the manager of the resort. No, he's more than that - he's my HERO, as, he is the one responsible for hooking me up with a cool rental while everything else was already so very sold out this holiday/cousin gettin' married weekend.

I smile and wave, "Hi Greg!" He confirmed my intuition by responding, "Hi!" I tell him, "I'm Gillian". "Oh! You made it! Awesome!" he says. He shakes my hand and guided me up the stairs to the office which is a little room at the entrance of his home! Money handled. Got the key, gate code, Wi-Fi password and directions to my unit which would be about a half a mile down the road to the south.

My incredibly awesome tour with Paul would end in the gated driveway of this beautiful blue and white home that I would soon find myself calling "my beach house"! Paul would then drive away and I'd forget to give him a gift I'd brought especially for him, a beautiful polished piece of Selenite. My intention was to call him during my trip and figure out how to get it to him.

My rental was amazing. It's basically a one bedroom apartment underneath the main house. The main house is owned by the owner of the resort, hence, they don't usually rent this out!!!

The whole house sits on the beach and feels and resembles ...a boat! A great BIG white boat with sky blue trim! Part of the unit I was in, was half way underground. While the front door was ground level, the back of the unit...was about 3 feet underground. So when I looked out the windows in the back of the unit, I would see feet walking by - that is... IF there were feet walking by...(the others!!! Lol). There never were, really, just painting a picture. Maybe a better description is like looking out a basement window to the sidewalk just outside... Actually what I saw was patio furniture and the gazebo and palm trees and sand.... But this perspective gave me the sensation of being in a vessel partly under water... Not a bad thing... just... a thing.

The WHOLE place was perfectly, tropically astounding in ground cover and plants and nosey geckos. The sound track was the ocean which, in all its glory, was RIGHT THERE.

I looked forward to nightfall. - Not sure why...but yeah. I hurried to unpack and settle in. I opened my computer and turned on my ATT airport for a signal. AT&T had promised me it would work. We looked on their coverage map and I was gonna be in good shape but...no. No signal. Not even half a micro bar! So grateful I had the Wi-Fi password for the resort. That totally saved me as I was able to connect to the internet for the remainder of my trip.

My Sprint phone, well, that is another story. They TOO had promised me a good signal on the North Shore. - It was spotty. And none of those 'spots' were INSIDE the house or even on the premises of my beach house!!! I had to go outside the property, outside the driveway and stand almost inside the neighbor's lawn across the street (more an alley) to get enough bars! Luckily, no one was home over there!!

It must have been about 6/6:30pm when the sound of water made me look up from my monitor. I looked to the right out the open front door through the screen and notice a tall, slender man. Very handsome. I wanna call him an 'Island Hippy'! He has long thick, wavy, salt n peppered hair he likes to sometimes wear in a ponytail. He was busily and happily watering the grounds. He'd been watering for quite a while, now. I thought about how lucky they are here not to have to deal with a drought like Southern California. He's just watering to his hearts' content.

Whenever I travel off my home continent, my mission is always, "Operation: Meet the natives". Paul was a white guy originally from someplace like...Florida, or something. So even though he'd lived in Hawaii for more than a decade, long enough to have a well-established business there - he kinda didn't count. Sorta! Lol! This man in my front yard, however, was a real born & raised, Hawaiian native! I got up and went out the front door to introduce myself! With his island accent he expressed surprise, "OH! I didn't know they would let anyone rent this place!" The miracle in getting this rental is now further verified. I guess I really was supposed to be here and the Universe totally made a way for it with grace and ease.

His name was Sturmah and he's a grounds keeper at the resort. At about 50 years old, his pride and joy, passion and mastery is surfing. August is off season for surfing in North Shore. The water is very calm now.... I was in town at the right time. Sturmah would become a very important tour guide!

He asked me if there was anything I needed. I got a big smile, "Yeah!" I expressed my needs which included a rent-a-car. He promised to pick me up in the morning at 7:30 and take me to the Turtle Bay Resort where there's a car rental agency. Yay! Everything was unfolding so gracefully.

Night fell on the steamy warm island. I wandered outside and around to the back of the house which faced the ocean. I could hear it...but ...it was so dark I could no longer see it. Knew it was out there, though. It crashed repeatedly against the shore... There was a LOT of sand between the house and the shore line. A LOT. I felt uneasy about going down the stairs with no flashlight and actually touching it. I decided that wouldn't be necessary! :) The only light came from the stars and a sliver of moon. For now, I would sit in the gazebo on the patio next to the stairs that lead 20 or so feet down to the sand. I closed my eyes and listened to the sea... and then I opened my eyes and looked at the darkness. It was so vast... and as I observed it, I was startlingly one with it.

I teased myself with contemplation of the emotional experience the LOST characters might have endured in the circumstance they were in. I dared myself to think...*what if.* My plane just crashed... I'm alive and I'm here. My family is separated from me by 'the veil'. I'm in a different dimension but I don't know it. It seems physical -like the earth I've always known. I stared as deep as I could into the nights' horizon. The wind blew against the palm trees. Suddenly - there was a BIG gust! The big palm fronds rustled loudly. BOTH of my eyeballs suddenly popped open wider! LOL! I looked up! -Looked left - right - up- right - left. House, Gazebo, plants, trees, ocean sound. Ok. I'm cool. No Black Smoke Jungle Monster. "Butchoo know what?! Let's go back inside!" I told myself. Off I went - the beach house would be my Banyan tree yacht haven!

I'm glad they did that LOST experience as a group and that they figured out how to light fires n whatnot cuz its friggin DARK out there by the water, yo! Add to that darkness, the thick layer of the unknown multiplied by endless possibilities and WOW!

Eventually I climbing into the coziest bed I've experienced in ...maybe forever! I had actually been anticipating it since Greg emailed me photos the week before the trip. It's a gigantic dark walnut four poster bed. -King sized with perfectly delicious and bountiful white bedding and down comforters. "I've got to bring Berson here. He's gonna love this" I thought.

There are many reasons I know that I've found 'the one'. For one thing, he's the only man I know who is cool with what happens next: I get up. I then proceeded to turn on the air conditioner, the overhead fan and positioned my meno-fan on the night stand so it could blow directly at my head/face. Ahhhh yeah! Perfect! Now with the room becoming 'icy' against my naked skin I make a mad dash for the bed. It's kinda funny. Almost a survival thing as I race to get under the layers of blankets and comforters and quickly bundle up feeling very Eskimo-esque! It's warm and cozy within the bundle. Somehow, with this chill and moving air, I am unaffected by hot flashes. Night sweats are a thing of the past now that I've got my routine!

One day on the phone Berson told me he turns on the fan in his bedroom at night when I'm not there, "not so it blows on me but so that I can hear it. It reminds me of you"! -Tear drop! -Like I said... He's the one! :)

Journal 8 -
DAY 2
Friday 8-29 -THE LOST TOUR
Guess I missed my ride this morning. Or was he just...late n then we missed each other?! Is this an 'Island Time', thing?! So I'm like, 'okfinewhatever' - I was determined to have a victory! I

started walking. Saw someone else on the path and asked about transportation. They pointed me the way to the bus stop where I waited a mere 5 minutes before one arrived. -$2.50 for the 10 minute ride to the Turtle Bay Resort where a lady at the car rental agency was waiting for me.

O M G the bus driver was SO nice! He was trying to help me cuz I mentioned I had to get to Honolulu by myself today! Freeways n whatnot from the North shore for the first time in a place where all the street names look like Kahoahoalanigula!!! And to further press my point - I could only understand every 4th word the bus driver was saying. His accent was so thick! Everything rhymed with something that I thought I might understand so I'd say "got it". But I shouldn't have said that because I really didn't "got it"! But God Bless him! I thanked him for his effort, took his hand and wished him a beautiful day!

A little more power-walking through a huge parking lot and I was in the open floor plan of the hotel lobby and car rental office. While helping the guy before me, I noticed he did a double take on his bill! His body language and inflection were like, "wait, HOW MUCH?!" While he searched for the right credit card I called the Doll House. I guess I was being overheard discussing some crazy staffing issue mixed with personality profiling, "Kristi & Aubrey do NOT get along. I really don't want that drama. You know what - Aubrey doesn't even like wearing the miniskirts so take her off. Put Mierra on instead. Then put Aubrey on the Mulholland party." When it was my turn, the customer service rep asked "what do you do?" I told her, "I own an all-female, private event, valet company" and about thoughts of bringing it to Hawaii. "Do women in Hawaii know how to drive manual transmissions?!" I asked teasingly. She was like, "hell yeah!" She was excited. Further into the process, since I'd seen what the previous guy went through I asked, "uh...how much is it per day for a semi cool car?" "Don't worry" she told me, "I'm gonna hook you up!" :)

I got a royal blue Jeep Wrangler for about $60 per day! - I was SO grateful when I realized THAT was half price! O M G! For a JEEP! Welcome to the North Shore! I dared not ask about a Range Rover! - I think the guy before me had made that kind of mistake! Lol!

I cruised back to the Ke Iki Bungalows. Greg had printed out copies of the release form I needed for the interview after the LOST tour. I've been texting Rey, fine-tuning details and am looking forward to meeting with him this evening to talk about his experience in LOST. Though he only had a background role as one of the temple guards, I know he will be a good interview. Nothing about this trip is for not....

From my schedule: Lost tour 12:30pm (look for yellow Hummer). Done by 6pm. Meeting with Rey 6:30.

I managed to make it to the Ala Moana Hotel in Honolulu by 11am. So proud of myself! Took myself inside for brunch at a Japanese restaurant then went outside to wait along the side street as I was instructed by my contact at KOS Tours. I was looking for a yellow Hummer. It was 12pm, now. I was early. -And it was toasty out with temperatures in the upper 80s, again.

I suppose for most folk getting a tan in Hawaii is a top objective. I.... don't need a tan, yo! I needed a parasol! I took out my meno-fan and let it blow hot air at me. I decided another quick call to the Doll House was in order.

Meredith answered the phone. It sounded like a busy day. She had a ton of questions, it was kind of becoming a blur as I thought to myself "I don't want to be drawn into this" - there was something about keys to somebody's Ferrari and then, with complete confidence she told me, "I'm gonna email you this quote request for Charlie Sheen and the other one for the Dulan party. I'll send em to the inbox and you can just do them a little later". Um...wait. What?! Lol!

I love these clients, ok?! Ok.

Now - OM   G! Did she really just delegate work to me?! It's almost funny but it's NOT funny!

Granted, I DID promise to help intermittently but not TODAY! I'm about to go on a 5 hour tour! And then there's the interview and the one hour drive back to north shore. I just TOLD her what I'm doing today! Translation: I'm swamped with R&R today!! It's the busiest day of my whole trip! The day I've been waiting for. I got on a plane and battled psychotic illusions to get here for this! Are you kidding me?! Come on!!! The disconnect in her was blinding me. Her request annoyed me to no end BUT verbalizing and further investing in being annoyed was not on my agenda. I made a choice to keep my cool, put on my emotional shades and simply verbalize some healthy boundaries. With a calculated calm I said, "MmmNo". There was a half second of silence and I continued, "That would mean sometime tomorrow -which is too late. I don't want to stress myself out about it. Please make it happen". Surprised at my answer I could hear frustration as she said, "O ... kay." Yes, there was a separation between the 'O' and the 'kay'. - Her way of passively expressing judgment about my answer. I knew she wasn't smiling and I knew she thought I SHOULD stop what I'm doing and help the office since it's MY company. Hmph! Oh - - - Well! I can't believe she asked me that question. And please know there are two other admins besides Meredith. They've been in training for this for months and in one of their cases, years. It's on, now. This is NOT a drill! They, seriously, need to rise to this occasion.

As if unaffected by her response and tone I perked up and announced, "I gotta go! I'm waitin' on a Hummer!!" "Well" she shot back, "THAT sounds like a PERSONAL situation you should have in PRIVATE!" We ended on an upbeat vibe! At least outwardly! I made a silent commitment that as soon as the Hummer arrived I'd turn off my cell. Which was a good idea since the battery was dying :(!!

The big yellow gas guzzlin' H4 arrived around 12:35pm. It was the only yellow vehicle I'd seen so my face got that 'oh yay! Here it is!' look which the driver noticed as he swooped toward the curb! "Is this for the LOST Tour?" I asked through the window. A handsome, muscular blonde fellow said, "Yeah". He hopped out and walked around to the sidewalk to meet me "are you Gillian?" His name was Jeff. I shook his hand and would be the first to board for the excursion. He went to open a back door for me until I boisterously declared, "I got shot gunnnn!" We both laughed and he moved to open the passenger *front* door instead! "I've driven a ton of hummers", I told him, "but have never gotten to ride shotgun in one"! That was my outward excuse. Truth was, I had taken my throne as first tour pick up, in the front passenger seat!! Plus - I didn't want anybody's big 'ol tourist hat wearin' head in my way! I am on a mission!

We stopped at two other hotels. First we picked up an adorable young couple and then, last stop, a cranky lady I'd guess to be in her 60s. Ironically, all three of them, now in the backseat, were from Ohio! That helped the cranky lady. Familiarity. Geographical kinship! They had a few streets and a mall in common! I was the only one from Cali, except for Jeff! He was excited to hear I lived in Woodland Hills. From Pacific Palisades, he was familiar with Greater L.A. The five of us would spend five hours in places where they filmed LOST.

I was so looking forward to meeting other LOST fanatics. While they were absolute fans, I quickly remembered that not everyone saw it or life the way I do. First angle of LOST conversation to come up was whether they were all dead from the beginning. "Actually", I said, "they were all still alive -but only because that's what happens after our bodies die - like theirs did in the crash. - they were in a different dimension and they didn't know they were dead because dead ISN'T really dead. Dead is... alive". I took a completion breath as the entire vehicle, which had been so fully a chatter, went completely silent. Eyebrows up, I looked around the vehicle one face at a time. No one knew what to say. The cranky lady was squinting at me. With his eyebrows bunched in concern Jeff breaks the silence, "they were ALIVE at the beginning. They died LATER". I looked at him and was silent for a moment - my eyes connected with his as my brain twirled...."Nope" I shook my head, "As YOU understand the word death - they TOTALLY died in the crash, yo". "They did NOT die in the beginning" he countered, "this is straight from the horses' mouth." "WHAT horse?!!" I shot back. "The creators of LOST SAID this. It's written", he replied. "Hm..." Unfortunately, at the time, I didn't know what I know now. Jeff was only 50% right! And even without having done any true research at that point, I came back with a declaration that I stick to, to this day, "I know they created it and they might have said that but...they're wrong". I giggled out loud deciding to just let them think I'm being silly! I was done with any talk of metaphysics and spirituality. I had a pen and a notebook and could just write my impressions and keep them private (til book time! :)).

So.... they did what normal people do... Gossip! -There became lots of conversation about the people who played the characters in LOST. I don't want to share that here. They had lots of who was temporarily dating whom and a plethora of other blahblah. That info is not the intention of this book. I would NOT be surprised, though, if many of the actors who had roles in LOST, met and worked with Soul Mates– people they've done many other incarnations with, while in the production of this series. But I wasn't about to share that with this Hummer load! And more than anything I wanted to see and do the things I ultimately saw and did on this tour.

Ya know that great big rippled, green Mac Daddy of a mountain they always show? Well, not always but... often enough this mountain is, like, a signature. (Season 1, Episode 1 @ 26:38). I got to see it. I got to...hang out with it! I kept taking pictures of it, as if I thought it would change click after click. No matter where I moved it was the same majestic beauty. I got to be IN the Jungle with all that green around me. I got to see BANYAN trees like the one Kate and Juliet, Walt & Michael, Boone & Shannon used as a life or death shield (Season 1, Episode 13 @ 25:35). I got to touch a few, hug them and blend with their energy field. They flipped use of the banyan tree on us when we found Charlie hanging from one (Season 1 Episode 2 @ 3:12).

Many Holistic Healers are familiar with Banyan for its medicinal properties ranging from chapped heels, boils and painful joints to a slew of other things including several skin conditions and ...I just saw 'on-line' Banyan tree extract also cures some venereal diseases!!! Didn't mention which ones!! But GO Banyan Tree!!!

I got to stand on the golf course that Hurley created (Season 1, Episode 9 @ 19:07)! It was actually kinda lumpy! Challenging golf course! I got to see the dock where the 'Others' brought Jack, Sawyer, Kate and Hurley as bound and gagged hostages (Season 2 Episode 24 @ 34:46). My stomach almost got the same knot when I saw the scene of them on their knees in complete submission to Ben and his soldiers. I say my stomach ALMOST got that knot – I couldn't get there because the dock was empty now! But I vividly pictured the four of them lined up in a barter so that Michael could be reunited with his son Walt in exchange for them. I saw the building where Richard lived with his wife before she died (Season 6 Episode 9 @ 6:10). Again, my mind raced as I envisioned him riding up on his horse in that storm. His victorious return, was too late. I walked around the grounds of the site where Sayid was building houses for the needy in the 'Dominican Republic'! This would be the same place where Locke came to beg him back to the island (Season 5, Episode 7 @ 17:07). We went to the tower where the bomb 'Jughead' hung (Season 5 Episode 3 @ 29:25). The tower was still there. Jughead was gone! Saw the village of houses where the 'Others' lived (Season 3 Episode 1 @ 2:41)! OMG -the field where Hurley had to pop the clutch on that old VW van! (Season 3, Episode 10 @ 34:34)!! Saw the beautiful jungle spot where Charlotte died of ...*time change disease* (Season 5 Episode 5 @ 33:10)! Drove past the church where everyone met at the end (Season 6 Episode 17 @ 3535) and lots of other stuff. The tour is truly WONDERFUL. Jeff was a fan-TASTIC, super knowledgeable guide who deserved every bit of the fat tips everyone handed him at the end! Great job! It was an action packed 5 hours.

I will say I did take notes to share from the 'gossip' that relate to the 'Creating Under the Influence (CUI)' theory. Apparently, the 'Hurley/Hugo Reyes' character wasn't originally in the script! My tour guide told us, the actor who played Hurley was auditioning for the role of Jake and they created Hurley's character instead! I can totally see that. He's so loveable.

My fellow LOST tourists thought I was a little over the top with my love for Hurley! They were talking about how hot Sayid, Sawyer and Charlie are. That's absolutely true. Especially

Sayid & Sawyer.... Like, I don't know which one of those is hotter! But I was like, "don't forget about Hurley! He's hot, too!" I understood Libby's attraction. His hair, his smile and … he wears his heart! "I could seriously hug Hurley for hours! He is just SO precious!" The cranky lady was squinting at me, again!

Jeff also said that the lady who played Sun was actually auditioning for the part of Kate and from that effort they decided to create Sun's character instead. In my humble opinion, that is more work by invisible forces influencing those doing the casting and those creating the script. I also was charmed to learn how many of the characters are 'best friends' NOW and how many choose to stay and live permanently on Oahu! I would get verification of that later.

My favorite parts of the tour were being in the Jungle. I clicked like a maniac on my new camera! The pictures turned out amazing! Here are just a few...

(See these in color on the Kindle version of this book)

SO beautiful. This photo pales by comparison to what this mountain feels like in person. As I look at the picture I'm remembering and re-experiencing the intense craving to…touch it, hug it and plaster myself against it in a wild crazy show of my love that would be met by massive love in return! Yeah, I've got a *thang* for this mountain!

So, since the journey to actually touch it wasn't on the agenda that day, I stood there and shared energy with it. For now, that was enough. I think I have a date in the future with that mountain!

The Hummer dropped me off in my starting point around 6pm. I turned my cell on and it immediately told me my battery was moments from dead! I didn't have a car charger. I was supposed to meet Rey next for an interview. Our plan to meet at this place down town, 600 Queen Street, where there would be what I can only describe as a 'food truck festival', didn't work out. There were SO many people. Parking was nearly impossible. I finally found a parking space but now had a dead phone. Long story short, a friendly Hawaiian person passing by on the sidewalk, let me borrow their phone! Um…would that happen in L.A.?! I tried to reach Rey but couldn't.

Rev. Gillian V. Harris M.S.P.

We communicated later and set up Monday the 1st! In setting that up, we decided we'd meet at the home of yet another LOST cast member in Kailua and I would interview them *both*!

DAY 3

Saturday 8-30-14
The wedding is today. 4pm, so says the invite. Up at 7a which made it 9 in California. I got dressed and headed out for a signal. I'd coordinated with Agent B. (Lisa). Our plan was to do credit card transactions this morning. I drove to a spot about 2 miles away where my Sprint signal was strong. I took notes as she gave me the information I needed over the phone. Back to my rental so I could do the transactions; emailed receipts to client - bcc'ing the bookkeeper. Then via email I gave Lisa transaction reference numbers so she could write the data on the hardcopy that I couldn't reach. Also told her what sent items to print. I couldn't get my remote connection to the office to connect with the printer. That was the only glitch. She handled it! We rocked that 1st time make shift system and handled a good 15 transactions. We both felt

victorious! I was comforted knowing money was flowing and the company was happily afloat even though I was on another continent hangin' out under coconut trees!

BTW; the rain in lost -was real!

Well, sometimes, anyway! It's an honest to goodness tropical rain forest, so... yeah! It rains intermittently despite the fact its 80-ish degrees! The humidity was delicious to me. And the intermittent precipitation didn't bother me at all. I felt very LOCKE about it (Season 1 Episode 1 @ 28:50) as I threw my head back, sometimes, and let the drops caress my face. I found it purifying in the most natural of ways. Tour guide Jeff said that (he heard) at one point in the filming they were stopping every time it rained. "But then, they just said fuck it! Let the rain be part of it". That totally makes sense. But of course, some of that rain we saw in LOST was absolutely manufactured and timed to scripted perfection! And sometimes...it was REAL or it was timed rain on top of real rain. Example: Season 5, Episode 4 @ 29:10 minutes. The ground is wet and there are clouds but...no rain as Jack and Kate watch the attorney go to Clare's Mom's hotel room. They presume this is the mysterious client demanding blood tests on Aaron. 30 seconds later @ 29:41 minutes, the attorney comes running out of the apartment and its POURING down rain! It's like that on the island. Thing is... they're SUPPOSED To be in Los Angeles!! It doesn't rain like that in L.A.!!

BTW; the sweat in lost was real!

Ok, now, I realize some of the sweat on their collars could have been sprayed on by the costume/make-up folk or whoever handles the 'make it look like sweat' department! HOWEVER - I am here to tell ya they couldn't have had to do much 're-applying'. It was friggin HOT out there, yo! I'd forgotten how much closer to the equator Hawaii is than California!! Hello!!! Hot! But different than So Cal hot. Until you get used to it, you just gotta be okay with sweat. Or stay in the ocean or a pool. Or stay inside with the AC (Boo on this last option!).

This sweat thing - takes me to the athletics required to have even been the actors who played Kate, Jack, ANY of the characters (including Hurley) who repeatedly WALKED and or RAN across the SAND! Are you KIDDING ME?!

4pm arrived. I drove the almost mile from my beach house to the main Ke Iki Bungalow resort, the epicenter of these nuptial festivities. My Jamaican family had gathered from New York, mostly. Aunt Angie (my Moms sister), Uncle George (Angie's husband) (and I don't call either of these people 'aunt' and 'uncle' unless to tease them, as, they are only about 7 years my senior!). There was also Cousin Phil (Angie & George's first born and Andrew's brother) and Aunt Gracie (my Moms 1st cousin, making her my 2nd cousin but I call her Aunt. Family dynamics, ya gotta love em!).

Rev. Gillian V. Harris M.S.P.

Everyone was gathered in one of the rentals. We sat around the table and caught up. "How's your Dad doin'?" they asked. I raved about his health, "He's doing amazing. He's great! He's just kinda pissed off about his license and the fact he can't drive his brand new car right now!" Knowing my Dad they were all like, "Oh my God, I know. Poor Roy!"

I met Bri's Mom and dad. Her folks are FROM Hawaii, so, she was home! Both Bri and Andrew have tons of friends who went to school with them at M.I.T. (Massachusetts Institute of Technology) where Andrew just finished his PhD. Their wedding party was nearly a dozen strong and then there were other friends. Their friends said yes to the invitation and made Hawaii their vacation timed with this lovely wedding. It was a wonderful gathering of really nice people!

I was early, it seemed. Not sure how I did that. I took pictures and spent time in the jeep in front of the AC texting Cali! Soon it was time for all to gather out on the sand where the ceremony would take place. I hadn't put my feet in sand in more than a decade. Tortola, I used to go there all the time. 2001 was the last time. Pitiful...

I knew from memory that it takes more effort to walk on sand and makes for good cardio. I THOUGHT I looked forward to this *opportunity!* The distance to the chairs where the ceremony would be didn't seem that far at a glance. Aunt Gracie is in her 70s and uses a cane. She has a condition in her hip which has severely affected her walking ability. But Gracie is a get up n go New Yorker (of Jamaican descent) so nothing stops her! Ever! But I'm thinking, OMG -a cane in the sand? I knew the right thing would be for me to offer to help her across. "Oh thank you", she said and handed me her purse. Right then, God stepped in (clearly) sending a GORGEOUS guy over named 'Wilson' to offer his beautifully tanned, muscular arm to Aunt Gracie. I was like, 'Wooowwwww'! And awesome! Now I could concentrate on getting my SELF across the damn sand. Ok... (deep breath) I don't wanna talk about this anymore!

I went down the 7 or 8 steps and there it was. A SEA of sand. Might as well have been quick sand, ready to gobble me up! I kicked my diva rhinestone studded flip flops to the side thinking I'd need all the muscle my toes could traction to make it to my seat in the front (farthest) row.

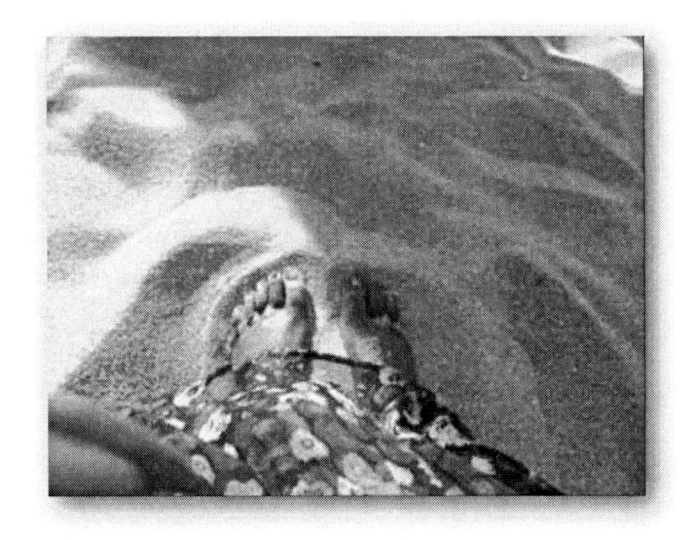

Know what?! Maybe I was wrong. Maybe this effort woulda been easier in the flip flops! Oh MAN. I ...really don't wanna talk about how every step was not as forward in motion as I intended. With every step, my feet dug down and almost back - instead of forward. Simple math: weight + gravity + sand = the moonwalk. I don't wanna talk about how my entire body was in the effort. Wearing a long flowy sundress and carrying only my camera, cell phone and Aunt Gracie's purse, I struggled to lift my hem so as not to trip and fall making matters even worse! I wondered if people could see the effort this was for me. "Hurley" I thought as I trudged, "Dude! How did you DO this?" O M G! I was deep in commiseration, now. I finally reached my friggin seat in the first friggin-fraggin row. This journey had been DOWN hill. I didn't even want to think about the end of the wedding and walking back UP to the reception area. OMG... My *pride* wondered how I was gonna pull this off without being a spectacle!

The ceremony was beautiful! The minister especially impressed me as he opened by blowing the big conch shell horn and then delivering a perfectly eloquent, memorized ceremony! He was phenomenal and I admired his skill. I hope to one day flow as smoothly - without copy - when I do ceremonies.

The end came and I'd already premeditated a plan; ' I'll need to pretend like my cell phone keeps going off and I'll stop intermittently to check it while catching my friggin breath. I coached myself through it, "Don't wipe the sweat. Pretend like you don't notice it... Look down and let your hair fall over your face so no one will see the sweat and the huffing n puffing. I GOT THIS!" The journey back, UP HILL across what felt like MILES of friggin sand went pretty much as I'd anticipated. You get what you expect! I forgot I could have focused differently for a different result. Instead, I planned for it being even harder than it was coming down. And so it was. I didn't have to worry about Aunt Gracie. Wilson was impressively on the job immediately after the family photos were done.

He escorted Aunt Gracie up to normal land where the party was. I trudged behind them, working for an Oscar as my goal was to make it appear I was taking my sweet time, ON PURPOSE! Lol. I occasionally glanced up at them and marveled at how much farther ahead they were than me, AGAIN! Oooh man. - Ya know what?! I don't wanna talk about this!

I guess it was a compliment that I APPEARED fit enough to handle this journey- so much so, apparently, I did not need an escort, as well. Or...maybe they'd just run out of escorts?! "Oh my GOD", I wondered at one point if it would be cool if I just stopped, turned around and faced the ocean and just sat down. Like... on purpose. -As if I was meditating like Locke liked to do! - No! Why prolong the inevitable?! "Where the hell's MY Wilson?? Willllllllllllsoooooonnn!" I screamed his name in my head and made myself laugh out loud as I thought of Tom Hank's character grieving his lost soccer ball friend named Wilson in 'Castaway'!

While I can find ways to entertain my mind during such challenges as this walk across the sand (did I mention it was UP hill?), the biggest truth is I was being smacked in the face with a lesson. Present tense. Loud n Clear. The Universe was talkin' to me. -SCREAMING at me with great seriousness and articulation about my need/desire/next-project-starting-this instant to get fit again and quick. - Because you NEVER KNOW when you're gonna have to power across some damn sand (Season 3 Episode 21 @ 16:31).

Native O'ahu
Day 4
Sunday 8-31-14
Sturmah had the day off so this afternoon, he had promised to take me to places where I can commune with those who walked the island before us. "You want to have a REAL Spiritual experience? I will take you" he said in his island accent. He reminded me to bring something with me I could leave as a gift for the Spirits. This gifting, he explained is called 'Ho'Okupu'. He'd said this word to me repeatedly. I was excited to gift the spirits and I was thrilled that I'd brought the perfect stash to pick a present. Before we left my beach house he asked again, "do you have your Ho'Okupu for the Spirits?" I assured him, "yeah, I got it!" I opened my purse and found a little silk pouch carrying the stones I'd chosen as gifts. Angelite, Citrine, Crystal and Chrysocolla.

Sturmah had also talked to me about the Ti Leaf which ya get from a 'Ti Tree'. The Ti Tree was introduced to Hawaii by the early Polynesians. It's a tall plant and has tightly clustered, deep green leaves that spring from the center like a fountain. The leaves are dramatically large! Oval and blade shaped. Each leaf can grow to about 4 inches wide and can be from 1 to 2 feet long!! I know you've seen these. I'm about to show you a picture and you're gonna say "oh yeah! THOSE!" These leaves have long been considered sacred. They were used by the Kahuna Priests in their ancient religious ceremonies as protection to ward off evil spirits and to call in good. In old Hawaii the plant was also used for many healing remedies as well as for shelter as thatch on roofs.

Sturmah found a Ti Tree plant on the resort grounds and pointed at the very, very center where there was one skinny shoot. "See that?" he said. Looked like a long blade of grass. "If you're ever hiking or something and you run out of energy and you think *oh no I'm not gonna make it -* you take one of these", he reached for the little blade "and you go like this" he said as he put it the sliver of green in his mouth like a (micro) cigar. "You'll get your energy back and you'll be able to finish your goal".

Sturmah, who also had brought a few shells to gift the spirits, said we should wrap our presents in a Ti Leaf then leave the offering. I got that the Spirits would appreciate the gift even more if I followed this advice from one of their fellow natives. I was actually very awed by the experience. I wanted to understand the people - especially the ones who'd since transitioned onward. I felt such intense reverence for that and those still playing into the creation of the energy I was experiencing. The history and those who lived the history physically on this island in the 1800s and earlier. I could feel them. They were so present. And in the midst of it, I felt like a kid on her very, very best behavior!

Sturmah took me to several areas, two of them were very alike. Mountains by beaches. In the mountains I could see caves like from Shawn's story. I understood their potential, now.

As I drove, Sturmah turned my attention from the mountains to the water. He told me his belief that when people "die" there, they are then in Spirit form and they have to wait to be able to move on. He said, "as the sun sets, all the spirits who are still here make their way to the west". He was directing me to drive us to an area along the beach where he said we'd see "stepping stones" out in the water. The effort was to make their way across the island in what felt like a chasing effort - to get there in time. Timing was everything. The Spirits then leap these stones and try to spring into their next step or life phase by way of the setting sun. According to my new friend, if they didn't make the leap at the exact, right moment... they ended up still in this dimension/realm for yet another day! Here to wander the islands earth with no bodies.... Here to contemplate their lives just spent, until they finally make the leap that moves them forward. Until then, it is, for many a purgatory.

Out in the water, see the "stepping stones" that spirits use and if perfectly timed, they can leap forward into their next stage of life.

When I saw the cross on the beach on the beach, I asked Sturmah if someone had transitioned or was buried there. He said no that the cross was most likely just a way to honor someone's loved ones as they do their work to finally be able to leave this lifetime by successfully 'leaping' into the next.

Sturmah wandered off as I sat on a bolder behind this cross. I closed my eyes "Creator of all life, all things thank you for today, for now. Clear and protect this space and my effort. Allow me only communication with those based in your Love. That or something better for the greater good. Amen". I hoped there would be someone to talk to. Very quickly, I was in communication with a spirit, a light and friendly female personality. She presented herself to me in her 30s. Long dark hair and a motherly energy about her, she was also just very social and hospitable! She noticed me and came over to me. She was curious. I told her what I was doing, praying for her and everyone else. She confirmed that she's waiting to cross, "I'm just waiting for my turn" she explained. I was moved to ask "do you forgive yourself?" "Yes, I do. I have made peace". I got that, she was waiting because it was, in her belief system, the 'proper' thing to do. I offered her blessings, "I will add you to my prayers tonight. I will pray that you are happy always and for your speedy move forward." She thanked me, I thanked her. She was the kind of person I would totally befriend, in the physical. I really liked her and would keep my promise in prayer later that evening.

As we drove to the next stop I shared this with Sturmah. "How LONG?!" he asked me with great anxiety. In truth she didn't say how long because she didn't know how long because that was part of her belief system. I didn't say that. "Did she say how LONG she has to wait?!"

His face showed concern. I felt bad because, though I had not asked her that question, my sense was that it was an indefinite amount of time. :/ - I didn't tell him that. I just said, "Shoot! I didn't ask her that!" To Sturmah, THIS is the key question. How friggin LONG will HE have to be in this limbo (as he perceived & believes it) after his body dies while he's trying day after day to leap these rocks for easy entrance into his next phase....?!

Soon we arrived at Pu'u o Mahuka Heiau State Monument. It's a monument now...but back in the day, this heiau was a functional epicenter of conscious and heartfelt intention by way of vibration and energy (sacred religious ceremonies) resulting in.....BIG BLACK SMOKE. Yeah! Makes you think about how 'the Others' used black smoke to warn Danielle that they were coming (Season 1 Episode 24 @ 1:40). Isn't that interesting!?! In LOST, the *Others* would make a proclamation/declaration via their smoke "We're coming to see you and it's not gonna be pretty". (Are you thinking C.U.I. - Like the history of the island played into a silent influence of the scripts creation?) It seems that sometimes the smoke rising from Pu'u o Mahuka Heiau was sometimes a warning. And just like in LOST, it could easily have been that *sometimes* 'others' in their paranoia misread the message of the smoke as it was ALSO used in ceremonies for healing and to give thanks.

A 'heiau' is a religious site or temple. Situated on a ridge with an amazing panoramic view of Waimea Valley and the northern shoreline of Oahu, this temple had ties with other heiau's at Wailua and Kauaí. It's reported that signal fires at these heiaus provided visual sign language between the islands!!! In times of war the heiau would be used as a sacrificial temple to insure success in the conflict!

You'll find this sacred place off Pupukea Homestead Rd (Hwy 835) from Kamehameha Hwy (Hwy 83) across from the Pupukea fire station, high in the green forest mountains that blanket the island. The tall pine trees ALMOST made me feel like I might be in Oregon or Washington State - but mixed with the tropics of Hawaii.

This particular heiau is the largest on Oahu. It covers almost 2 acres. Pu'u o Mahuka is translated as "hill of escape". This temple played a huge role in the social, political and religious system of Waimea Valley which was a major occupation center of Oahu.

At the top, the area is flat.... and there's a gigantic rectangular section bordered by rocks. Sturmah told me that when this Heiau was being built, workers walked these rocks up to the top, one rock per person, at a time! Not sure of the elevation but it was a steep, curvy climb even for the jeep! And that's a lot of people- a train of people carrying rocks for days and days until they were done creating the stacked walls that ranged from 3 - 6 feet in height and the interior surface that was also paved with stones. Within the walls were structures... What I could see was a large flat rectangular surface that is maybe a fifth the size of the entire external rock rectangle. From the look of the burned rocks, sometimes the whole entire gigantic rectangle was on fire. Sometimes it was just sacrifices on the smaller rectangular surface where the offerings would lay and ...burn.

I was awed to be standing in this place where so much focused intention/energy in life and death situations, took place. I was so moved I choose not to take many pictures. Something about photos in this space…felt inappropriate. The energies experienced here, the power of will left a vibration that was clear and overpowering yet I struggle to find the words to explain. What must it have been like to experience the magic of that time? I didn't know who (spirits) might still be hanging out at this heiau but I wanted to show my respect.

On the hood of the Jeep, Sturmah and I prepared to individually offer our gifts.

(All photos in dazzling color in the kindle version of this book!)

THAT is a Ti leaf! And my stones were Angelite, Chrysocolla, Smokey quartz, Citrine and a few shells I'd picked up at a previous beach where I'd talked to the lady spirit.

Angelite (big blue ball and near the center of the cluster of rocks on the leaf)- This blue stone is awesome for inner guidance and astral travel. It helps with the connection to angels, spirit guides and an individuals' higher self. Its energy assists n converting fear into faith. It is a powerful stone for healers as it provides protection for the body and the environment it's in. I thought the spirits there might appreciate some Angelite!

Chrysocolla - (colors of chrysocolla range. In the picture here Chrysocolla would be the stone closest to me as I took the picture. -The darker navy blue one with marbled turquoise running through it. This stone is way up on my cherish list. It's a stone of communication. Very 5th (throat) chakra as its essence is expression, empowerment and teaching. The colors discharge negative energies. This allows a calm which allows truth and inner wisdom to reveal itself and be realized. And it's like the peace pipe....without the carcinogens as it emphasizes the power our thoughts, words and actions have on our environment and those in it. It's a compassion stone. I thought the spirits might appreciate some Chrysocolla!

Citrine - There are two small pieces of this golden stone in the picture. They are behind to the left and right of the angelite. Let me tell you - CITRINE is the MAC Daddy of stones in my book, right now. I have such high affinity for it I insisted there be citrine amongst the diamonds of the promise ring I wear.

Citrine is of service for multiple purposes. It multi-tasks harder than your average Light workin' stone! As I studied Citrine I learned it was referred to by several different nick-names:

The Protection Stone

The Sun Stone

The Success Stone
The Mind/Emotion Stone

Citrine is extremely powerful at expelling any kind of negative vibe be it from a person, place, thing or situation. Its energy plays into the resolution of negative situations. If you MUST be in this situation, this stone will help you through it!

Then there's the fact that this stone, Citrine, has energetic qualities of the Sun! It assists in energizing and invigorating the Spirit Body and how you feel emotionally while also adding to the vitality and power of your physical body. Citrine is a comfort stone, warmth and nurturing - just like the sun (minus the ultra violet rays!). Citrine has a subtle way of encouraging self-confidence and elevated esteem of self.

Citrine is a potent stone when it comes to benefiting our mental capacity. Its energy sooths anger, fear, self-doubt, anxiety. It is a tremendous aid in the healing through grief, emotional trauma and depression. Citrine is your 'don't worry be happy' rock. Happiness, joy and optimism are its main ingredients. That being said...

Prosperity, abundance and success (especially in business) are strong characteristics of the Citrine energy trait. I like to mention this last because 'true success; is not just a bunch of money in the bank. Citrine is in alignment with this truth as it aids us in all the areas necessary to bring your goal line wins to fruition. Self-discipline courage and will power are potent citrine energies as this stone emanates good fortune and wealth. I use citrine in meditation to help regain my center in peace...and when I'm working affirmations to aid in manifestation. Citrine is perfect for the effort of shifting energy for the purpose of consciously designing your life so...I figured the Spirits might appreciate some Citrine!!

Speaking of stones, you might remember a few scenes where they were part of the story line in LOST. Jacob sent his brother a stone - not sure what it was except that it was off white. (Season 6 Episode 9 @ 31:39) I read that as a gift of light and higher consciousness. -Because of its color, its properties are in alignment with the upper chakras like the 6th and 7th (3rd eye and crown). I was especially taken with the scene when the original island mother (as I have decided to name her) was laid to rest in the cave, alongside the body of Jacobs' brother and a little pouch containing two stones. While the writers may have been using two stones, one black and one white to symbolize the two brothers, both stones actually have similar qualities.

You can see the stones pretty clearly when Jack and Kate discover the decayed bodies in the cave (Season 1 Episode 6 @ 12:59). One stone was Selenite, the other was Obsidian (which I recently learned is made from molten lava!). Both have strong protective energies. Selenite is also a great stone for protection grids. I often leave one per room at the close of house healings. Selenite is also a powerful intuition, psychic awareness & clairvoyance tool through its influence on the third eye chakra! You can also access past lives and do past life work and healing with it. But of course, we are learning in these pages by 'past' we mean 'other'. Other lives - not past but present tense in a different dimension! The other stone (black) assists in the clearing of psychic debris in the aura (energy body). The energy of Obsidian is protective in that it will shield you against negativity while releasing it from your field. Perfect for this womans' passing. She was a friggin MURDERER! (Scene 6 Episode 15 @ opening scene)

My ho'ukupo

I wrapped these stones along with a little ball of crystal (another multi-purpose energy/intention enhancing stone) along with a few shells Sturmah had handed me after the first beach stop, "here, this is for your ho'ukupo". I think he'd forgotten that I'd brought something but I graciously took them anyway. I was all ears, all heart, completely open and wanted to learn. There was a terrific sensation of 'respect'. No... I'm not saying this right. The energy I was experiencing was breath taking and left me wide eyed. I didn't really know what to do.

After wrapping the stones in a nice little ti leaf bundle, I held them in my hand and said a silent prayer to bless all who were there, to bless our efforts in this ho'ukupo. I then opened my channel to receive Reiki energy thereby clearing and enhancing the stones and the ti leaf wrapping. "Love". I focused the radiant light of love into the stones. Then I wandered over to a grassy area where there was a massive bolder calling me. It was an easy 4 feet high and at least as wide around. Pitted and acned from fire and years of weather, it sat there in all its boldness. I was almost afraid to touch it. I had the sensation of not wanting to touch ANY thing. Like a kid in a really expensive house as a guest, - like I might break a bolder or something!

I gently placed my gift on top of this huge rock next to a stone that it looks like someone else left previously. I sat down on the grass next to the bolder. I let the busyness of the day melt away... I felt...watched. In a kind way but watched none the less. But no one (spirits) talked to me. In fact it's like they got really quiet BECAUSE I was around. I felt ...very observed. And ...that was ok. I just hoped they accepted my gift with the spirit in which I intended it.

I thought it would be a good idea to sit and maybe go deeper...or just be and see what happened. I had a hard time relaxing as first. I thought it was because I so buzzed from all the activity on the trip. At least that's what I thought at first!

Finally, I relaxed and settled back allowing my mind to get quiet. In a meditative calm, the hyper mode I'd been stuck in, dissolved and my inner self got still. That's when someone came near me... A male energy. I felt him above me to my left. A father figure... A large yet patient presence, observing me. I sat and I felt myself kind of swimming in consciousness other than mine... I realized there were more spirits but they were back ground. He was their leader, this male consciousness who'd come close to me. A penetrating communication transpired that went beyond and was without words. And when I say "penetrating" - know that this was not necessarily ...comfortable. It wasn't the warm fuzzy moment I was looking forward to. All I can do to explain is tell you through my clairsentience what transpired and even that is linguistically tricky. It was like being in a room full of people who were suddenly, quietly staring at me. I felt judgment! But at the same time I felt like those observing me understood my intention, Love, which was at full force. They understood that AND... they really didn't care that much about it. I was...a nuisance. Like...suddenly everybody noticed a GNAT at the dinner table! And...I wasn't sure whether they appreciated my gift, either. The ti leaf wrapped bundle, by this time, had fallen off the big bolder where I sat it. When it hit the ground it startled me a bit. I sort of jumped in alignment with not being fully at ease in this situation... I opened my eyes and looked down at it to my left. "Hm..." I thought, "I... wonder what that means?" I deliberated about whether to put it back. I decided to leave it where it was, beside the bolder on the ground in the grass. "I hope you like my gift", I told them. "I wanted to find a way to honor you. I love your island. Thank you for what you do to make it like it is! Peace and blessings to you..."

Ever been in a situation where even if you didn't intellectually know the history, you could FEEL it!? And I also felt...ego! Could that be right?! It was an understanding of their own...royalty. - I felt like a pauper who'd gone to visit the Queen's castle! Before I knew it', we'd been at the heiau more than an hour! When I got back to the car I quickly jotted notes, thoughts and impressions and this pretty much ended the long day. Time to get back to my beach house!

I later read that this very heiau we visited ceased functioning in 1819 when the traditional religion was "abolished". Read that on-line. When I saw that word 'abolished' it really stuck out to me. I was like, "Abolished? Can they DO THAT??" Can you 'abolish' a religion?! .... I think one might TRY but I don't think it's possible! Just sayin'...

The sun was setting as we were in the 8pm hour when the electric gate allowed me into the driveway at the house. I parked next to Sturmahs pick up. It was time to say farewell to my new friend. Monday would be busy and my last day before my Aljira flight - I mean Hawaiin Airlines (lol) flight would carry me back to L.A. I was so grateful for all that he'd shared. I had wanted to go hiking deep in a green, green jungle. He was going to take me but we ran out of time. Next time!

Suddenly I felt…the chunk of Selenite I didn't give to Paul, MUST have been for Sturmah. I went and got it from my suitcase and handed it to him. He was floored. "Wow! I have NEVER seen anything so beautiful! Where do you get all these stones?" I was surprised at his surprise and delighted to bring him so much joy. I told him about my 'rock shopping' addiction and about the properties of Selenite. It's an amazing, amazing stone. Another of my favorites. I use it extensively in Reiki healings. Even distant healings have profound results with selenite. It's a purifier. It's the only stone I know of that can cleanse, clear and charge other stones and crystals while doing the same to itself. Selenite doesn't needs to be cleansed or cleared ever. That would be like trying to wash some soap with … soap!

I hugged Sturmah good bye. Time to plan the next day.

Journal
Monday September 1,
DAY 5

My last full vacation day in Hawaii has arrived. On line with the office I see a client is seeking sudden service for TODAY. In an effort to expedite the quote I must head out to seek a beloved Sprint signal! The owner of the resort had returned home. We met each other in the driveway. Its 8am Hawaii-time and he's in his robe. He extended his hand, "Hi Gillian, I'm John" "Hello! So nice to meet you", I said. "Thank you so much for these awesome accommodations!!" "Our pleasure" he smiled and looked at me fiddling with my cell. "Crisis in the office and I gotta catch a sprint signal which will be right over there in that front yard!" I pointed across the way at a neighboring house! He laughed, "Ya know, there's a landline inside the house beside the couch!? I told Greg to tell you that!" My eyes met his as my jaw in dropped! Still giggling he said "you probably would have liked to have known that five days ago, huh?!" "Oh My GOD!" I laughed hard! It was too funny after all the contortions and TRESPASSING I'd been through! "I know NOW! Thank you SO much". I made an about face!

I thought about what I'd gone through a few days earlier, Saturday, with Sarina (an admin of 3+ years who I sometimes struggle to communicate with. I often say, I won't fire her because …she feels like my daughter from another life petal! We care for each other like family…and like family sometimes I know I'm being…..tested!) I could have just done this quote myself, in 15 minutes but…I had vacation stuff to do! Steadfast, I was determined NOT to write this estimate! Instead - I spent TWO HOURS of back and forth via email patiently trying to employ the right words that would get Sarina to understand the prescription (how many valets/shuttles/where we'd stage etc.) - A location that she, herself, had once scouted! She kept revising and sending it to our inbox (for my review), SO askew! Finally… I had a schedule to keep and enough time had been gobbled, so… I did it myself! LOL. - Wow – and there was a phone in the house this whole time! I think maybe I should be more observant sometimes!! I'd never …relaxed enough to sit in the living room! I guess I was too busy!! If I sat, it was at the dining room table at my computer. Sad… Oh well! It was now a NEW DAY!

I handled office business lickity split. Wrote the quote, talked to the client without static, took their deposit and deployed valets all within about 25 minutes – and I felt very bionic! Tia was in the office, today. I updated her and she took it from there. Tia is pretty sharp. Knowing that this party was handled and in process, it was back to Googlemaps. I needed to be in Kailua at 1pm.

I figured the freeway was faster. I'd take the H1 from the North Shore and head south. Continue south on the H2 and then connect with the H3 for the eastbound travel to Kailua. Ultimately, I would end up at a house in a beach community off Kalaheo Ave… Here's the thing - I should have looked at the map closer. The H3 tried to kill me! - No, seriously!

Did I ever tell you I'm afraid of heights?! Ahhhh yeah. I become…*undone* when in those moments. So, I'm drivin' along and all of a sudden I realize *holy shit, I'm in a predicament*! I can't turn around - it's on. I've got to…get to the end, however far that is.

I found myself on this…this… freeway that is basically a very high, extraordinarily long bridge! Way not cool. I don't do bridges, yo! And then there was the tunnel. For six miles I'm traveling deep, deep, DEEP within the innards of the Koolau Mountains. Did I ever tell you I'm somewhat claustrophobic?! Ahhhh yeah! This was about 16 miles of psychological torture! Look up the 'John A Burns Highway' or 'Interstate H3' and see the pictures! See them and feel me!!! I've been trying to find numbers. How many hundreds of feet above the ground is that bridge/freeway?! I'd guess an easy 1000ft in some spots cuz it feels like the 57 freeway where it passes over the I-10 in Diamond Bar California. One day on the air in L.A., before a traffic report, I decided to call and ask Cal Trans to tell me how tall that freeway was and they said "1000 feet". A freeway like that traveling over the San Andreas Fault! Are you KIDDING me?! And just like that ridiculous freeway is in Quakeville Cali, as I'm traveling this H3 monster I'm realizing…Hawaii has earthquakes, TOO!! Just like California, Hawaii has dozens per day! Granted, most of 'em are teeny weeny! But once in a while they get a good one! I admit, the fall here might be a smidge more pleasant as it would be into a rich, lush, thick jungle below.

Rev. Gillian V. Harris M.S.P.

Some people LOVE this kind of thing and I must admit, I would have been taking a million pictures if I'd been a passenger because the beauty was truly breathtaking. Thing is - I was NOT the passenger and I was having a different kind of breathtaking experience!

The fear - if I let it -makes me a little ... light headed. I was fighting that side effect with EVERY thing in me. When I realized I was in a bit of a life n death pickle I quickly threw white light around the car. Protection. Found my (spiritual) grounding cord and made sure it was firmly connected with the center of the earth. I had a very short, to the point convo with God, "Thank you for helping me. I know you're helping me with this and that all is well. Thank you for getting me to my destination safely". I then turned the radio up really loud and sang really badly -to stay grounded. Don't know the words? Change em and make the words 'I got this' work in the melody!

Took em 37 years to build this freeway. THIRTY SEVEN! And it's still kinda new! Opened for use December 1997. Lucky me...

With deep gratitude, I made my exit off that crazy highway! I'd made it to Kailua - alive and still within the same incarnation!!!

John & Rey

Photo: LOST Actor Rey Payumo in one of his many classic cars!

The past doesn't matter. Like, yesterday was yesterday. Every day is a new opportunity to recreate yourself and your life.
Paraphrased quote from LOST; Jack talking to Kate
(Season1, Episode 3 @ 38:38)

    I wanted to talk to someone who'd been part of LOST just to know what the energy was like. I wondered if the lessons of the LOST story affected them personally. Beyond that... I really wasn't sure what I'd ask them. Again, I wasn't interested in gossip. In harmony with that, these two wanted to make sure "dirt" wasn't what I was looking for. I assured them, this book, "is SO not about that!" I am so very endeared by the time I spent with these two LOST actors! It was the energy... Warm and exciting as they found the words to share their time in the TV series.

I was early into Kailua so I had time to shake off the scary H3 near death experience! I arrived at John Reyno's house (different John from the one who owns the Ke Iki Bungalows) at about the same time Rey Payumo pulled up in his long 1965 Chevrolet Impala convertible. (I'd learn this was one of many classic cars he has.) Their stories are both follow your heart/ step outside of your comfort zone and live -kind of testimonies. And by way of this, they both end up in Hawaii and part of something so awesome it will serve as one of the highlights of their lives - FOREVER.

For having such profound experiences, both of these actors joined the show in a late season, like 5 or 6. Neither really knew that much about LOST before becoming part of it. Though their parts were not starring roles, their experience in LOST is spoken of with such fond memories and are spotlighted as turning points in their lives! Thanks to taking a chance and following their hearts. And don't get me wrong, these guys were already living exciting lives in island paradise!! But as a result of their time in LOST, there was evolution within. And another gift is that, now, they are both dear friends with some of the actors who played leading parts. I don't mean just acquaintances, I mean heart to heart friends. They spoke highly of the men who played Sawyer and Hurley. When Rey talked about hangin' out and playing basketball with (the actor who plays) Hurley, I was like "WOW!" How awesome and how wonderful to know that the kind, loveable energy I got from Hurley on LOST wasn't just his acting! And this trend was LOST-wide! Many of the actors we enjoyed in the series are dear friends now! I believe these people are also friends and otherwise associated on other life petals. They met again, in this incarnation for the production of this TV Series. Further, it was an agreement they made in the realm of the 'unconscious', to reunite at this time, in this place, and do this TV show. Rey and John are perfect examples of life unfolding so that this plan could take place.

Rey stands about 6'4"! He's got long black hair down his back. Of Philippine decent, his look blends well with the native Island look so he was perfect for LOST. He'd been a US Postal carrier for 20 years on the mainland, when he visited Hawaii. Shortly after that vacation, he got a *random* opportunity to transfer to Hawaii! Next thing ya know, serendipitous events lead him to acting, LOST and several other shows. For LOST, he got 3 months off from the post office to film while he played one of the big mean LOST temple guards. Prior to his role, he didn't know much about the show. He knew it was about a plane crash on what he called a "hyped up Giligans Island".

He talked about the culture of the island and how it influenced the cast "they grew into it and a lot of em still live here". There were 3 or 4 guards in the temple scene, then they added John. Other than the through-the-roof FUN he had during filming of LOST John says the biggest thing was "the friends I met. To be friends with some of these actors is....unusual. -Wouldn't happen in L.A".

It is my contention that these new friends are actually old friends from other times and these people had a reunion, as cast and crew in LOST!

John Reyno grew up in L.A. with the film industry all around him. He viewed it with disdain. He says he used to call the industry "silly and superficial. I didn't want anything to do with it". Life goes on and eventually John went to Hawaii to relax and enjoy the fruits of his previous labor. He met a mountain climber guy who became a great friend, Dave. Dave got a gig on LOST but couldn't do it. John says Dave suggested HE do it instead, "he says, I think you'd fit my costume!" So John met the producers "they loved me". He met the casting agent and got the part! They'd already been filming for a couple weeks so he says he felt awkward at first "you're wearing these rags. Then they give you a gun - I've never held a gun before. So I'm holding an AK 47!" he laughed hard at the insanity of HIM holding a weapon – let alone, one like that. He explained a scene where he was to stand guard as the lead actors came out, He didn't know where to point his gun. The director told him, to just pick somebody! So... he pointed it at KATE! More laughter. "It was a fun gig. -About as fun as I've ever worked. The camaraderie set the bar for anything I'd ever worked on. It was such a family. We worked together so much and we all looked forward to being together".

Despite the connection to doing the show - watching it was another story! John had watched some of the first two seasons (that's more than Rey had seen!) but then he says "as soon as polar bears and black smoke came out I was like -Oh No! -Too metaphysical for me!" He also says it was hard to concentrate on the story once he was in it. Even in review he was doing a critique, "like noticing I was chewing gum in one scene!" So it was hard for him just to enjoy it.

John and Rey told me how talented this cast was. "They hardly EVER had to do retakes", Rey said. I wanted to know what lessons they'd gotten from their experience in LOST. What has changed?

REY: The way I live my life. -I take advantage of every moment. Opportunities. With LOST it reminded me of -as a kid in my parents back yard pretending we were pirates and soldiers stuff like that. I took that as a kid and did it on the show... And don't care what people think - just enjoy!

JOHN: Sometimes in life you have these preconceptions about things. My preconception was that the industry was a certain way. Even though it *was* the way I thought it was going to be, I took something positive away from it. It was a grow thing and every time you do that you conquer one more fear. Go with it a little bit, let your life unfold. It's not going to hurt you... you can always back out - I didn't back out and it was a great experience. Enjoy the ride and let the doors open. And so, now, I do other auditions too!

I hugged them both a hearty thank you and promised to be in touch when I was done writing!

My intention now was to get back to the North Shore by taking the long way around the island. Go sea level and coastal this time. Thing is... I was so moved by my time with Rey and John that, deep in thought, I missed a turn and was soon horrified by the realization I'd done it again. I was STUCK on the friggin H3! I COULD NOT believe it! Man! I tell you what, though, I will not let that happen to me again!! EVER!

Finally back in the north shore, I ended the day driving to the Wailea Falls. I followed Shawn's verbal map to reach the sacred burial grounds. The entire way I was exhilarated by the energy, the beauty, the plants and OOOOH the Banyan Trees! They were everywhere!! So majestic! At one point I stopped, looked around and thought, "I've died and gone to heaven".

17

"And the drawing near of Death, which alike levels all, alike impresses all with a last revelation, which only an author from the dead could adequately tell."

Herman Melville (1819-1891)

Lori & Raina

Interview date 9-9-14

As you know by now, one of my dearest friends/confidants/sisters in spirit is Channel and Multi-Dimensional Healer, Lori Board Camacho. THIS incarnation we would meet as valets. It was before Valet Of The Dolls, though. Back in my days RIGHT after radio I was working for another valet company both in the field as a valet and in the office learning for the days to come!

Lori was Lori Board then. Camacho would come with her awesome husband Brandon, later. Lori and Brandon own what may be the largest and most popular businesses of its type in Orange County (Ca), Awakenings Center for Conscious Living in Laguna Hills. Along with an amazing metaphysical bookstore, stones and jewelry, there are classes and workshops as they live out their mission statement which is a dedication to "providing resources that teach, uplift and inspire individuals to love themselves and their world deeply".

About 15 years my junior but it didn't feel like it. We are kindred spirits. I remember being on a party with Lori one day, a Tuesday afternoon. It was a tea party in Beverly Hills. During the miserably long downtime, we sat on the curb between a Jag and a Bentley and killed a couple hours with conversation about metaphysics. I don't remember much of the specifics, but I remember part of the beginning. Somehow... someone must have said something that lead me to say, "I don't believe we die". "Me EITHER!" Lori said enthusiastic to find a like mind. She actually knew more about me, at that point, than I knew. She kept a lot of what she knew to herself that day. Later she told me, "The first time we communicated was via email. I knew THEN that you were important to me! And then the first time I talked to you, I heard your voice and I knew we were from the same spirit family. I knew immediately."

Soon enough we would become incredibly close friends. One day going down the 101, Lori was driving and as a good mentor she'd encourage me to use my intuitive muscle and to go deeper than just a fleeting message. I got a picture and a feeling and told her what I then knew, "you're gonna use your gifts to help people for the rest of your life. Like, it's gonna be your livelihood". "REALLY?!" she said beyond excited! "Yeah!" I confirmed.

Our life story together, this incarnation, would have us severe our friendship in 2003 and then come back together with love and forgiveness in 2008. By the time we reunited, Lori had blossomed in so many ways I almost didn't recognize her. She'd grown an amazing, ever blossoming business. Personally, she had healed and transformed, evolving from a bartender who was so connected to the universal unconscious that she was tortured by it to a place where she was at peace within and all the monsters had dissolved into nothingness. With her own healing done, she could now help others. She'd gone within to resolve issues and the result was a loving clarity and freedom that allowed her to, with much grace and ease, master her natural abilities.

As a twin, Lori and her sister would have complete telepathic conversations when they were growing up. So she started early. Now, with her intention and path clear, she followed a natural current that lead her to where she is now. Lori takes hundreds of appointments per year in an effort to guide others to their healing. Much of the path traveled in these treatments, is multi-dimensional. She crosses dimensions with grace and ease and also has very close, grounded relationships with those on the other side, in the spirit world, who assist in getting the work done. In the truest sense, she is a multi-dimensional healer.

Lori ...sees dead people!

She sees em. Hears em. Talks to em. I'm cool with it NOW but it used to be so incredibly unnerving to have a friend who would ...*behave* like this, regularly! Lol! I'm playing here but seriously - back in the day, she had a habit of intuiting random people around us. When we'd go somewhere - shopping, to dinner - anything, she'd always tap me and then whisper something she learned about someone around us. "See that guy right there? (Referring to an employee of the establishment where we were.) He's worried about a report his Dad is going to find. He knows his Dad will eventually find it and he has to figure out what to do. He's scared to go home". Sometimes the stuff she'd pick up would be serious, and sometimes just hysterically funny! And sometimes again, in anticipation of this habit she had, we'd approach the door to a place and I'd say, "Lori - no psyching anybody in here, today, OK?!" Lol!!! She'd promise and do her best to refrain! Sometimes successful, sometimes she just couldn't help but tell me something! "See that girl right there..." Lolol!

I remember one day sitting in my living room her stare moved from my face to just beside me to my left. One of those moments that made me look to the left to see what she was seeing but…there was nothing there. Um… or was there!? "There's a tall, thin guy standing beside you". EYEBROWS UP! I was SO undone by that. Man!- Do you remember in the LOST series how Richards eyeballs were buggin' out when Hurley was explaining that Richards wife Isabella was standing next to him?! (Season 6 Episode 9 @ 41:20) Lololol! Touching scene but just focus on his eyeballs for a moment! While I worked hard NOT to look like him, I FELT like him in that moment!!!! And Lori continued, "he says he's really glad you're doing the work you're doing with mediumship". At this point, I'd barely decided to crack the book on that part of me.

Lori is the first of several people to tell me, "you're a natural medium". While being a medium certainly sounded like a cool thing - I was sure these people were sweet and simply mistaken. That is…until I, too, started seeing, hearing and talkin' to folks on the other side! I won't say I talk to dead people because as ya know by now, I'm past that. Nobody's friggin dead! But yes, multi/inter-dimensional communication, indeed.

Along with being a multi-dimensional healer, Lori is gifted with the razor sharp tools of clairvoyance, clairsentience, clairaudience, channeling and mediumship! I can think of no better way for you to understand the literal depth of her work than to share with you the experience of a conversation I had with her regarding this book. This spine chilling banter takes place prior to her going into trance for the purpose of allowing me to interview 'Raina', her closest Spirit Guide, who comes through with an AMAZING interview later.

Just like the buddies we are, we were just shootin' the breeze, first. Catching up! I think along the way in the beginning she forgot I was rolling tape (I just dated myself by saying 'rolling tape', didn't I?!) and just like it is when we're hanging out, we were just chit chattin'!

CAUTION: The rest of this section moves from easy to read, great information to…seriously not for the meek or faint at heart. When you see "Zzzzz" know that what happens next is CRAZY and Dark. Crazier than anything you saw on LOST and absolutely real rather than TV. So, again, when ya see the "Zzzzz" brace yourself, or just flip the pages past it til you get to the interview with Raina on page 297!

I know this portion of the interview is unsettling because the NIGHT I was listening back and transcribing it (luckily I type about 100 wpm) the friggin Valet Of The Dolls phone would intermittently ring and I would JUMP out of my skin! Why I picked a busy party night to do this I D K! O M G! I finally figured out I needed to finish transcribing this part during daylight! So, I moved to a different portion of the book until then!

Though only via internet, it was awesome to see Lori! We hadn't laid eyes on each other in a couple years! That would be when I started Bless & Clear ™. Lori was very instrumental in the energy and momentum of that company's first year in 2012-13.

I guess what made this conversation even scarier is that... it was about metaphysical reality.

Please know that with three full time jobs; career, mom and being a wife, Lori doesn't have time to watch T.V.! That's never really been her, anyway. I took comfort in that. And, in the beginning of our conversation, I was refraining from telling her the inspiration of this book was the TV show 'LOST'. Needja to know - there is a super sweet innocence about Lori. She doesn't lie because she's awful at it and she's awful at it because she doesn't get why not just tell the truth!!! Isn't that beautiful? OMG! This authenticity about her is a quality of clarity so pure that she sees past the reasoning for what others (like ME) would see as time for a perfectly good ...truth inconsistency! (- Like the long con I did to one of my employees! Tell you about that in a bit!) Consequently, if I need a friend to help me with a sneaky moment....I'm calling Lucy not Lori! Lol!

Just mentioning this so you have a better sense of who Lori is and her authentic way of being.

As I'd done with Shawn, when I originally contacted Lori I told her I wanted to interview Raina to talk about multi-dimensional existence; parallel lives n whatnot. Vague. But in this moment, now, with the record button on, I decided to say the 'L' word - just to be sure. I went ahead and popped the question:

Me: ....so, girlfriend - did you see LOST? (I did NOT stutter.)
Lori: What?

Me: LOST!

Lori: .... Um no. What is that?

Me: Ok! Perfect! That's BEAUTIFUL! (I giggled) Let's just talk!

Lori: Ok!

Me: So...You came into my little hut in the woods back in 2003 - Malibu Canyon... you and Clarissa. It was that teeny weeny house where I started Valet Of The Dolls and you were saying how busy it was in there and there were, like, three or so other beings there. They had their own scenario going on and you said the woman was being held against her will.
Lori: Oh wow - I don't even remember this at all.
Me: Yea, you guys noticed stuff right away. Then you stopped and tuned into this lady. She was being held against her will and I was like O M G! Noooo! I didn't want this to be happening in my space. I was like tell her she can just GO and you said it wasn't like he had her physically bound and chained. It was like her decision, her

choice. Psychologically she was going through something. So you saw this and you communicate with her a little bit - you told her she could split and she's like "no I can't". So the first thought that happens at this time is like.... 'So ...are they using my furniture?! Are they using my kitchen?' (lol!) If you could, please explain in your words how it is that they have their own environment going on within my space!

Lori: Yes that's true. I vaguely remember this. I don't remember all the details I got at the time but, in terms of spirits occupying space, that is a total dimensional thing. You're absolutely right about that. So their dimension is really close to ours its right next to ours. So things look relatively the same in their dimension. Some things are in different places though. They do have their own environment. They have their own furniture. It might be your furniture but it may be turned around. It may be in 3D for them. Almost like you're looking in a mirror.

Me: Wow! But at the same time could it also be a situation where... here's your house and then ...here's a freeway... In the other dimension there's a freeway running through your house in THIS dimension - or a hospital or an airport?

Lori: It can. Yes -So in that case I would call that a vortex. So in a Vortex sometimes there's several realities existing in one place at one time depending on where each being is vibrating. There could be like 10 channels hanging out in one place. So you shift to this channel to see what's going on, shift to that channel to see what's going on. But they're layered realities. There could be a hospital there, a freeway there... absolutely.

Me: Okay so there are layers. So between the layers, some people use the term 'the veil'. My contention is that the veil doesn't really exist that it is an illusionary word.

Lori: Okay so, I have not had that experience, I've seen the veil. But I've also seen the veil lift. And I've seen what it looks like it's very, very, thin. In terms of what you're saying about it being an illusion I think it probably is an illusion. Raina might describe it better but how she's explained it to me is 'time'. Like our concept of time actually creates the veil. So those two things kind of exist together but when the veil is lifted you see other realities. And it's thin, like I saw it when I was in labor with Bodhi. The veil lifted so he could talk to me before I gave birth. That was a cool experience.

Me: What did he say?

Lori: He took all the pain away from this crazy contraction I was having. He dropped in and he said today is my birthday!

"But when the veil lifted for him to come in all the pain went away and he was able to communicate within my soul almost - is how it felt. So I've seen the veil on several occasions in near death experiences and then in medicine experiences. It's not an illusionary word. I don't know if it looks different to other people though. To me it looks like this shear almost white-ish material. -Like a see through sheet almost.

Me: Someone said to me once, there's no such thing as a ghost. The person who said it... -I really respect their opinion, so much. I let that simmer for a minute and I now agree because to call someone a ghost is like them calling you a ghost just because you're not in the same dimension..... Cuz there's no such thing as dead....

Lori: Yeah. True. Well I guess I think of them as not having a physical body...

Me: Or so it seems here on this side. Right?! Because in their dimension they might be having a more full experience and may have solid stuff, right?

Lori: Possibly. It depends on whether it vibrates higher than the earth, they have physical looking stuff but they can go thru it. But there are also lower dimensions than ours that are very physical too. (I thought of LOST and the Island)

Me: Ok so lower dimensions than ours that are also very physical ... So that would mean not as evolved - spiritually? Um - no. What's that mean?

Lori: Not necessarily. I'm literally talking about the way particles vibrate that make things solid. There are other realities that have that look so things are very dense and become solid matter.

Me: So like us

Lori: Yeah, like us. Exactly.

Me: I know you didn't see it but...to me, that's what I'm talking about was happening in LOST.

Lori: Ok. Yeah. And I've heard them be called inter-dimensional realities.

Me: How's that?

Lori: Kind of like inside the earth or like almost as if you opened up a portal and walked inside our reality and then you found another one.

Me: RIGHT! That is EXACTLY what happened! THAT'S what happened!!!

Lori: Awesome!

Me: (I fell into my deep southern accent!) -They were on an airplane mindin' their own business n then... the airplane fell OUT the sky! Ok - wait- FIRST it broke in to pieces n - no wait FIRST there was turbulence, n then the back fell OFF. Then the front kinda cracked n poured a buncha people out (season 3 Episode 1 @ 3:01) n then it went summer saltin' through the jungle n shit - Okay sooo... (back to my normal speech) what I loved was when Jack comes to, he's lying on his back. First thing we see - his right eyeball opens and then ya look up and all ya see is the bamboo trees moving in the wind. And then something rustles in the leaves to the left and it's a golden retriever. N then his hand is kinda moving and then all of a sudden he gasps. In my perspective of what's happening in that moment it's like his soul has caught up with the movement into this new reality.

Lori: Yeah. Right!

Me: And so now he's suddenly fully conscious to it and he's wearing the same body that he had in the other dimension. So he still looks like him and he can feel his wounds on that body as he fell out of the airplane n hit some bamboo trees n got scraped up n whatnot. So he's bleeding and he can feel all that. And he's got the little bottle of liquor that the flight attendant gave him. So they transitioned and they just happened to be in the same earth suits. And then he takes off running.

Lori: Right...

Me: Did you see 'Ghost'?

Lori: Yes.

Me: Ok so remember when Patrick Swayze's character gets stabbed by the bad guy and he gets up and chases after him? Bad guy gets away. He goes back and he realizes his body is on the ground...dead and his girlfriend, Demi Moore's character, can't see him. Remember that?

Lori: Yes

Me: I feel like that's what happened with Jack.

Lori: Ok

Me: And I feel like in that dimension - it is as solid for them there as it is on this side.

Lori: Right. I've heard both things. It totally depends on where their mind was when they crossed.

Me: you mean how solid it is where they go?

Lori: Yeah

Me: Ok. Does it also depend on what they need and their level of enlightenment?

Lori: Yes. And when someone ... You know the idea of not knowing they're dead OR if someone hasn't grown spiritually when they're here...when they leave they are more likely to get caught up in a continuous world and that will seem very dense to them.

(At this point in the interview I thought - HOLY Shiznit Batman - a continuous world was ex ACTLY what LOST was. I thought of Richard, Charles Whidmore, Jacob & his bro the Black Smoke Jungle Monster and even Ben who had been in this crazy Island whirlwind of drama for ....SO LONG! Juliet and James who got cozy there for a minute...)

Me: That's what happens in LOST! It's a bunch of people with unresolved issues.

Lori: Right so they needed a lower vibration.

Me: Time. I am totally counting on other people to explain time. Cuz all I can find for words to explain it is: I have complete knowingness that all time is happening now. The clock is just a tool for this dimension and it's not really, really real.

Lori: Right and it creates the illusion that time is real but it's not. -Exactly.

Me: Other than what I just said, I can't explain it. Cuz... they do the flash backs, flash forwards - sideways - which is parallel and to me, it's all relevant and is what we experience. And it's not sci-fi. Its real, and all of it is happening in this one moment.

Lori: Everything is happening now but time gives us the perception that it's linear. SO it happens in the past or in the future or parallel - that's a whole other thing. The parallel life that's going on. So this is how I would describe it; You are a movie theatre (she didn't say you are AT a movie theatre, she said you ARE one) and you're looking at the choices. You can go to this movie or that movie, or this one... Then you decide which movie you want to go to. But anyone can go to any one of those movies at any time cuz they're all happening at the same time so they just pick their movie.

Me: So - so you can you can pop out of that movie and go into another one before the first one is finished?

Lori: Exactly

Me: Do we do that?

Lori: We totally do. And I can give you a very good example. So I've had people come and visit me before death. So part of them has left their body and come to tell me that something is happening. The first times this happened I thought this person MUST be dead if I'm feeling them this way. But they had a very different feeling to them. So, the feeling was like they were HERE, around me. Like, I could feel them in a denser way than I feel a deceased person. One of them is this girl that I probably hadn't seen or spoken to in probably 20 years. And she wouldn't leave me alone either. (She giggled) Like, she followed me to my class that night. She freaked out a couple of my students cuz she was hanging out in the hallway.

"So finally I talked to her and she explained to me that she had a Vicodin addiction and that it was going to take her life very shortly. She told me what she looked like. And she said to me "I'm not allowed to tell you my name because you'll try to stop this from happening and that's not what this is about". And I'm like "okay that's new!" Then two months after... I get an email from a mutual friend letting me know that Heather had died of a Vicodin addiction and this was an invitation to her funeral. Hit me like a Mack truck. I'm like "Oh my God that was her". So she's very naturally blonde, she describe herself that way. She was someone I hadn't talked to in like 20 years. Every single thing she was - it was absolutely her. So a part of her separated from her body to come and tell me that.

Me: But she wouldn't tell you her name?

Lori: She told me she wasn't allowed to - as if there was another being blocking her from being able to do so.

Me: Like maybe the Creator and her - like part of her master curriculum plan?

Lori: Yeah and that I would try to stop it and that I was just supposed to know. I went to the funeral… and what was strange was last time I saw her baby she was 2 years old. Now that baby was 15 and she was the spitting image of her mother.

"I've also had it happen with a couple of clients, too, where a piece of them has come to tell me that they're dying or that something is happening before they even leave their body. And they feel much different as if they crossed over."

Me: So remember when I told you about the house clearing I did in Glendale where I had that physical sensation. I was in the bedroom of the client who'd been experiencing the phenomena and …the entity zipped through my abdomen. I felt it like…. zipped through the fat part of my belly and it felt like 'ZZzzzzzz' like electrical. What was that?

Lori: That's funny cuz I just had one recently – it's someone who owns a 'new age, Zen Restaurant and performance center in another state - outside of California and they needed me to fix a problem. Others had tried to fix it but no one could. So I would have to get on a plane and fly there and it was WINTER… Kind of a long story but about a month before he asked me to do this, something held me down to my bed and tried to sexually assault me -energetically wrapping itself around my 2nd chakra and holding me down.

Me: Got it.

Lori: It was not alive. - I mean… it was alive but… it wasn't human.

Me: Right.

Lori: And…it freaked me out!

Me: RIGHT!!

Lori: - Woke me up! And then I fell back asleep again and it happened again. I've had that kind of thing happen before. Then I went back to sleep and dreamt that there were all these bats on my back porch and I had the door ajar and I was kicking them all so they wouldn't come in and suck our blood. And I thought… what the hell is that about? I'd never dreamt about bats before this! And then I got that I was gonna have to deal with the underworld. That was the message I got, 'you're gonna have to deal with the underworld soon' and I thought….. THAT makes no sense. Then my friend calls me and he says "I really need help".

"I've never had someone ask me to do something where I felt like possibly I cannot do this. I don't know if I can do this. So I fly out from John Wayne Airport. About three hours later, I land. They pick me up. I go to their new Restaurant/theatre which was in a new location for him and he was planning a lounge area where people could get readings before or after dinner or a performance. He had great clientele at his old location. He needed a bigger space so he had moved and now was having trouble.

"I walk in and there's a SEA of people. Like I have to get past someone who's at the front door even, to get in. And... a bunch of em come and are talking to me. A LOT of them didn't know that they had passed. - You know how funeral homes have a feeling to them?

Me: Yes.
Lori: So... the building he acquired had been a mortuary for 70 years. And I said, "uh... you want me to clear something that's been housing dead people for 70 fucking years!?! How am I supposed to do THAT?
Me: (I laugh deeply)
Lori: This one lady flies up to me and she says, "what's goin' on here?" Like, she's looking around. She gets that I'm there for a reason and she wants to be part of the show or whatever's happening. - I get that she doesn't know that she's crossed over!
Me: Right.
Lori: So I deal with her first and I say, "well, you're dead". And she kinda got in my face. I said "you died in a car accident. Your family brought you here and this is where you had your funeral and your viewing" and she said "WHAAAAT?!" (Lori's voice squeals high as she impersonates the sound of this disincarnates reaction). And then she flew away from me. So that was how that one went. And then I had a whole bunch of em look at me and say "we're not leaving until you deal with the problem in the back". And I thought, ok... So I go to the back which is where the morgue and the embalming room were.... Never been in one of THOSE before! I couldn't even go in the embalming room, it was so bad. Like, I couldn't breathe. It was the most physical feeling I've ever had anywhere.
Me: And what was this room NOW?
Lori: A huge room with several candle lit seating areas for, you know, metaphysical things [like readings] to happen however there's problems. And other well-known mediums and channels wouldn't step foot in his new location. And then he's getting inconsistent readings because not all of his readers are mediums. So, all those extra beings are flying into rooms and messing with all the readings.

"So, the embalming room - I literally felt like I was gonna be sick if I stayed in there. So I set up outside of the embalming room and Raina created a portal, this very thin portal where certain ones could come out of the embalming room to the middle of the circle (portal). And then we set up a physical portal with selenite in the corner and opened up a portal for them, basically, to leave the earth. They had all been playing out their scenarios in the embalming room. And there were a couple culprits. -By the way, it took me seven weeks to do this.

Me: Wow! You went back how many times?

Lori: I only went back three times. But it was a total of 7 weeks of me energetically holding space for this. And the night before I went back, they all filled up in my house in Laguna and I had to say, "uh get the fuck out of my house! I'm not there yet." And I had a horrid headache the next morning - through my flight and all the way until I got back to the location.

"This headache thing lasted and the problem... cuz I thought ok, this was a mortuary, I get it. But why are they all still here? What's the problem? There has to be a problem... Well, when it was a mortuary, it was owned by the same family for 70 years. And all the men in the family had a problem ... called necrophilia.

Me: (My eyebrows go up like, "what?")

Lori: Yeah. And...they had a TYPE. They're type was young women and girls, some of them were children. A lot of them were young women, teenagers and women in their 20s and a lot of those women had been violated in their life, died young and then got violated again in death and couldn't move beyond the embalming room because they were afraid, *if this is what death is about I don't want any part of it.* So... I saw some crazy shit in there... some *crazy* shit I had never seen EVER before in my life.

Me: Wow... you mean because you saw what was going on.... AS it was going on?!

Lori: I saw it going on as it was going on and the main culprit who was the newest one - So... it's kinda like I had to go through these layers. So, the first visit, 'Roger' came out. So, Roger was not sorry. He had no remorse. Zero remorse. -None. He LIKED it and so... he would TRY to have remorse and then he would start cracking up laughing about it. And he also molested children. He just wasn't sorry. So, I watched and... Remember when we talked about the 'black angels' when my mom passed away?

Me: Yes

Lori: The black angels came. I've never seen the black angels in a clearing before. They detained him against the wall away from me. He was not allowed to come near me because he wasn't safe. And then a lot of the girls that he had violated kinda came out of the room very afraid like, "what's going on?" Raina had to get them to come to the center of our circle and they had to talk about what happened in their life. And what proceeded and resulted in them coming to this place where this happened to them. And then they would go down the other portal to where the selenite was. So I did this several times with a lot of them.

"What's interesting is that the owner of the restaurant has been very, very sick for several years. He almost died. And he has some sort of mystery disease. A couple of the [deceased] women were past lives of HIS that he needed to heal and release which is why he acquired this building. So his physical healing was contingent upon [getting and] healing the space. So that was fascinating.

Me: Wow... (I thought about how what we learn in one life affects our other selves in other incarnations...)

Lori: And then - so you're gonna love this - So Raina brings in, like, this team of angels, to line the portal - for some reason releasing the ones who were particularly attached to the owner - allowed the other ones to come out and find their way to the light through the portal. And she [Raina] said it would take several weeks and that we [me and the business owner] wouldn't meet again until that process was complete. And then she gave a few directions.

"So, they needed to burn frankincense and myrrh in there, every day and play a singing bowl to help the release continue. Then they brought Roger to the center of the circle in his detainment and... I've never seen this before - Raina explained to him that he could not cross over as he is because his soul would repeat his behavior again in another lifetime. So the black angels had these 'bags'. These black bags. And they separated his soul into five different parts and put him into bags and crossed him over that way. They went to different places, different dimensions. Each bag to a different place so he wouldn't repeat his behavior. But what remained afterwards was the part of him that had been wronged as a child so then we got to see what happened to him. How did he become this way? You know, like there's a REASON for that. So there was still something left over ...it was like his spirit without his soul or something."

Me: Hm...

Lori: And then THAT crossed over. And when I left, my headache left immediately. And, as soon as I walked out the front door, the Sushi Spa next door - the cooks are, apparently all these people have been going over there, fucking with them at night while they're in the kitchen cleaning up. So they're all freaked out. And then, so I go home and I think to myself, is this even happening? What's going on with this? Did all that just happen? I get back to Laguna. I go to sleep and I dream all night long. I see all these women walking out of the embalming room and one by one, making their way through the portal. But before they walk through the portal they look back at me and telepathically thank me "Thank you for helping us". It happened all night long. And then at the end, like, right before I woke up my Moms gay best friend who died last year, remember 'Dennis'?

Me: Right!

Lori: He says, "Your mom and I want you to know that we saw what you did today!" And I said, "How can you see what I did?" And he goes, "oh you know me and your mom. We're just hangin' out on the earth plane talking about everybody before we cross over". (Lori is giggling now) - Which is totally something they would do! And then I woke up, so...

"And then there were several weeks where I couldn't bring myself to make the trip again. Couldn't even log onto the airline web site to book a ticket! And there was snow there, too. I just couldn't do it! And he wanted me to come out for some big events they were having and I was like 'no, no, no'. And I said "are you guys doing the Frankincense, Myrrh and the [singing] bowl every day?" He said, "Yeah. We are!" And about...two or three weeks later I decide its ok, I can go. I can handle this again. I mean it literally made me physically ill.

"So I book a flight and head out. Land. I get to the Restaurant and it's worse than the first time! MUCH worse than the first time. So they bring out what is probably Rogers great grandfather. And, he was the first violator who acquired the mortuary, created it. He was really well known in the community. He was really outgoing. But he was a homicidal necrophite. So he used his place to also, kill. - That's WORSE! That's much worse!

Me: He'd kill people in order to have sex with them dead?

Lori: Yeah. Exactly.

Me: Oh - my GOD!

Lori: Which lead me to have to research this whole necrophilia thing because I was completely fucking disturbed. Really disturbed. And I found out that 57% of morticians have this problem. And in *other* countries. - Other countries KNOW this and so... if a younger woman dies they will not send her to the mortuary for three or four days because they know that this might happen. Our country's so disconnected they have no idea. There isn't even a law against it here.

Me: Really?!

Lori: Oh no. They call it a victimless crime because the body is dead.

Me: Oh my God...

Lori: It's NOT! The women didn't leave the embalming room, they were like trapped in there because they got violated at that point. They weren't even allowed to cross over appropriately - so it is NOT a *victimless* crime.

"Anyway, I also got that this guy created... He was very into ...creating rituals with his... shit that he was doing. I got that there were bodies buried all over the place which freaked me out. And the whole time I was walking around I felt like I was walking on top of bodies. And I got that he created some sort of portal, himself, with us. So I don't... I don't know what I'm supposed to do with that but it explained why I kinda felt...I felt like I was bombarded.

(Suddenly the video of Lori's face freezes mid word. Her mic is dead. Crazy timing!! We are DIS-connected! I wonder if my face has frozen on her monitor in such a crazy way as hers has frozen on mine! I say a series of bad words and in about a minute, she logs off and in a minute more logs back on.)

Lori: So I get that this guy is doing all this stuff... It was worse than the first person. What was strange, too, was when we were in the circle and had to bring him to the middle - and the same thing happened with Roger - all of our heads hurt, really, really bad. And they had to do the same thing with him, they had to pull him apart and cross him over in separate pieces and places. And then, again, I got told we have to keep the portal open to keep this moving.

"So then, like about a month went by four or five weeks. I just -again - NO desire to go there. It just wasn't time. Then he texted me maybe a week before I actually went and he said, "I feel like it's time to finish" or something. I said, "Ok". And I had been feeling better anyway. So -back to John Wayne airport - I flight out again -a 3rd time. Land. Get to the restaurant and ... I feel like I've got to deal with the front now, so this is just the entrance, waiting area. This is not the main area the restaurant, kitchen, reading areas and all the rest of it. And I walk in and there's a bunch of them and they're relieved and they're ready to go. They weren't the ones who were violated in the back, they just knew about it. A whole bunch of em left pretty, you know, easily. And I was amazed by... -(interrupting herself for clarity) So, my Buddhist friend had done this mantra thing with me - and it worked, like I didn't get a headache anymore. They didn't come into my house anymore."

Me: Wait. What mantra thing?
Lori: Okay so, after the 2nd time flying out, I went to my Buddhist friend who knows a lot of Mantras and he's really good at it. So he came over and put his hands around

me and said, I'm gonna do a protection mantra for you with this so that you don't get pulled down into the muck. He said, you're kind of walking into this really dark place, it's like a planet and you have your light so you can sustain for a little while but at some point you would get pulled down in it.

(I thought of Clare, in LOST this character was originally a light worker, too. Read cards, had her cards read and knew how to do astrological charts. Yet, she got pulled into the "muck" of the island.)

Lori continued: Anyway it worked. They didn't come into my house. When I went in there I didn't get a headache. Nothing. It was awesome. So I go back and there were a whole bunch of em who were ready to leave. There were three that I had to deal with who really liked being there. There was this grandma lady who would pose as grandma in readings but she wasn't really the person's grandma! There was this younger man, 18 maybe, who had killed himself and one other one. So I had to deal with their main shit. They angered the front of the spa. And then there was this thing that wasn't human, at all, ever. It was like a collection of everyone's emotions (I thought about the black smoke jungle monster - except that he was human at one time) Like a poltergeisty kind of thing. And it was having a whole lot of fun scaring the shit out of all their employees at night. So that thing would come out at night. So Raina, like, released all of that from the front of the building. And then I said "oh the back of the building"! I wanted to go see what the back of the back was like. This is behind the restaurant where the theatre and reading rooms would be. I felt like it was done back there but like maybe we had to do one more thing?! So I go back there and I was SHOCKED, Gillian! Shocked at how CLEAR it felt.

So the embalming room had some kind of energy in it still and so when I went into trance, all it was, was anger. It was anger from all the people who had been violated. They kind of left that behind. And it really came up and out of the room and released. And THEN I saw all these MONKS walking around. And I saw that the construction of the place was gonna considerably change and be, like, some sort of a new age performance center or something. I said [to the spa owner], 'they're asking that you honor the Buddhist Tradition back here. And he started laughing and he showed me these plans that he had been creating to totally remodel the back so it doesn't look like a morgue anymore and it's going to be a totally healing Zen theme! The food, the music, performances, interior design - everything.

Me: Wow!

Lori: And then, this construction worker comes in afterwards and he kinda walks around and then he comes up to the owner and he says, I don't know if you know this but, you cleared a whole bunch of spirits out of here. I was really considering not coming back.

(Suddenly Lori switches gears, reminding me of how this part of the conversation started in the first place!)

Lori: My answer to your question is this -

Me: (laughing): Shit! I forgot what I asked you!

Lori: I got it! I'm circling back now. The reason you felt something very physical [during the aforementioned house clearing - getting zapped in the belly "Zzzzzz"] is because when someone has a whole bunch of dense emotion; anger, hostility, all those things make them a denser energy. And so they're able to affect you physically more. So that's my answer to that. So that, the more not nice a being is, the more they're able to make you feel things.

Me: Well that makes sense!

Lori: I was supposed to keep that one to myself but...

Me: Well THANK YOU!

Lori: And also while this was a huge learning experience for me my friend [Zen Restaurant owner] said to me, you know Lori, you don't understand, I've had every well-known healer...house clearing people here - he even had a bunch of Monks come! They [the Monks] wouldn't go inside, though. They stayed outside the perimeter and they chanted for, like, an hour or something like that. He said nothing worked, like NOTHING. He said "you doing what you're doing... -Nobody did it that way, either and it's the only thing that worked."

Me: So it worked because you went in and communicated with them?

Lori: Yeah. Not like just go to the light! There's a problem!

Gillian: Yeah, I agree. I have a little discomfort asking people to *go to the light*. I don't, anymore. In fact, the last several house blessings & healings have been about an energy/ person rather than just um...emotions or something being left somewhere. I just wanted them to kinda ...scoot over! Like... to take that...

over there! Ya know?! (We both giggle). I just really don't think it's my place to tell them whether their curriculum here is over and what they're supposed to be doing but since I can communicate with them, "on behalf of these folks who live in this house, could you just...scoot over and out of this particular place?!" Just scoot... Over! And... it's worked.

Lori: Yeah!

Almost 1 hour into our conversation, we take a 5 minute break. Lori comes back and takes a few minutes to go into trance, clearing her brain and body space for Raina's use. Raina enters...

Raina (Soft, feminine voice with strong accent. Irish I think. Raina often refers to herself as 'we' a collective consciousness): Alright. Greetings there, dear physical angel. How are you?

Me: I'm good! Thank you!

Raina: We're most excited to be here to answer these questions that you have to ask. If you don't mind, we'd like to say something first.

Me: Absolutely...

Raina: .... (Long pause).....alright. One of the things that we want to say is some of the things that you're asking has to do with whether or not reality or realities are real. Are they real, meaning, are they tangible realities. Can you touch them? Can you feel them? And we would say there are different ways to touch and to feel. We have our way of touching and feeling however it does not contain a physical response from a body. So, yes, there is that. However whether or not a reality is tangible or real also depends on how it has been created. Has it been created over time? Has it been created in one reality and projected into another? How does it exist? And we will leave that at that for now and pick it up gain in a moment with some of your questions.

Me: Ok, One of my questions is about Time. How do I explain that all time is happening now?

Raina: Well first we need to speak about the illusion of time. It's not something that really exists. It does not exist at all. It was created. It's something that was created by man so that they could measure years. Someone figured out, alright, well we're here and we age. That happens. How does that happen? And here is the reason for it. Without time everything - everyone would eventually step over the veil. Everyone would find their way through their spirit. Through the world. In order to create an illusionary world something that is tangible and real and has egotistical reality along with it, it has to have time measured. Time creates fear. Fear creates age. At one time on the earth - before time existed, age did not measure itself in the same way. However, there are experiences where it did not work exactly. It did not become tangible enough for each human being to create an experience - a movie in which they learned about their emotions. They learned about love. The only way to do it, that worked, was to create and measure time. It created a sense of fear, a sense of purpose as well so that they felt as if 'I only have this certain amount of time here' I must immerse myself in the egotistical reality. I must immerse myself here in what is material to make something of myself. But through that some people find their spirituality. They find it and then time also begins to sort of disappear. -Also known as creative people who seem to never show up on time. There is a reason for that. They're also here measuring time in a certain way, however they begin to live differently and so the time stretches out a little bit differently. So it creates the illusion. It also helps to create matter. Matter becomes much harder when time is measured.

To answer your question about time and it not existing or existing all at once... as you move into dimensions, as you move into the higher vibrating dimensions, time becomes something different it becomes measured differently. There is a way that spirit beings can measure time in order to come through to this reality. For instance, when you have an appointment at 9:30 and you need us to show up - we have to measure time. When is 9:30? There is a place a portal that we can go into that gives us the illusion of the earth's time. And that is why a spirit will show up for an appointment a human has made. Otherwise, we do not have a sense of it. We must sort of step down into that reality to feel it. As you go into the higher vibrating realities where bodies do not exist and they are made up of mostly energy, there is also a bit of an illusory time difference, however it is not measured the same and is a bit difficult to explain in linear words. We do not measure years, necessarily. But we will measure, let's say, ages. So there is an age, of what, 100 years or so or something. You measure it in years we'll say well that age was about this ___ and that age might be a snap of a finger for us. But for you it was 100 years. So it does not exactly relate to the earth. And moving on to higher vibrating realities ...the higher the vibrating reality, the more there is no time, period.

Yes, you are right, everything is happening now. We will explain it this way, if you were 700 feet tall, if you were to grow all the way up to your higher self and you look down at several realities at once, as a multi-dimensional being you would feel it as if everything is happening right now. There is no time. And that is the truth. None at all.

(I was wowed by that analogy)

Me: So tell me this, I'm very grounded in this incarnation that I'm talking to you from right now. Let's say I'm in an accident and my body stops ...my heart stops beating in this body. So I pop out of this body. If I have curriculum that I have not finished in this incarnation would I create or co create a place where I could go to work on that curriculum before moving on to the next? So -

Raina: So, what you are asking is where *does the soul go* to continue learning? If you have not finished it here, your soul will choose many successions of lifetimes on the earth. So there will be a choice. You will leave your body, you will hang around for a bit. You will see what has happened to your body and then at a certain point someone on the other side, a guide a friend, will come your way and help you move into the deeper reality that is the spirit world so that you can access what is next. (This is what Desmond was doing Season 6 episode 17 @ 4:08) You will spend some earth time there accessing what is next. For some people, that time is not any time at all. They may go there for maybe on earth day and decide that they need to choose another earth lifetime immediately. If they choose that, they will immediately go into a baby's body. They will go and they will choose another parental unit, another family pattern that can provide them the same learning experience or continued learning experience. There is a place where you can kind of try on your family. Alright if I go to this family I will have this experience, this is what they have to teach me, until some choose and move immediately back into the earth plane. That is one way to do it. However, you are not forced to do so but you are encouraged to do so depending on your development. If one spends many lifetimes in spiritual development while on the earth, their choices are broader. They may have a choice to either go into another physical incarnation or to try something new. That is sort of where we are now. We're not fully experienced meaning we have not made our journey all the way back to our higher self per say, but we are finished with our incarnations on the earth. We no longer choose to learn through a physical form. So, we are in a dimension where we have learned enough to not need the earth plane and we can assist human beings but we also, have our own jobs, our own things that we do. But none of them consists of physical form.

Me: May I interrupt you for a second?

Raina: yes

Me: That makes me wanna ask you if that is …interesting. Because you know… it would seem to me…And -I interrupt myself to say… *how you respond or how you react to the problem is actually the problem.* Okay so…what you just described as not needing the physical anymore - that just doesn't sound exciting to me!!! That's a problem! Are you SURE you're having fun?!!

Raina: Yes! We are having a lot of fun. Part of the reason for that is that we are still focused on the physical. We are choosing to channel through this one (Lori) and we are

161

choosing to make communication with the physical world. We are creating in a different sense but still focused on the earth.

Me: I hear you saying you're being of service and that fills you up.

Raina: In a way, yes. However there are other things that we have here to experience as well. So we will focus here on the earth plane with our channel and the others that are here, yes in service in that way where it is about love. We also get to experience, for instance, this physical body right now. We just do not have to stay within it.

Me: Okay so when people leave, say, my buddy Gary has a car accident, his body's heart stops beating so he pops out of his body. He had a ...er..uh...alcohol addiction! So, he goes to a place where he can work that out - but he doesn't start over, like from a baby. He picks up where he left off. Is that possible? Where he's in the same body that he was in before he hopped into his car and had the accident? And then, let's say it's a PLANE CRASH!!!! Or not – it's a BUS! So the whole group of people that were in that bus that fell off the bridge or in that plane that fell out of the sky and a bunch of them end up in this place where they can live for a minute while working out their curriculum in sort of an in between dimension. Is that possible?

Raina: Yes and there is this idea that religion has created 'hell' we do not like that word but to some degree that is the idea ...it is more of a parallel reality.

Me: Okay but tell me this

Raina: Yes

Me: So... I believe that there is a being that is greater than and one with me.

Raina: Yes

Me: I like to refer to this creator as God. It's just an easy, one syllable – Omnipotent - Bam! So, I believe that God hooked this up, this whole system. And that this place where these folks would go is a God created place and if it's a God created place it's ultimately out of love, made of love and any experience to the contrary is an illusion. I personally don't believe in hell. But I do believe that there could be a place where there's, like a.... a retreat, ya know. A place where they are getting extra doses of ... God Shots so that they can do their healing. Do you know what I mean? Like where they're taken out of this dimension so that they can go focus on their particular stuff. Is that possible?

Raina: Yes it is, in a way. And we do not believe in hell either. We are using it just as the idea that humans have created to explain it. There is not necessarily a negative place to go, not at all. However, it is something the soul creates. So each soul on that particular plane crash for instance, is creating the next place. -When a group of people come together in that way and they all create a place - again, in a multi-dimensional manner, with another part of themselves. Which is what we would refer to as Source or the Divine Infinite Intelligence or God. Yes. It is being created that way. They are creating it together and it is the idea, we would say, of God not necessarily something that is separate from you. Right? So this God is creating THROUGH you. You are the creator. You are God. So yes, from that perspective that is happening. However, because of the multi-dimensional reality and ability there are still ones who will peer into that particular reality to hope to change it. So we're not suggesting that it is bad, either. It is just... well, we would explain it to be a bit of a lower dimension however not negative not bad. Is it helpful for them to be able to do that, yes. But at a certain point when they realize what is happening - there's self-realization - there is enlightenment and then, there is a way out of the place that they are lost in. There is just an additional....... pathway. A pathway to be able to leave that particular reality. It is not ideal to stay in it but what you are saying - is it God created yes- but everything is. There is nothing that is created in any dimension that is not God created.

Me: I have two more questions for you. One is - babies are born in these curriculum in between life time dimensions, yes?

Raina: Hm... Good question/And there was something else we wanted to touch on as well.

Are you saying that not everyone is born into a small baby body? Yes. True. There's also the idea of a 'walk in'. Someone who steps into a body that has had some sort of traumatic event. They acquire the person's memory so to speak to move on to go on as that person but is also very clear that they are not the same soul. That is also another way to learn. Have you heard of this?

Me; Yes. (That ended up not being accurate! I lied! But at the time I didn't know I'd lied!).

Raina: Ok. So babies being created into this scenario. Let us have a gander at that one. (slight pause) Yes it is possible, absolutely so. It is a consciousness peering into that reality to help them to work something out much like the earth.

Me: Makes sense. And so then, let's say - everybody in this group - for whatever reason, they all wanna go at the same time - same busload so to speak - So, they work out all their stuff and some of them help each other to get the growth and learning - evolution and now they collectively realize that they've already transitioned and everything that they experienced was real and not for not. All important and significant. And they're in a space where they get all time is happening now - they see it all and they get it and they make this decision to move forward now. And they're going on...but they're going on to another incarnation. Is there white light to proceed this? And do we feel like we're ...*dissolving*???

Raina: Alright - there's something that we have to think about before that. You are speaking of contractual agreements between souls as well. SO, there are groupings of souls that agree to come into an incarnation to work something out. However it may take them several incarnations in order to work out that contractual agreement. They have agreed from another place, another dimension on the other side that they will work this out and will continue to reincarnate until they work this out. That is also another reason for them to move into such other dimensions where things look relatively the same and play it out that way. Then when that contractual agreement is over and they have a choice to move as you are saying, into the white light. Some have the experience of the white light but not everyone does. It is what they need to experience. One may need to experience Jesus coming and holding out his hand. Another may need to experience the tunnel and the white light. Where another can dissolve or simply transition into the next place. So some may feel as though they are dissolving and we would say - is that possible? Absolutely. Where another may disappear from one dimension and appear in another.

Me: And appear.... in the same body they were in before?

Raina: If that is necessary, yes

Me: Like if it's a baby they seem to stay in baby form. Like if a fetus is aborted it would start over in the same spot right.

Raina: yes but it also will grow and at a certain point in the spirit world there is this idea that we are all about 29 or 30 years old and that is what we look like and that is true as well, so when a spirit crosses over and they look the same age initially, depending on where they are, they will also go back to that ideal age. And it is ideal in a certain sense because there is wisdom that is there but you are also aware, your soul is aware that it can look anyway it wants. So it tends to choose wisdom along with enough youth to look a certain way. However at the same time it is not that important.

Me: Wow Raina, well I can't thank you enough.

Raina: Yes you're so welcome. We want to look at your book for a moment. Can we do that?

Me: Yes please!

Raina: Alright. You're going to have several helpers who will be helping you from the other side as included. So when you sit down to write you will be able to channel certain things from us. We are giving you our permission in this way. And there will be other spirit beings who will do the same. You will have a team with you who will bring through certain types of information. So when you find yourself saying' maybe I should have asked that unseen friend that question' know that your ability is the same. If you hear us in your head - we sound like this and we are speaking to you while you are writing this because we are channeling through you and we are helping you. Do not discount that ability.

Me: Thank you. Very much!

Raina: You're quite welcome. This is something that is needed. This is something that is also a contractual agreement between many beings that will come together toward the ending of your project. And many years thereafter.

Me: Much gratitude. Raina I look forward to talking to you again.

Raina: You're quite welcome and we will do that. Love is given without constitution, dear physical angel. Good night.

Journal 9

October 21, 2015

Just did a wedding in Palm Desert this past Saturday then proceeded to have a glorious time with my parents who came with me to the desert. I left them at the Agua Caliente Resort while I did the nuptials at a house not far away. We stayed two days. Before leaving them at their house in Riverside my Dad almost made me cry when he said, "Oh!" I turned to him, "huh?" "Thank you", he said. It was a very deep from "the core kind of thank you". Being able to take this time with them was not only huge for me, it was huge for them. They never want to get in the way of my work and they know Mondays are predictably grueling. It was beautiful to show them who/what is more important to me as I, without even flinching, moved work to the back burner. Those in the office were handling it. I was delighted not to think about work.

Also, I was touched because he had made <u>ME</u> SO happy by accepting my invite when I turned the desert wedding gig into this family road trip opportunity. Back from Hawaii a month now, I am feeling myself release some of things that have stopped me from joy and bliss. VOTD is delicious …in moderation. Too much drains me. I am achieving new balance by spending more time with myself & family. Gratitude.....

All is well and Dad got his driver license reinstated!!! A notice came in the mail while we were woopin it up in Palm Springs! Ecstatic, we encouraged him to get the keys to his new Lincoln and he took me n Mom for a victory spin through the neighborhood! What a great weekend!

18

"I maintain that the human mystery is incredibly demeaned by scientific reductionism, with its claim in promissory materialism to account eventually for all of the spiritual world in terms of patterns of neuronal activity. This belief must be classed as a superstition...we have to recognize that we are spiritual beings with souls existing in a spiritual world as well as material beings with bodies and brains existing in a material world."

Sir John C Eccles (1903 - 1997)

Shawn & Torah Part 2

A week or so after interviewing Lori and Raina, 1:30pm on a hot So Cal afternoon I left Meredith to man the Doll House while I had a visit at Shawn Randall's office/classroom which is, luckily, close to me in Woodland Hills. It had been a while since Shawn and I last saw each other. I gave her a hearty hug. She sat in her favorite armchair from which she does all her channeling during class. Instead of a dozen additional chairs set up, there was only one. I sat directly across from her.

She asked for a refresher, "What's this about again and what made you want to write about it?" Hm... I didn't really want to give that all away. But I figured since I was in her space, she'd either seen LOST or she hadn't and she definitely didn't have time to watch a few episodes prior to the interview because, I'm HERE! "Did you see LOST?" I asked.

"Lost?"

"Yeah"

"No!" she giggled, "What's THAT?!"

I spilled it in a cryptic brief: it's a TV series I was late on watching. Found it on Netflix. Six seasons. Loved it. I got to the end of it and realized that the characters had died in the beginning and we were watching life after life after life. There were all these awesome metaphysical multi-dimensional things that happened that are absolutely plausible when you consider that *'all time is happening now'* but I don't wanna be the only one to say *this is so* - I need someone from another dimension to come here and tell me about it. Tell me about consciousness, time, reincarnation and parallel dimensions.

She understood. "Well that is definitely Torah's field of expertise", she said. Our conversation went immediately to 'consciousness' and especially communication inter-dimensionally which is in the realm of the 'Unconscious'. This realm 'the unconscious', is touched over and over again in LOST. But if you don't know what it is - you'll miss the magic! This conversation plays right into how CUI works. The process of Creating Under the Influence of non-physical beings and energy- including the influence of our own experience in other life incarnations is all in the realm of the unconscious.

Shawn started by talking about 'crop circles', which she is very, very into. Yes, there's a lot of 'hoax' material you'll find over time and on line about them but then there are also regular cases of crop circles that science can NOT explain. Those are the ones that have peaked Shawn's interest for decades. She talked about the (non-human) intelligence that creates the circles and noted that it is, "other dimensional. It is multi-dimensional and yet there's some degree of physicalization". She talked about the creation of these crop circles and how they are often direct responses to requests from people on the earth plane. That would be an inter-dimensional experience - an inter-dimensional agreement, even.

Shawn: I gave a workshop with Torah… He's been talking about how an in-between dimension of rapport and communication just beyond our human thought, not our normal everyday waking reality, involving other dimensions such as ghosts and non-physical consciousness, somehow has to do with the human being's *experience of their own unconscious*… In other words there's a level of our minds, as human beings that we can connect with that is part of a linkage to 'other' if you will. It is involved with one's unconscious mind.

Going to personal experience: I had a profound event in a crop circle years ago. It was early in the day and I was the first one in the crop circle at a hillside field called Liddington Castle. I kept thinking, "the last consciousness that was here were the circle makers." And that took me into a zone. I wasn't in full trance or anything like that. Yet something was different. Torah later identified it for me saying that in my experience I was tangibly aware of the presence of my own unconscious mind. My own unconsciousness.

Me: The unconscious is different than the subconscious?

Shawn: Yes. It's deeper. The unconscious level of mind holds and includes…all your lifetimes, all between lifetimes; and it exists outside of space and time. Whereas the subconscious is related to one's current life - what you had for breakfast when you were three years old, your tenth birthday. All memory data and current life conditioning is held in the subconscious. Belief systems from this life are subconscious. It can include certain carry over pattern, Dharma or Karma, from past lives... *(Did she really just say "Dharma?")?*

But an interesting thing about the unconscious and the subconscious distinction is that most of the time people aren't aware of which they're dealing with. For example, when you get a 'flash back' of a past life experience, or pattern - that's the *presence* of the unconscious mind being experienced consciously. We are becoming more conscious of our unconscious experientially! It is part of our evolution as humanity, that we can have an interactive dialogue between our conscious mind and our unconscious mind.

All kinds of phenomena that we're talking about, ghosts and the like, involve crossing from one dimension to the next and engaging the unconscious mind. - Going to LOST, one can only fantasize that the characters of this story are living in a zone of their unconscious mind very consciously. That is what happens to most individuals when they cross over to the other side (i.e. when they die). They have to deal with what's in their unconscious mind - not only what's in their subconscious from the most recent life they just left behind.

There are so many cases of people on the other side, *dead folks*, who retain or are locked into the lifetime memories or identifications they've just left. Torah has done a mediumship session, in which he has talked to somebody on the other side who recently crossed over and is still using a walker in their new reality though it is no longer needed. Some people still stay stuck in the trauma of how they died. It is like a dream they are having from which they cannot wake up. If, however, Torah is talking to someone who has been on the other side a while and is fully adjusted to their new unlimited reality, they've passed by any personal discomforts. They've learned the illusionary limitation of their subconscious and they've moved out of that....

Going back to the presence of your unconscious - this is one of my new campaigns: to study what the presence of the unconscious is and what it feels like to be in it while alert.

Me: (Kind of a tangent thought to the purpose of my interview but I had to ask -). Who ARE the crop circle makers?

Shawn: They are multi-dimensional consciousness. There's no name you can attach to them. People have tried. Some people say, 'Oh they're from Andromeda...or, 'oh they're ETs from from Arcturus'. You have to take all assumptions out of the contemplation process. Because any such ET assumptions are coming from our limited human projection. If you project a simple ET agenda onto the crop circle phenomena it takes away from what's really happening and narrows the mind. However, one thing is very clear - the wisdom in the formations, the sacred geometry in them, and the meanings of numbers. Sometimes incredible wisdom is uncovered in the analysis of a crop formation years after the formation appeared.

Slowly but surely there's a telepathic rapport being built multi-dimensionally between human consciousness and the crop circle makers. I believe that rapport definitely involves our exploration of the unconscious.

And with the 'channeling process' (learning to channel), a similar rapport happens. Think of all the meditations you (Gillian) had to do in class. You know, where you're getting comfortable with your altered state and your unconscious mind gains access to your non-local self – (non-local is not rooted in space time) the non-local realm is engaged. And that makes for a good channel, a good psychic etc., etc."

Shawn and I talked a little more. She suggested I read a book called 'Conscious Universe' and then bid me farewell as she centered her body, closed her eyes and relaxed to go into trance.... In a couple of minutes her relaxed body suddenly perked up. Energized by another presence/being, it adjusted to an absolute upright posture...

Torah has an accent. I'm not sure what it is... very proper, kind of British. I really need to ask but if he were to pick his own clothes, I imagine it'd be a dark tweed suit with a red vest and blending bowtie! And he might wear glasses! That's how he feels to me!

He refers to himself as 'we' a collective consciousness/personality. His energy is very light, warm and welcoming:

Torah: Alright! And so we say greetings indeed to you, Gillian.

Me: Hi Torah!

Torah: A pleasure to be here with you. How would you like to begin? Do you have some questions?

Me: I would love your explanation of dimensions. Like... there's this one and there's another one on the... 'other-side' and there are parallel dimensions. What's your take on dimensions?

Torah: Well dimensions basically are a matter of frequency and let's say mutual agreements also. If you look at the frequency factor of subatomic particles (and there are so many that have yet to be discovered) that can help individuals understand how there are two dimensions, three dimensions – and even more dimensions than that. So it's about frequency but also consciousness and collective agreements. So, of course there are non-physical dimensions and there are physical dimensions. And what did you want to know about that?

Me: So they exist?

Torah: Oh yes. Other dimensions do exist - as do parallel universes.

Me: And so, like, I Gillian... can be living several of these at one time?

Torah: Yes you can! You can actually be living more than one lifetime on the physical earth plane, at the same time.

Me: I can... live more than one human lifetime... on THIS earth plane... at the SAME...

Torah: At the same time!

Me: That's amazing Torah. I wanted to veer away from asking that question because I thought it was crazy.

Torah: It's not crazy. It takes a lot to wrap ones head around it and even consider the possibility. But it's a very different you, of course, it's not you as you know yourself to be now. It (your parallel lifetime) may be on a different continent, different race, different mentality, everything.

Me: When I was a little girl, I used to have repeated experiences when it seemed like in physical time it would be a split second but inside me I felt like I was gone for ... half an hour. All of a sudden poof - I'd be somewhere else. I could never remember where I went but it felt like I was there for a half an hour or an hour. Then all of a sudden I'd be back. Standing on the field where I was playing baseball. I'd pop back into my body and I'd feel so strange. I knew I'd been GONE. And I'd look at a friend nearby and say, "Hey...did I look really weird just now?" And they'd say, "no". But I was convinced that I went SOMEWHERE. I would love to understand what that was.

Torah: Well let's rule a couple things out. First of all: had you had any childhood trauma or abuse of any kind?

Me: No

Torah: None what so ever?

Me: No. I mean... Yeah! - Getting grounded n stuff! Absolutely!
(We both laugh!)

Torah: No, that doesn't qualify! But what you described is often what multiple personality individuals feel. Or some that are approaching that state of mind. The split off of the consciousness, the ability for part of the consciousness to tune out is there with an individual with multiple personality disorder. The part suffering a trauma may split off and become another personality as a protective mechanism. This can happen in extreme cases. It's called dissociation.

So there is a definite psychological phenomenon in consciousness called dissociation. Now we have to ask you some more questions about what you experienced when you were 'gone.'

Me: In terms of my body n stuff, the word I wanna say is I went blank.

Torah:	What did you feel or think?
Me:	And I remember a black space. Not a white light, a black space.
Torah:	Coming back from the black consciousness and becoming aware and conscious again were you thinking to yourself, 'I went somewhere...'
Me:	Yeah. Around the same time I remember sharing with my math tutor another experience. I said, so... sometimes I see this guy. He's got brown hair. He's wearing a leather jacket and he's walking along a walkway... along a row of bushes. My tutor asked me if I knew him. I said, "I AM HIM".
Torah:	And so you were able to flash, to crossover, to a parallel life to see this. You were able to shuttle back and forth?
Me:	Yes. I would always see him doing the same thing in the same place so I thought it was flash back.
Torah:	A past life...
Me:	Yes.
Torah:	If it were a past life, you would have something to bring back by way of behavior or thoughts or feelings or emotions from the past life. A phobia for example, a gift or ability.
Me:	I didn't bring anything back... So it wasn't a past life. It was parallel?
Torah:	Yes!

(I sat with that and was wowed for a minute...)

Me:	I heard a quote once... I can't remember who was being quoted but it was in response to a plane crash that killed a bunch of people and he said something like, "do you know how hard the angels had to work to get those exact people on that particular plane at the same time?"
Torah:	How many guides do you think worked during 9/11?
Me:	How many?
Torah:	Oh, countless. Because [we're] talking about the unconscious mind. But it wasn't your guide saying 'ok, let's go! Herd your way over here...make your way over this way'! The individual unconscious minds of most of those individuals had, let us say, former agreements. The agreements were not at the level of the conscious mind but, rather, at the level of the collective unconscious.
Me:	So ... a plane crash just a few hundred people...is it possible that say...50 of those people needing the same environment to live out particular...unfinished life curriculum - lessons and growth in whatnot...in a dimension...
Torah:	Still living out – while trapped in their plane or something like that?
Me:	Not necessarily trapped in their plane, but they're still in the same bodies with which they got on the plane or so it appears - same bodies it LOOKED like they had while they were at the airport. And now in this place, this city, this island

- whatever - they're doing the things they needed to handle. Like, if prior to getting on the plane they had abandonment issues or self-worth issues - now in this place, they could work that out, while the person who was sitting next to them can work on their alcoholism so...they'd do it in -like, a group. Is that possible?

Torah: Yes, it is. It's not as common as *individuals* finding their own participation in an environment. It would be rare that more than one individual would collectively experience an environment like this, but it does happen, yes. And also if there's an inter-connectedness like the channel mentioned, (hypothetically) a car crash into the water and when they crossed over to the other side the trauma and terror is so great they could stay stuck in that trauma and terror of trying to get out of the car.

(*At this point my brain was flashing to the last episode of LOST where this phenomenon was depicted in the characters transitions from a life incarnation Season 6 Episode 17 @ 46:10: Kate's crossing while being stuck on being an outlaw, Clare crossing while stuck on being pregnant and giving birth to Aaron, Charlie also exiting an incarnation while stuck on being addicted and on stage and Desmond, anxious to complete his transition from that incarnation is crossing as he still shares his gift of understanding to help them all complete their transitions….moving on.*).

"So let's say, sharing that experience together, would be part of their *becoming*; a way of loving each other, of helping each other, of saving each other - whatever interconnected growth purposes the souls may have. So there can be interconnected purposes. If such a thing occurs there is usually a shared illusion; a delusion environment due to an interconnected karma of some kind. An interconnected drama. Interconnected purposes such as helping each other, understanding each other, or forgiving each other - whatever it may be.

Me: So...are there stages to an incarnation? Like, right now... I'm in this stage. Let's say I transition out of this dimension but I'm not done with stuff so I go to finish stuff in another dimension and I still use this same body. Can I create a whole family? -Like, say I was younger - can I make babies? - Can I - am I finishing curriculum before moving on to the NEXT incarnation?

Torah: Not exactly. It's not usually done that way. It's usually done so the individual for themselves sees their incarnation they just left and they are seeing it as the illusion that it is, the story that it is, as the very real dream that it is - and their guides and teachers help them to get the wisdom they need. Sometimes that can be done with guides but sometimes the carryover of the issue, as you say, "resolving the issue" is intense enough that the guides can't get through. In that case the 'issue' will be carried over to the next lifetime. So you wouldn't be living it out, so to speak, in a story fashion, on the other side, but may be experiencing it. We'll give you an example:

There's was a man we knew when he was physical and when he crossed over (to the other side) we communicated with him for his widow. He came showing himself in his home office. We explained to the widow 'he's recreated the office he had at home. We described the room and a certain piece of art hanging on the wall. The widow confirmed, "oh yes that's his office exactly" including the art on the wall. The man had recreated his office as a way of being comfortable in his new environment with elements of the old environment in the physical dimension. He was also completing his purpose and seeking greater safety, realizing he had it within himself. That also helped him to be comfortable in his new environment, his new reality in spirit. He also felt a certain upliftment that came from the work that he did in that office - a sense of family with his wife and all that goes with that. But he wasn't there in this scenario with other people interacting. Is that making sense?"

Me: Yeah. Got it.

Torah: You see the difference from what you are postulating?

Me: I do....

Me: You know how you mentioned the trauma of the event of that transition - This thing I'm writing is based on a plane crash which is pretty traumatic when that happens.

Torah: You mean the unexpected death and the shock of the death itself?

Me: Yeah – so would that then be more plausible for a group of people...

Torah: Yes! A group sharing the dream. Sharing the delusion.

Me: Right... until they're done with that.

Torah: Well now. Until they WAKE UP! Until the teachers and wise ones and guides and elders help them to wake up; and that could happen very quickly. It's not often that it would take a long time or that more than one person would stay stuck. That is because everyone is different in his or her subconscious and unconscious. It would be unusual, yet it does happen, that a group experiences being 'stuck' together in an experience or frame of mind.

Me: (Thinking of the Black Smoke Jungle Monster) and so... how do you explain fear and projections? Like things we're afraid of so we focus on them and BAM it happens. Or we're afraid and we then create a crazy scary scenario. Like you didn't fear the exact thing that happened but you were in fear in general, and then this wild crazy scary thing presents itself.

Torah: What you are saying is related to one's participation in the collective unconscious. Act of nature - for instance, fires. One could ask: why did a large group of houses burn down except *one is okay?*

Me: (I thought of Rose and Bernard living peacefully on the island while all that craziness was happening for everybody else! Season 5 Episode 16 @ 29:13)

Torah: ...the individual unconscious of those individuals – as well as their Higher Selves their Souls – provides a complex interweaving of dynamics that would go into them creating that their house is ok (in this hypothetical situation). It could be seen as *resonance causation* ... You're right, fear can lead to a manifestation, "*Oh my house burned down!*" or "*Look, my house didn't burn down and the other houses did!*"

Me: (Thinking of my C.U.I- Creating Under the Influence theory) How about influence of guides and whatnot in the creation of *brilliance*. I've often heard myself say, "I don't know where I got these ideas from but whenever I get them from there they are always brilliant." Where is *there* and how does that happen? I believe that the creators and writers of LOST were influenced by.... sources outside of themselves that they couldn't see...like they channeled what ended up being the 6 seasons of the show.

Torah: Absolutely. It has a lot to do with *permission and willingness* given by the individual to *receive*. Albert Einstein got some of his best ideas while in the shower! And a lot of his ideas would just come to him. You couldn't say it came from mommy and daddy ET per say - no, no! Not like that. A kind of wisdom-of-the-Universe channeled to him and then through him by his permission and willingness.

Intuition is really a very magical thing. Sometimes it's only one self. Sometimes intuition opens a dimension to other crossover consciousness of the non-physical dimensions and other realities. It depends on each individual case. You could ask: what is the influence? Is it one's own intuition? (Which is in itself quite magical) or is there other dimensional consciousness involved? You have to take it on a case by case and investigate.

The writers of LOST, what we feel about that...(pause) It looks to us that they would have brain storming sessions, where they'd all sit around and talk. When they would do this...they would go into a certain collective consciousness field that they would co-create themselves just by being together and brainstorming. Collective thoughts might have gone like this: "We're going to go into a certain pretense about...and what could happen to the people. Let's pretend that they are in another dimension. Let's pretend that." At that point the writers would collectively be in a very open place of permission and willingness to receive a multi-dimensional concept or truth. They could entertain the 'what-ifs' with the help of their Guides whispering here and whispering there into their minds. Yet a lot of what they agreed upon for the show was from their own intuition, their own consciousness and, again, a shared awareness field they co-created - AND what intelligence their consciousness field may have attracted as a source of ideas or information.

One can learn to be sensitive to the source of the input when a thought comes in. *One can learn to sense whether the information is from one's intuition or whether it's from an outside influence such as a guide.*

Be conscious of thoughts coming into your mind and say to yourself, "Something's coming to me and I want to pay attention to it. I want to focus on it." Be aware of it coming in then dialogue with it. Ask of it, "OK, I'm getting this idea, this thought, where is this coming from? Me?" Answer: Yes or No. Maybe. Go down that short list in a process of elimination. If the answer if 'no, it is not from me (my daily conscious thought-mind)' then ask: "Is it coming from my Higher Self? Unseen friends?"...Ask until you hear the answers clearly in your mind. It's really about *paying attention to the multi-dimensional thought zone/thought universe* in one's mind. Learn to pay attention to that area of thought.

We find it very interesting: people can be in a store talking on their cell phone. They're totally focused into that thought universe, with the other person on the phone, and totally not relating to what's around them or any other people around them. You've seen that. It's very common, right? People are very capable of tuning in: ring, ring – "Hello, here I am" to that thought universe of conversing with someone on the phone. Imagine this now: imagine simply having that tuning in ability with other dimensions, intuition and guides. Imagine just being able to say, "Right now I am tuning into multi-dimensional messages coming to me." Imagine you can do that just as well as making a call on a cell phone. And, by the way, *you can learn to do that.*

What fascinates us is the fact that people are learning how to focus their consciousness and compartmentalize their consciousness very well with technology. Now if they'll get the idea that they can do the same with other dimensional consciousness, we're really getting somewhere, yes!

Me: (Still trying to find a 'title' for Richard and Jacob) Gatekeepers. Can you define those people?

Torah: There are many kinds of 'gatekeepers'.

Me: So I am asking about not only the kind of gatekeeper that I would go to for channeling or mediumship but also, would there be a kind of gatekeeper who would help folks in their transitions?

Torah: Absolutely! Just as there are gatekeepers who help people come *into* physical existence. And that's a very interesting topic because many people in an early life regression can remember being coached by their guides or their unseen friends or a higher consciousness of some kind. They often remember beings helping them stay with their new little baby body (giggle) and what that all means. So, oh yes, people can easily remember such events with a regression experience. So, there are gatekeepers with you to help on both ends of a lifetime.

Me: How do I describe what a gatekeeper is? ...An escort?

Torah: Well in the case of the moments of coming into the incarnation and going out of the incarnation, we would, in addition to the term gatekeeper, we'd call such a being an usher, a companion, a...what was the term you used?

Me: Escort.

Torah: Escort! Ah yes! That's a nice term! A very, very *wise* escort! We call them gatekeepers but escort is a very good word! Assistants!

Let's hypothetically say someone comes into a lifetime with a very, very, strong intention, say, to be President of the United States. And there is a very strong sense of the unconscious mind of that individual.

It is well-focused based on agreements made with their Higher Self and their Soul (subject to review and discussion with elders on the non-physical plane).

So, let's just hypothetically say that person comes into physical existence with a strong sense of a certain purpose, a higher purposeful good. Let's say they're going along and going along in their life then, bam, they're in a terrible car accident. Let us say, another person drives by, sees the car that has rolled over, and their attention is called to it; "Go retrieve that person and get them out of the burning car!"

That strong directive may come from a gatekeeper that is the gatekeeper for the higher purpose of the individual in the car. It will also be assisting the higher purpose of the person saving the life of the person in the car.

Yet, a lifetime is all subject to change. There are, I'm sure you've heard the term, 'exit points'. Exit points in a lifetime (near death) in which one can go either way: stay or go - stay or go. In certain cases a person's gatekeepers might let them go, let them leave the lifetime. Or they may help them stay. And when they do help them stay, oh, there are some miracles that can happen. Every now and then a person gets into a lifetime that, for one reason or another, they're not up to the task of what their Soul had hoped for within the lifetime. So they leave prematurely.

Me: (I thought of Charlie and how DESMOND was his gatekeeper and saved him over and over again. (Season 3 Episode 8 @ 40:23) And even in the end, he hated letting him go and only did so because physically, there was no other way. But in that exit, Charlie was a hero! And then look at the life Desmond lived in a parallel where he went around beating up Ben, hitting Locke with his car, having himself thrown in jail to be with Kate and Sayid. He was a gatekeeper! (A gatekeeper by any means necessary, it seems!)

Me (to Torah):   So, as I understand it we do a lifetime and we learn lessons and then once we learn the lessons eventually we move to a level where we don't need physical lifetimes...We may still be learning lessons but it's not physical like this...like where you are. IS that fun?

Torah: (laughs, as if to say 'of course!')

Me: I mean, I'm having so much fun in THIS (physical) existence...

Torah: Good! You'll have even more fun in the next one.

Me: Really?

Torah: Oh yes! (He's smiling) MUCH more fun. As long as you're willing - as long as you're willing …and of course one's definition of fun grows, changes and evolves.

Me: Am I gonna like it?

Torah: Well, you rarely hear those who've crossed over say, "Oh I wish I could go back!".

Me: What's it like? Why is it fun?

Torah: Well first of all, the discovery of the power of one's mind is an amazement. The discovery of the power of one's consciousness - is extraordinary. It's a bit like human beings taking a drug! So, imagine a human being takes LSD and thinks they can fly - and just loves the feeling, "Oh I can fly, I can fly". On the other side it happens to be true. *The discovery of the extraordinary creative power of one's mind is beyond description.* And then at the same time comes the responsibility for one's consciousness. This involves the realization of the responsibility of, and the power, of choice.

Also on the other side there is the power of being with others. You're not in a vacuum when you're on the other side. One returns to one's Soul Group. It's a great reunion! Its old family and the shared experience of each other, which is without words.

On the other side there is the creativity of not only being able to fly, but to (for example) dash your imaginary arm into the air and create a colorful brush stroke. Everyone becomes ultimate magicians. Love is all around if you wish to see it.

Me: You, having had many, many, many life times…

Torah: Oh! We don't talk about it that way…

Me: OH! Ok. Well, you've had uh…uh…ENOUGH lifetimes and in those you've had Moms 'n Dads (we giggle) and so now in this other place, in this great reunion, the person who was your Mom or Dad - or other beings in your Soul family - do you recognize them? Do they recognize you?

Torah: Yes but in our case we're past that. Oh, we don't do that anymore. But *you* will recognize them. It will be a passing realization flash. Because then what's behind that? They might just sort of flash a recall of what they were to you in a past life of yours - but generally there won't be a feeling of human attachment. If there is any remaining intense relevance between you and one in your Soul Family, it would come up to reincarnate again. It would be investigated further in a future shared lifetime. For example: (hypothetical) *remember that time when your father and you beat each other up and, now, how about let's settle that terrible friction in the next lifetime and learn more from it?'* - That kind of thing occurs.

Gillian, you might really enjoy reading 'Journey of Souls' by Dr. Michael Newton. It'll give you a taste of the infinitude of life.

Me: Thank you so much Torah!

Torah: You are most welcome. You have a unique situation where you have had an experience of a crossover with a parallel lifetime. That may lead to more discoveries on your part. We'll just leave it at that for now. Much love to you dear Gillian. We support you in your wonderful project.

A little reflection on my time with torah:

1. My heart sank with what Torah said about recognizing family and other characters in our physical incarnations, once we're at the level he is. But I am comforted to know that prior to that level... At the level where we are now, when in between incarnations, we DO see our loved ones again. These loved ones, say a grandmother (for example) may be the first one to come meet you as you begin your transition. And she can do that even though she may presently be in a NEW incarnation, herself. AND she is totally real as she meets you and escorts you to a reunion with other loved ones as you make your way across. This is all real. (As real as Jack's Dad was to him at the end). Our exit out of the physical and into the Spirit world seems to be very calculated in steps designed for purpose. The re-entrance by a spirit into a new physical incarnation is much swifter!

2. It occurs to me that Christian hovered in earth realm and waited for Jack. This also happens! In fact, in another conversation with Lori, coming up, you'll hear (or –read) me say that's also my intention if things go down a certain way! There is actually a term for what souls are doing when they hang out in earth realm BETWEEN incarnations. I took Torahs advice and read Michael Newton's book. He uses the phrase "Hovering Soul Syndrome". His work, through a plethora of NDE case studies, chronicles what happens when we leave our bodies! Fascinating! Not all souls who hover are angry! That'd be me! The family Casper :) -Ha! But seriously, unless one of my guides or someone had something SUPER persuasive to say to me, I think I would opt to have the hover syndrome. I would want to be here, close by to constantly love my family through the rest of their incarnations. And there are lots of people already doing this! My Granma Sue (my fathers' mom) is hovering here. And she's not an angry spirit!! I also know my Moms friend who I call 'Aunt Bev' is still in this realm. Though she's waiting for her daughters, she and I talk sometimes! I LOVE seeing Aunt Bev. She presents herself to me, always wearing white (she was a nurse) and in much bliss while in familiar Jamaican surroundings with friends and family who crossed before her!

3. It also occurs to me that, when someone transitions after another person, and friends or family say, "well, they're together now" - that may only be true energetically as we are all one. But they may also be in other dimensions/ incarnations/playing different

roles so that neither of you realize the person who is now your ...family dentist is also your loveable MOM in a different incarnation!

4. After this interview with Torah, I feel more than ever that I am oh so correct about the creators of LOST being influenced. While consciously, they may have been thinking they were writing something totally IMPOSSIBLE in real life terms - they were actually writing what CAN and does HAPPEN in some group transitions! In this case, many of the people on the island (lead characters, anyway) were in the same Soul family. Or 'Spirit family'. - The epitome of 'kindred spirits'. This was a group of spirits in unconscious agreement to engage each other in ways that fed their individual learning and evolutionary processes.

19

Flash Forward

As I watched LOST the 2nd time, I made a lot of notes. Around season 5 I'm scribbling stuff about a "Lady Marshall". Poor Sayid! Gettin' his b'hind wooped AGAIN by a gorgeous woman (Season 5 Episode 10 @ 31:24). Sexy moment gone terribly awry! Lol! The 'ol, *take off my boot,* trick!

I didn't really take note of her name until faces came together for me. And what's interesting is her face and essence did the same thing to me this time, as it did the first time. Only thing is- it took a figurative minute. I probably took subconscious note the first time through LOST but now I was watching it all over again.

We first see this character with Sayid Season 5 Episode 6 @ 29:13. .... At that point I still didn't recognize her. Season 5 Episode 6 @ 31:10 we see her again with Sayid inside the Aljira plane. I'm seeing this and I'm like, "la laaaa" I don't really notice the connection but I am, at the same time, very familiar and I'm thinking the level of comfort is what made me just... ignore her for a while. I mean, I REALLY didn't like the way she was treating MY Sayid :) but other than that...

Finally after the Aljira flight had already crash landed and they were on the beach by the big foot statue (Season 6 Episode 2 @ 38:20) it suddenly HIT ME! Like WHAM! Her face on my screen merged with the face of the student with whom I'd had that uncomfortable moment in 2010! Yes! I paused the video. Out loud to an empty house I'm like, "I KNOW HER...I know - Oh my God - is that... Ze? Ze Robinson??!!" I stopped everything and Googled the cast to be absolutely sure. Zuliekah Robinson. I exhaled as my heart kind of sank a bit. I was suddenly so bummed to put the pieces together. The emotion hit my solar plexus as I now understood her reaction that day. I'd THOUGHT it was something like this. Wow!

I had been right about my sense that she didn't want to be recognized as an actor while in school. I TOTALLY commiserate with that but she didn't know how much. It's ok. There's WAY bigger news here!

So, the woman playing one of Jacobs comrades, Ilana Verdansky, was in my graduating class at USM. I remembered her - from the FUTURE (and maybe beyond)! THIS is the woman I was talking about earlier (page 12) who I told how familiar she felt to me but instead of going forward with trying to figure it out we got through our project and went our separate ways! I get now that she thought I was one of the 2 million+ viewers who'd seen LOST or maybe something else she'd done on TV or theatre but nope. Not I. Not YET, anyway!

So, the great big observation is this – at the very least; in 2010, I was remembering ...2014. That's basically time travel through unconscious territory! This was different than just intuition, though. Her being was Déjà vu familiar to me. When I intuit information about a person, place or thing - it doesn't affect me PERSONALLY. I don't FEEL it like I felt my first meeting with Ze. It was a personal connection. It leads me, to wonder if there's more. Based on the warm energy I tuned into upon our first meeting, I sense that we may be in another incarnation as friends or some other very amiable association. When we were in the classroom meeting for the first time over a project, it was a total Jack & Desmond moment when, while on flight 815 when it doesn't crash, Jack is trying to place Desmond's face (Season 6 Episode 1 @ 5:05). Why she is familiar to me is still a mystery as I sit here today but I get that this mystery doesn't need to be solved.

At the same time, given the subject matter of these pages...I do see the Ilana/fellow classmate thing as being kind of a super cool development though the time span is only 4.5 years ahead. A blast from the - future!!! DUDE!

Ecstatic about this realization and wanting to share the development with her I shot Ze an email. I take it she doesn't use that particular email address anymore because I've gotten no response and it's been a few months! What's interesting is, the same way I felt when she sort of put an energetic wall up with me (MY perception) in school, I felt rejected again as she was not responding to my correspondence.

I left her a voice mail end of February. I haven't heard back (It's early April as I type!). Hm. Definitely the right number because on the outgoing message a female voice said something along the lines of, "Hi, this is Zuliekah...". All the students were given a contact list of all the other student's emails and phone numbers. I didn't stutter when I dialed! - You know what I think? Seriously... I honestly - fully think, SHE thinks I'm a LOON! - Just another LOST fanatic who is also CLEARLY psychotic -suffering some kinda crazy delusions about multiple dimensions and a book n whatnot! I can picture her maybe saying something like, "OMG and she has m'damn phone number!"

It's also possible that she read my email and heard my message and is simply not on the same wave length and finds my fascination... *odd!* Suddenly I feel like Hugo must have felt when he laid out the whole flight 815 and island saga to his mom (Season 5 @ Episode 2 @ 29:50). I agree, if you don't 'get it' all this stuff I'm writing can sound kinda craycray! So... I was going to call Ze again but ya know what? Naaaah!

20

CURSING! There is no such thing!

"I'm going to be VERY busy in the Afterlife.
The list of people I plan to haunt gets bigger every day."
Anonymous (found on Facebook!)

I take that back. Let me put it like this; all curses are self-inflicted. Not trying to lack compassion for people suffering from what they feel is a curse, like poor Hurley. The thing is - it's not possible for someone else to do that to you unless you allow it. It's another case of the Law of Attraction at work. Don't forget, you are a unique expression of God! Can you put a curse on God!? No! Not EVEN! So...there's THAT!

Further, hearing an inner voice telling a person to do crazy, destructive stuff to themselves and or others is not outsourced! It's not a demonic entity. As Michael Newton writes in his book 'Journey of Souls, "Negative forces emanate from our self." And further, he says "all souls are held accountable for their conduct in the bodies they occupy." He details accounts of near death experiences where part of the process is with guides who do a *review* with you of the life just lived. Read that last sentence again and then repeat after me, "uh oh!" My guides tell me this review is of 'feelings' primarily. How you 'felt' when… *How someone else felt when you said or did*_____. Oh yeah! :) And NOW – how do you feel about how they felt?! To make this 'review' experience less harsh, I personally work to take responsibility and ownership for what happens in my life and process all negative feelings to a place of neutrality. And I'm not done until I can get to a place of compassionate self-forgiveness and the easy ability to energetically wrap the entire experience and all its parts and characters in Love. Any parts where I'm courting resistance on getting to the neutrality and Love are just more life curriculum but I'm not going to stop until I'm done! Handle it. Because…the REVIEW is coming!

That's what time it is. I've had several people come to me for energy work or a clearing because they say someone, "put a curse on me". They are pretty forthcoming with a list of curse symptoms. Ultimately, it's KIND of like hypochondria in that the 'curse' doesn't exist. HOWEVER the hypochondria can play into the energy of creating or maintaining the symptoms on their list. But bottom line...Nobody put a curse on you! Even if they actually WANTED to!

In another conversation with Lori she agreed, "oh yeah, I even have something on F.A.Q.'s (frequently asked questions) page on my web site about that because so many people are told that and there are psychics who are unscrupulous who will tell you that you're cursed and you have to pay $10,000 for them to remove the curse! It's like a classic con artist thing".

I thought about Clare who went to see that shady psychic (Season 1 Episode 10 @ 12:25 & 24:37 & 27:50 & 36:21)! SOOO shady, this guy! It's because of HIM that Clare is on flight 815 on her way to L.A. to meet an adoption couple arranged by the psychic! Of course, we don't find out he's a quack until he spills his own beans while talking to Echo who was, at the time, a priest (by default). The fake psychic guy's daughter had had a near death experience and in blowing it off, he explained to Echo how he gathers intelligence and then uses it to exploit his client's needs (Season 2 Episode 21 @ 2346)! He planted information in Clare's mind and she lived it out on the island BECAUSE she believed him! That's not a curse, it's a 'Projection'.

Projections are REALLY important to understand. They live inside each us -a perception and belief that is then mirrored into our life. A projection can be good or bad. Beautiful or ugly. Cool or unacceptable. In other words, a great way to spot whether you've got a projection going on is when you hear or experience yourself in 'judgment'.

Positive projections can be identified when you, for example, admire something or someone. That would be a positive projection. To identify a negative projection notice what disturbs your inner peace. Once triggered, what are the feelings you're having and, where do they REALLY come from!? Projections are incredible and accurate roadmaps to self-discovery and healing. Projections originate from within. Anything that inspires and lifts you, whatever it is, already lives inside you. So when you have high affinity for someone - the qualities you admire of that person are already part of you! Realize that! Conversely, when something irritates the BLEEP out of you or you have judgment against something - look to how it is leading you to 'feel'. In the process of focusing on your emotions, notice that you are no longer so focused on the trigger. Good. The trigger really has nothing more to do with it than being a blessing to lead you down this road to healing. Goal: Identify the emotions and work in that arena to bring ...neutrality and compassionate self-forgiveness for the judgements. Not saying you should advocate...a CRIME, for instance. But to get to the *healing* is most important so that your life is not imprisoned by misperceptions. To figure out if possibly you were in harms' way as the result of a belief would also be mega helpful so you could ...realign your path for the future! Just sayin'....

Rev. Gillian V. Harris M.S.P.

If you're considering doing this kind of inner work, consider guidance. Life Coaches with Degrees or Certification in Spiritual Psychology are ideal along with Light Workers who use one of many healing modalities that adjusts energy patterns in your Spirit body.

There is no such thing as a curse. Lori cut right to the chase in defining a curse to simply mean "a person needs to take responsibility for their shit". So I tell her about poor Hurley; wins the lottery with a set of numbers (Season 1 Episode 18 @ 2:37). Same set of numbers is on the hatch door (Season 1 Episode 25 @ 30:23). Same set of numbers is needed to reset the clock every 108 minutes inside the hatch (Season 2 Episode 3 @ 00:41). Same set of numbers were on the odometer in the old refurbished Pinto (Season 4 Episode 12 @ 26:16)! BUT, as said before, Quantum Physics - thoughts create stuff!!! "And some people" Lori says, "are really powerful manifesters and they don't know it!" Hurley, as we saw through the six seasons of LOST, slowly grew into his gifts. At first though, he didn't know WHAT was going on!

My feeling on Hurley is that he suffered greatly when his father left when he was a kid (Season 3 Episode 10 @ Opening Scene). His Dad handed him a candy bar before riding out of his life on his Harley. Hurley unwrapped the candy bar and took a bite and it became part of coping with that moment of sadness as he knew his Dad was not coming back. From that moment forward (Season 2 Episode 18 @ opening Scene) he used food sensation as comfort and as a coping mechanism. - Did you know that the intake of carbohydrates actually triggers the release of (feel good) endorphins in the brain?! Dude!!! That's where carb-addiction comes from!

Where was I?

Oh yeah!

So, even though he won the lottery, with an undercurrent of low self-worth, he inadvertently unleashed energy that would destroy all that was great in his life. If anything bad happened, he felt it was because of the curse. His Grandfather died (Season 1, Episode 18 @ 5:46), Mom breaks her ankle and the house he bought her burned down (Season 1 Espisode18 @ 1139), he goes to Australia and on the way back his plane crashes (Season 1 Episode 1 @ 5:28)!!! Dang! Then -words are powerful so Hurley kept saying "I'm cursed. I'm cursed. I'm cursed." - multiplying the effect of the belief, like turning up its volume to which the Universe replied, "ok! Copy that!"

The important thing in Hurley's story is that he created that lottery win, as well. And when things got really bad (crashing on the island) he also created his rescue. But in the plane crash incarnation, he just couldn't hold on to the benefits because of his belief system regarding self-worth. That was the key for him. His work was to find peace within so he could enjoy a life petal where he could keep the money and have a more joyful incarnation.

LOST actually showed us two Hurley incarnations. In the scenario where the plane doesn't crash he has a totally different perspective telling Sawyer he has a perfect life and nothing bad ever happens (Season 6 Episode 1 @ 13:10)! In this incarnation, we also see Hurley being confident (except about women!) and compassionate as the best boss and philanthropist ever named Man of the Year (Season 6 Episode 12 @ 00:46)!

While curses are only self-inflicted by way of belief, there IS the reality of energies and entities attaching to people, places and things. Like lint on your clothes, wads of useless, potentially havoc wreaking negative energy could attach to our energy bodies for a ride.

WAIT! First a recap: Black Smoke Jungle Monster - An energy being - a consciousness not limited to a physical body. As crazy as the show made him look it/he was really just a love source gone awry! Frustration and hurt had caused him to express as black smoke or forest moving wind. When you think about phenomenon that violently haunts buildings - the Black Smoke Jungle Monster was just...another entity expressing. One of my favorite lines from the Jungle Monster after one of his temper tantrums which probably left at least one person dead, he reappears as John Locke and calmly says, "sorry you had to see me like that" (Season 6 Episode 1 @ 34:35). LOLOLOL! He actually says that a couple of times!

JUST like he hopped into Christians body (since it was vacant and available n whatnot) it's just another way to express and for some reason he was attracted to Christian and took on some of his memories and characteristics while impersonating him (cells of the physical body hold memory). Now imagine the Black Smoke Jungle Monster didn't take over a body but stayed non-physical - he is still able to move around and affect his physical surroundings. And when he was angry or simply annoyed - you know the term "knock you into the middle of next week?" Well, without showing you his face he could hurl you into your next life time (Richard: Season 6 Episode 16 @ 19:06/ the Pilot Season 1 Episode 1 @ 36:06 / Echo: 3 Season 5 @ 39:03).

Folks who stay in earth realm LONG after departing from their bodies are sometimes angry with many unresolved issues. This poor guy had SO MUCH unresolved stuff goin' on... His real mom was murdered by the woman he called mom! What?! Yeah (Season 6 Episode 15 @ opening scene). And from a young age he knew from a clairvoyant experience that his mother was not the Island mother (Season 6 Episode 15 @ 16:03) He simply wanted to live a normal life (Season 6Episode 15 @ 8:14). He was working on it and the island mother - who had killed his biological mother - destroyed everything (Season 6 Episode 15 @ 2510). Not clear on her motives for that. She SAID it was because she loved him so much she didn't want him to leave (Season 6 Episode 15 @ 36:31). Hm... And all he wanted was to ... leave...and live...like a normal friggin person! Only once Jack –with help from Kate - killed him (Season 6 Episode 17 @ 54:56), did he have that opportunity. Unfortunately, he leaves that LOST dimension with issues still unresolved from the insane chapters he lived on the island. -And he did mean things to other people. He'll have to face that at some point....

The other thing that can happen is ENERGY imprints created by emotion can gravitate to and connect to a building or with someone's energy field. Much of the house healing work I do is to clear energy imprints. Reiki is a great way to detach those and clear your physical body's energy field. Clear intentioned prayer also does the trick. But until something is done to remove these patches of darkness, they can feel ...like a curse. I recommend everyone get attuned to at least Level 1 Reiki so they can self- administer this healing life force energy on a regular basis. 'Energy Hygiene', I like to call it! Should happen every day, like brushing your teeth!

This is an area of work Lori Camacho definitely excels in and has been blessed with the opportunity to assist hundreds of clients living this circumstance. I asked her "what IS it when someone or something attaches to another's body?"

Lori: That is someone holding a certain vibration and an entity sees that vibration and says "oh! I match that vibration" and so they come in. So that is what a disincarnate would do who is lost. And it's just as created by the person who is living because they're vibrating there. So, if they have a lot of anger that they're suppressing, not dealing with or taking responsibility for they will attract an angry entity.

ME: Can they attract a happy entity if they're happy?!

Lori: It doesn't generally work that way.

"The other thing is when it's NOT a disincarnate. A lot of things are not disincarnates that are literally entities created by the person again because of their lower emotions that they're not dealing with - or events - traumas. So, trauma because it's compartmentalized, when they put it somewhere else sometimes it's something that they don't remember at all or it's something they prefer to forget but their soul needs to create wholeness and heal it. And so it'll create an entity that's in their face to reflect and show them *listen you have to pay attention to this*. And so sometimes people will start their healing process BECAUSE of something like that!

"I encounter those probably more than actual disincarnates. But they go together. So sometimes there's conglomerates of energy that people will say are demons - A demon is literally a collection of a lot of different negative energies that someone has been putting to the side over and over. - Or a collection of people in the house have been putting to the side and not dealing with and it'll create something that's not human. It's not a soul it's just an entity that's been created by emotion.

Me: Got it! So - let's talk about this walk on phenomenon. Is it a 'walk on' or a 'walk in'?!

Lori: Walk in!

Me: IN! Got it. Ok, how do you see a walk-in as a basic definition?

Lori: Well I've only met three, ever. And the third one just recently came to see me in the last two months.

Me: And when you say the third one, the third one what?

Lori: The third walk in

Me: Meaning the third person who is having the walk in experience-

Lori: Yeah.

Me: -of having walked into this incarnation ...from another one?

Lori: Yeah.

Me: Got it. G'head!

Lori: Okay so, when I first did readings and I had no idea what a walk in was, that was when I first met one! And she did not want to tell me anything. She wouldn't explain anything because she didn't want to color my intuition and what I was gonna receive. She wanted me to get it on my own and I did. But ...I was quite confused! (She giggles).

"I saw that there was this other person who had killed herself, who had slit her wrist and left. She released. Then I saw that this woman, walked into that body. She said, "Yes, that's what happened to me". She said, "now that we've covered that let's move on to some other things". But she didn't want to...color my experience with it.

"And so I did ask her some questions about it and she said, "Well the girl who was in this body before me, she just didn't wanna live anymore. So when she killed herself, she died. She left and I came into her body". And she said, "I do have her memories so I'm able to kind of pretend around her family". But her family does recognize that she is a different person now. They just don't understand that she really IS a different person now because she's a different soul. A totally different soul walked into this body."

Me: Ok (Southern accent kicks in) now - just....Hold on there one minute! The body that she walked into... had expired? - Dead - Gone. ?

Lori: Yes.

Me: And then it (the body) came back?

Lori: Well I'm sure someone took her to the hospital or something like that happened but... yeah. She died. She was gone. So her soul left.

Me: (I'm back to regular speech!) The humans around this experience, people around this body of the person who committed suicide are thinking that she had a...near death experience - but ACTUALLY she DID die and moved on?

Lori: Yeah and so the soul that woke up in the body was not the same soul.

Me: Shut UP!

Lori: Yes! And families will report "Oh my God this person is a different person" it's because they really ARE a different person!

Me: Right!

Lori: And for a walk-in, they're aware of it almost immediately. So rather than being born into a baby's body they come in this way instead. So that's my understanding of a walk in.

Me: Alright! That's amazing! That's ...AMAZING! Now... I've also heard it mentioned... being in two incarnations at the same time in different places, different bodies - same soul having two incarnations in the same...time period!

Lori: Ok

Me: So that I could be living one of my incarnations - like the guy I used to see all the time when I was a kid and I knew that I was him and he was me. That was most likely present tense. It felt present tense.

Lori: So my understanding is that is called a parallel lifetime-

Me: Well - but - they're all kind of parallel because they're all happening at once.

Lori: Yeah but we have this linear understanding of past present and future and so that's a reality of its own once we're in it. But when you're outside of it you get that they're all together.

Me: Ok, I hear you on that. So like, within the same CLOCK mentality that we live in this earth dimension we have yet another incarnation; parallel.

Lori: It means that there is another flesh and bone body on the earth with you having another incarnation at the same time. And then there's also, you could be having an incarnation here and another incarnation somewhere else that is NOT earth.

Me: What's THAT called?!

Lori: That's called your really fuckin' busy!!!

Me: Well yeah but aren't we?! -There's a guy - Eben Alexander - renown neurosurgeon brainiac guy who experienced his very own NDE and he brings up a point that I completely believe; that part of what the brain is supposed to do is filter out the rest of the true reality - like the magnitude of what life really is.

Lori: I TOTALLY agree!

Me: There's SO much goin' on. I think each individual is SO friggin busy, dude! Like, Oh my GOD!

Lori: They are!

Me: Yeah. When people are quote brain dead, they're BUSY!

Lori: Yeah

Me: Way! Like, when Christian was telling Clare to unplug her mom. I say DONT unplug ONLY because it's been a long time and you think they're in misery because they're brain "non-responsive". They're not even THERE. If anything, they probably pop back over to earth realm intermittently and grieve the fact they can't tell you not to cry, that they're ok.

Lori: Yeah

Me: And now that I know what I know, especially in the near death experience area, let them have their choice. The Spirit or Soul of a person, a Consciousness is whole and perfect even without wearing a human body, I say leave the comatose person plugged in! I mean, I know I'm generalizing. Every case is different but in GENERAL, I say, let them decide what they're gonna do as long as they need to do it. Even plugged in, if their bodies are ready to turn off, they're gonna turn off. So to let their body do its natural thing, while the person's consciousness handles their curriculum and goes forward without their body, or comes back into it.

Lori: Yeah and I've never done this but there are healers I know who will go and try to get them. Cuz sometimes they don't understand that their bodies are still alive. And they can be confused the same way a disincarnate can be confused. Or they can come back and forth and they describe the cloud where the person can't…they can't get back through, somehow. And so there are healers and intuits who will go through the cloud to find them and let them know that their body is still living and they come back into the body with them and then they'll help actually bring them back so they can wake up.

Me: Wow awesome! What GREAT work! -Makes me think of Clare's Mom. In a coma for at LEAST 8 months - minimum. She shows up at a memorial like *la la* ... 4 months or so after being in a coma for the better part of a year - like nothin' happened. And she's doesn't say much about it. In her lines there's very brief mention. I don't know… it's SUSPICIOUS!!

Lori: Oh…

Me: For a while, I thought she'd done a walk in, which at the time I was calling a 'walk on'! (I laugh) My definition of this multi-dimensional walking was that I was thinking of a situation where she just came back, in time. -Like, post funeral in stuff… like walked back in. Like BAM! She just materialized! (More laughter) I had explained so many things and I couldn't explain this part! And I was thinking she did this on behalf of her grandson.

Lori: I have heard of that happening but with the yogi's. I've heard that they're able to materialize after death, like, in complete flesh and blood! - Which is… I don't know! I don't have an answer for THAT one!

(We both laugh! Sometimes that's all you can do!!)

Me: But walk-in's-

Lori: Yeah. And There was a while when they did news pieces on walk-ins on shows like '20/20' - it was a THING for a little while. A long time ago. I was in my 20s when I heard about it. Then I didn't hear about it again until I did that reading for that lady.

Me: Right. And so you have three people. You described one, can you describe another?

Lori: Yeah, well, let me finish with her really quickly because there's something that's different about her from the other two, for SURE! (She giggles)

Me: Ok!

Lori: She also wanted to know when she would be picked up to go home. And I said what exactly do you mean? And she said, "Well, I'm not from here and I wanna go home soon". And I said do you mean you're an alien? And she said, "Yeah!" She said, "I'm from another planet" and she gave it some sort of name - I don't remember what it was.

Me: Right...

Lori: So for her, she came into this body but was not intending on staying here as a human being.

Me: What was her intention, do you think?

Lori: I think that she needed to be here for some reason and then go. And I could tell that she was not... -When I have some strange experiences with people, sometimes you can just tell that they are just...off mentally. But she really wasn't. At all. She was actually speaking the truth and that was very wild for me!

Me: Right!

Lori: The other two... Well the 2nd woman was from Australia and she was visiting our store. And she was also a walk in, same thing and I can't remember how the person died but same thing where this woman died and then she took her place. So she was just having a really hard time adjusting to being here but her intention was to stay here so she was definitely a human being with that type of a soul. But she was having a hard time because the other woman had a husband, also! And she said, "I don't know this man and I don't want to have sex with him. I don't love him. I don't want to be with him:

Me: Okay but wait - hold on. So she was Australian or she went into an Australian body. Where did she come from? Like, where was she before that?

Lori: Just ...on the other side. She doesn't have that much memory about that as the first woman did. She just knew she was born into an adult body and that's how she put it.

Me: Wow!

Lori: She talked about it being her birth into this world. She just didn't choose to come through a baby's body. But she woke up in this adult body and this woman had a husband to attend to. So her husband was coming to see her at the hospital, like "oh you woke up" and she was like WHO the fuck are YOU!?

Me: Right!

Lori: And then the family... She said she started getting some of the memories of the woman and so she was able to kinda pretend; okay so this is my sister and this is supposed to be my mother. But the hard one for her was, this man - "I don't have a relationship with him".

Me: Got it! Ok that's 2, tell me the 3rd one!

Lori: The 3rd one came in almost 2 months ago

Me: Came into Awakenings by coinkidink – like to shop or they came to see you?

Lori: Came into the store specifically to see me. She made an appointment on the phone.

Me: Wow. Got it!

Lori: And she had, like, the lowest vibration... Like there was just a lot of negativity surrounding her. And hers was interesting - and it took a while to get to it. She came into her body when it was 5 years old. So she was a kid and what happened was the kid had been raped and murdered - and then she walked into that body.

Me: Oh my Gosh! So, how long after the body was murdered did she take it over?

Lori: Right away. In each instance, it happened right away.

Me: So for the non-metaphysical thinking person; the paramedic, the doctor, the police or whatever, they're thinking if they hadn't gotten there when they did - she would have died. But actually, she did!

Lori: Right! And for her, she remembers the whole transition. She says there was a really big motherly angelic being there to help with the transition. So that angelic being took the child that was killed and then gave her the go ahead to take over the body.

Me: So, I feel that the person who took over the body and the person who left the body, had an agreement.

Lori: Right. I agree with that, too.

Me: And that they also have a very close relationship on some other life petal. Like this was a plan. She kind of saved her from having to go through that - or did she? Now there are TWO beings dealing with this awful assault and murder!! But for the soul who took over the body, she saves the original from living the rest out at that time.

Lori: She did but now the BODY is having a lot of disease problems. I could sense the trauma in her body. Her body is still holding that trauma. And so it was her path to work that trauma out. And my own feeling about it is that I think sometimes when a person chooses to take their own life - and you know how they have to come back into the same circumstances because they didn't finish out their lifetime? I think sometimes this is given to them as an option. -So that they don't have to start over-over because she definitely has to work out the trauma as if it's her own trauma.

Me: That makes SO much sense. So now she comes into this circumstance again and has to find the resolve, return to her authentic state of peace within. And that's where you came in?

Lori: Right. And she had a lot of anger and resistance that had nothing to do with THIS life time. And I remember sensing *Oh! This is why you ended your life before and this is why you came into THIS body. You haven't been able to work this out.*

Me: So that was 2 months ago. IS she still seeing you?

Lori: No. I only saw her that one time. I haven't seen her again. What's interesting to me is that the very 1st person I saw was literally within the first week of me doing readings professionally at a store. The 2nd person was about 7 years ago and then the 3rd person is now. So I got one in the beginning of my career, the middle and one now. It was like they were sent as a reminder that, yes, this is real -yes this happens and this is something that needs to be addressed somehow. -Because there aren't a lot of people who talk about it.
Me: -Cuz it sounds all crazy n shit!
Lori: Yeah!

21

The Hatch

Things with my parents were shifting. Dad got his driver's license back in time for Moms sciatic pain to flare miserably out of control. In so much pain, she could barely walk sometimes. One thing that helped her was my massage and Reiki treatments. I tweaked my schedule to get there twice a week if I could, once a week at minimum. We also found Jenna, a family friend who is a massage therapist in Riverside. We arranged appointments one every other week, which helped in the event I had to cancel one of my visits.

Now more than ever, I needed my office's support. While being with my folks is urgent, so is Valet Of The Dolls. I needed to limit my part to 60 hours per week, down from 90+. A challenge that required my team's participation. What I'd learned from my trip to Hawaii and the weeks subsequent to it, is that Meredith was the most able minded admin in the office and she didn't like that. I don't blame her but I was still buying into the false belief (shared by many business owners) that smart, dependable employees with skills for the work we do, are hard to find. The other admins were miles behind Meredith in know-how and basic business sensibility. Even my beloved Sarina who has been with the company and working in the Doll

House for more than three years, didn't come close to the kind of salesmanship and business logic Meredith has. Did I mention to you I was paying her almost DOUBLE what I paid anyone else in the office because of her abilities?! More money than I've ever paid ANYBODY administratively and that was in exchange for what she was now revolting against. Even if there wasn't that much work to do, Meredith wasn't interested in working the Doll House solo. Ever. -That made her feel like an 'employee'. With a razor sharp tongue and edge against authority, this just wasn't working out.

On top of that, her husbands' wealthy Brazilian Great Grandfather had passed away (at a young 106 years old!) and left them a lot of money shortly after she returned to the Doll House. So she wasn't as hungry for the work and pay as she had been when she originally pitched herself for the position which would replace two part-time jobs! She and her husband, Emiliano, planned to start their own Vineyard and restaurant on family land in Napa California. They are now ahead on the money they need.

All of a sudden, the ONE admin out of 4 who had the confidence necessary, was pretending like she misplaced it or it (the confidence) was on strike. No matter where I was, I was being interrupted for really simple questions which after answering I'd hear "Oh I know how to do it! I just wanted to triple check!" For a while I figured the Universe was just giving me opportunity to practice patience, so I did. But, this meant I was working when I was supposed to be working and I was working when I WASN'T supposed to be working! As a matter of fact, as it was panning out, with Meredith on board, I was now working much more than I had been without her! Go figure! The D-H was feeling like the constraints of the friggin hatch on the Island (in LOST) and its proverbial *button*!

One of the bottom lines, also, that I didn't realize until it was too late, was that Meredith came back out of an affinity for me. In fact we BOTH enjoyed each other and I believe we are kindred spirits. But I was not looking to hire her back for the sake of a social friendship!

For several weeks I was doing great and enjoying the balance of days off and then there was Hawaii and more weeks with at least one day off per week! Feeling like a 'normal human' I was in heaven! And don't get me wrong, while I found myself still putting in an easy total of 7 or so hours on any *day off*, being able to do that at night and still get out of the office and spend the day with my folks during a weekday was a golden gift. I am grateful to Meredith for the time off her presence DID allow me to have. Very. With this time I was also being fed something I'd been deficient in; Self-care & the opportunity to regularly rejuvenate.

As it became October, my days off would be less and less regular as Meredith would call in sick more and more often. I know a few of those times were hangovers. She only admitted that once, first emailing me to say she was sick then writing immediately back, "Oh what am I doing? You're so psychic you're gonna know I'm lying. Ok. I drank too much, for too long, last night. Now I'm sick, embarrassed and feel like shit, inside and out. I am SO sorry".

It became November and I looked forward to my days off with baited breath not knowing whether they would happen. (First set up for failure was my mind set, as I was deep in 'doubt'). My parents were now used to me coming and handling groceries and whatever errands I could for them. I loved it and they loved it. I kind of craved the experience every week being of service to these beautiful people who have done so much for me. PLUS it was just a ... GOOD TIME! My parents are a hoot! The consistency of the visits was nurturing all three of us. It would break my heart when I would have to cancel. My Mom would try to sound like she was okay but sometimes she couldn't mask her disappointment.

I admit that as I type, I am clock bound as I see my time with my parents as limited while at the same time fathoming the idea of doing any part of this incarnation without them somewhat destroys me. I hadn't felt this kind of emotion about this subject of my parents' human mortality/Spiritual eternity in SO long. I am proud of myself for having immersed myself in living and not the fear of bodies' dying. But now I was doing a bit of a rerun or feeling like I was back sliding into fear as my families' story was flipping pages and new chapters are being experienced.

By November, it IS <u>December</u> in full swing for Valet Of The Dolls with dozens of quote requests per day. As that race took off, I found myself in a frightened funk. I am fortunate to have grown to a place in my life where I don't stuff my emotions -AS IF they're going to disappear. I would rather face, process & release them than (suffer the consequences of) not. I would rather experience it and grow through it in an effort to gain back my authentic emotion which is a state of joy. Until I'm there (joy), I have work to do.

At this point, I would cry myself to sleep, cry myself awake and intermittently throughout the day, I ....was SO incredibly SAD and afraid in anticipation of something that is bound to happen one day...maybe 10- 15 years from now or ...maybe tomorrow. My mom is 82... My Dad is 79. How much longer do we get to do this physical incarnation together?! It feels like a race inside me as I want to be sure I'm absorbing & expressing all the time & love with my parents I can. The illusion of the clock and its friend, 'the illusion of separateness' were kicking my emotional ass.

So still needing to run VOTD and knowing I just needed a little time, 1 day, 4 maybe 5, I decided to move my operating position from the center of the Doll House to one of the little offices which has a DOOR! I closed it. I worked in there for about a week. It was like working from a remote location as I initiated phone communication and email rather than face to face. I needed to be able to work and cry sometimes simultaneously. A part of me was proud for having come up with a solution and for keeping up with the fast pace of operations. I filled my waste bin with tissues and plugged along like a machine.

I had explained to Meredith what was happening with my parents. It was like she got it in her head but not her heart. She was very disconnected in terms of how this reality was affecting ME on an emotional level. No, it was more than that. She didn't feel emotion was appropriate in the workplace. That's funny to me since we ARE emotion. But, to a degree I understand. So her problem is with certain KINDS of emotion being expressed. Certain kinds should be left in the car. For the most part, that's exactly how I am! But sometimes life throws you a whopper and by jove, to me, that's what this was! Unfortunately, Meredith didn't get that.

The incident

I love Meredith very, very much to this day but our chapter in the Doll House didn't end well. I mean... not for HER, anyway. For ME, I got layered opportunities starting with the ability to release something that had been haunting me for years. A life threatening contract that I later learn has been in action several incarnations.

In radio, as an artist/entertainer I worked solo. I created my work and performed it solo. So, radio didn't give me an opportunity to work on these areas, like Valet Of The Dolls regularly does. When I birthed VOTD I got a new challenge. And I can't ignore the nature of our company. Intensely female, we're one big bubblin' pot of estrogen! I acknowledge the experience with this company, on this level is priceless and I wouldn't trade it as much of my learning has centered in 'self-worth' issues! Workaholic overachievers tend to have self-worth issues as the mistaken catalyst that keeps them racing.

My outer experience is (always) a reflection of my inner reality. If nothing changes then... everything stays the same and if everything stays the same then..... One belief I would immediately work to edit was that *super smart, fun to work with people who have strong work ethic, are hard to find.* Lots of business owners and managers say this. I am no longer one of them. I now KNOW super smart, fun to work with people who have strong work ethic are EASY to find! :) That feels good to acknowledge!

Back to the incident - The incident where someone basically decided, we didn't need to push 'the button' for the rest of the day and this was going to lead to our very own version of an *electromagnetic anomaly* – exactly and precisely like what happened on 'The Island' in LOST – only different; This week of working in emotional quarantine was very productive in anticipation of Friday being my day off in Riverside. My goal was to work so hard and get so much done no one (Meredith) could complain of being overworked. I did pretty much everything. Other admins merely needed to maintain it while I was gone.

Friday around noon, I got to Riverside. Meredith was in during the morning until 2pm. At about 2pm she wrote me an email with a few notes about tasks she'd done and what she couldn't complete. She wished me a great weekend and signed off with a double XO. I thanked and xo'd her back. Then I focused on my parents the rest of the day and hit the freeway back to L.A. around 8pm. I felt bad that I hadn't checked in with Aleena who started at 2pm but figured no news was good news!

Back in the Doll House I sat down at my computer at 9:45pm. I started scrolling and noticing how much stuff got missed. Long story short, no one was in the office during the afternoon. For the 2nd time in our nearly 15 year history (the first being when my Dad was in an ambulance), the office was empty for several business hours but THIS time - it didn't have to be. - Seriously?!

There were several quote requests in the inbox and 9 voice mails requiring attention! I sent emails to all the admins (4) asking what happened?! Why were so many things missed? I gave examples of important emails 2:22pm, 2:49pm, 3:03pm, 4:18pm.... That's when I learned no one had been in that afternoon once Meredith left. Aleena had cancelled a few days earlier. I didn't know this. Meredith knew this but SAYS she thought I was cool with the office being empty. - OMG! What?!!

The most telling part of the story is that there was another admin who was ready, willing and very able to fill in that afternoon! Tia was like, "why didn't she call ME?" Meredith's decision to let the office go empty that Friday afternoon was to spite me. She had been getting more and more frustrated with the fact that the office didn't run like it used to years ago. With a small army of admins, it ran well but <u>without so much of Gillian</u>. She was NOT okay with letting this trend continue.

So, the empty office Friday thing has happened, it's now Monday. I've spent the day in my secluded office space – THIS time because I want to temper myself, as, I'm deeply annoyed and there's too much work to do. At the end of Meredith's shift, I decide to approach her about what happened. Still secluded in my office with a door, I used the phone to call her and entered the conversation just making sure there was clarity about my intention regarding the office never being empty during regular business hours. "I realize I made a mistake with the schedule and didn't catch Aleena's cancellation but if that happens again, could you just back me up by bringing it to my attention?" She was silent. "Backing each other up IS part of the job description. I mean, didn't you think it was kind of weird that no one was going to be here?"

Rev. Gillian V. Harris M.S.P.

I guess I put her in a defensive position because that's how she responded. "I'm not taking the heat for this, Gillian". There was something about that which read to me like, *neener neener you should have been working.*

"But Meredith, Tia was available and WANTED the hours!" I guess I was challenging her, now. Very self-righteously she came back with information I didn't know. She felt like she was the only one in the office smart enough or as she worded it, "I'm the only one worth their weight to be IN here running this with you! I CAN'T BE THE ONLY ONE, GILLIAN!" She yelled while implying she was overworked (5 hours a day, M - F, with a firm start/end time - which is the schedule she insisted on when taking the job - and she's over worked!). I was now so hurt and frustrated -tears were streaming down my face as I realized she would not support me. She couldn't see me since I was in another room but she might have noticed I was so upset I could barely speak. We'd had heated moments years ago when she worked here before but never, EVER, anything to the degree that was percolating to a boil right at that moment.

Something I had stuffed for years was now a saturating echo in my head. I honestly tried to resist but in the back of my mind I kept hearing "just SAY IT. Tell her". I gathered up hurt from nearly 10 years ago before she quit the first time. Out it came, "One day when you worked here before you said something to me. In response to my fatigue with no days off n whatnot you said, *you're the owner, you're SUPPOSED to work harder than anybody else.* Pretty inhumane but you said it".

"Heeeey!" Meredith protested in a loud knee jerk, "THAT was a LONG time ago! I've grown up since then". She continued with a high volume rapidly worded revolt which I interrupted with a whisper so intense it demanded she stop speaking to listen, "Meredith....." She silenced to hear me. Spinning in emotion, now, I fought to get each word out. I didn't stutter but my sentences were broken in a fragmented rhythm - each word separated by emotion welling up in my throat, "I hope....that karma ....is real. ... I....WANT you to get your Vineyard business going .... I want this for you and I want it soon." I could sense at this point that she thought I was saying something nice. I wasn't. I continued, "I want your employees ..... to have the exact same psychology and philosophy as you." She bantered something back in defense. -Exhausted with it all I countered, "Meredith, I have always....found you to be incredibly ...selfish". I hung up the phone and picked up my purse. -Time for me to leave the building. Meredith met me in the middle of the Doll House, "Wowww. THAT was JUST.... AWFUL", as if scolding a little kid. She tried to tell me something about being here as my friend and the sacrifices she makes to be present for this job. I corrected her, "You are HERE, for the money". Maybe I shouldn't have said that. That was anger (a.k.a. hurt) talking but I also was just done. AND I hadn't put pieces together yet. Her financial situation had changed -she really didn't need to make the nearly 1 hour (1 way) commute to do this anymore.

Before releasing my truth, I realized that I could be losing my strongest person at the BUSIEST time of the year but ya know what, I also figured I'd live through whatever! There was an edge about Meredith that had always been part of her, I might have even adored it at some point, but now it was vibrantly UNCOMFORTABLE for me and I couldn't be around it.

I drove away kind of in a state of shock. Like, post-traumatic stress - with an almost catatonic sense about me. I didn't know what to feel, exactly. What had just gone down was WAY intense and yeah, awful. I had, indeed, wanted to confront a difficult situation but no way did I anticipate all of that.

I did a walk-in (ha!) for a nail appointment and watched my phone blow up for about an hour. Meredith called and texted but I really wasn't ready to talk to her. Not right then. She was busy demanding a recant because her feelings were hurt by the word "selfish". "You owe me a big fat sloppy apology! …When a FRIEND tells you their feelings are hurt, you apologize", she wrote via email. Well now, if that ain't the pot calling the kettle black! Out loud to myself I countered, "You're right. I'm sorry. I shouldn't have said you are selfish. You're not. You're SELF CENTERED". But that didn't mean any less love for her, if that makes sense. I was sad… At the same time, a severance was in order.

I didn't want to fire her - preferred she quit so to ensure this, I did…. The Long Con! Yes I did! Thank you Sawyer! Lol! Most of my emails back to her were authentic as I kept offering olive branches. She kept coming back angrier and angrier and angrier because while I spoke of love and friendship I wouldn't apologize for expressing my truth earlier. I even wondered in one email what she and I were doing in a parallel life that might be playing into the energy we're experiencing now! - THAT didn't go over very well! Lol!

I understood that something had deeply disturbed my inner peace. That it was now my challenge to go within and work on bringing healing to that area. I also get that though Meredith seemed like the problem, she was merely the trigger for my reaction to the problem which was ALREADY within me. That's how it works. And I get that I had an agreement with her to come into each other's world and be part of the material we were now playing out. This was merely a path to inner work we each needed to do. Key: the issue was immediately (like while getting my nails done) no longer Meredith. I knew that once I went within (myself) and found resolve, my outer experience would begin to mirror this new inner reality. So inward I marched.

For me it was easy to let Meredith go, energetically. Even at that moment I knew she and that incident were blessings to me. I thought I'd already done a lot of this work but clearly there was a little more to do. The remedy was to go within. Later that evening via email, I expressed this plan of how I would go within to tend to my emotions and suggested she try the same. I shouldna done that! - NOT right then! She let me have it using words like "rhetoric" and "bull shit" all in one sentence. To her, I was talking my way AROUND the bottom line which was that I owed her an apology. Period. >>>>huge sigh<<<<

While I hoped (still do) there would be a way to salvage the friendship, for the time being, I didn't see it being comfortable for her to work in the D-H any longer. At the end of one of my emails in an exchange that lasted about an hour I started my Long Con by writing "I know your jury may still be out on whether or when to return to work here. If you'd like to give it a day to deliberate, I totally respect that". She took me up on that and seems to have spent much of that day writing her resignation letter which she pressed send on bright & early Wednesday morning November 19. That's a 48 hr long con! Not bad!!!

Not bad except now I'd need to hire someone else and I'd need to seriously get on my p's and q's to prepare to pull off 100 parties over the 30 days of December as the only mastered Sales Administrator. By the time she sent her resignation I had already scheduled several interviews with new candidates. Thing is, my focus now was on being three people, the two I already was and now Meredith as well.

Meredith quit Wednesday morning. All was well until the world almost started to spin Thursday afternoon around 1:30pm. I was light headed and suddenly panicked as I realized I hadn't taken my blood pressure medication that day. I was terrified of a repeat of what happened in 2009. That day (in 2009) I got so dizzy (from my elevated blood pressure) that, in fear I was about to pass out, I dialed 911 and welcomed in a house full of gorgeous paramedics. To avoid that THIS TIME, I reached for my meds which were right in front of me and took my dose.

I'd been on the phone when this happened, with a prospective new admin, by the way! "Oh wow..." I told her "I'm really light headed". I didn't want to freak her out, "I haven't eaten" I said and stayed on topic regarding her process but I also cut the conversation short. Once I got off the phone I took my blood pressure (BP); it was 171/89. Just SEEING those numbers took my BP up another notch. I called my doctor Marc Lavin with whom I am an MDVIP member which costs extra but lets me do really cool stuff like see him when I need him - not two weeks later. I talked to his nurse and told her what happened. Dr. Lavin came to the phone and got details then asked what time I could come in. We coordinated and I headed over around 4pm. By the time I got there my BP was 118/75! So all was well! I left feeling like I just needed to concentrate and not FORGET *myself* again. OMG!

In 2009 those cute paramedics actually took me away in an ambulance! Once again, within an hour or so my meds kicked in and when my BP reached 140/80 the E.R. released me to call a taxi and go home. I remember the gratitude that day five years ago as I stood outside of the hospital waiting for my ride. I'd been given more time in this incarnation! I got that. Bliss! I also get that life continues and that there could be other stuff even more exciting than this outside of this incarnation but I am here to live this particular life to the fullest. NOT to have a stroke that I can avoid. This light headed dizziness thing is one of the symptoms of a stroke on the verge. Hello! Now, 5 years later, here we go again? Seriously? "Gillian please keep it together" I scolded myself. I suddenly pictured myself in a hospital bed and needing to give Meredith that great big fat sloppy apology she wanted...

Needing my life partner, Berson, I called him later that day. We connected for a walk. Two Gemini's, this is usually our time to talk but I wasn't my normal loquacious. I did tell him about my BP scare earlier that day. He already knew about the incident with Meredith.

With every power walking footstep I was deep in thought. Reflection... For so many years I'd struggled to create an administrative system that worked. Before I could do that I'd created a monstrously successful company. Talk about putting the cart before the horse! And 'I' was the horse!!! But that was then. We got it all flipped appropriately around and now all systems are seriously a go. It's like I'm at the end of the tunnel but this last stretch is UP HILL!

Then there's the power of words and especially the power of BELIEF. If I say and believe its "uphill", then the Universe says, "uphill, it is"! Feeling victimized by the multitudes of people *I mistakenly hired* who were genuinely incapable of doing the kind of work required in the Doll House, I was overwhelmed. I felt stuck. I'd started this adorable athletic type company because I'm an adorable athletic type person. But now, glued by workload to my desk for sometimes 17 straight hours at a time, though still adorable - I gained a lot of weight and I had said over and over again, "this job is going to kill me. - It's gonna take me out early". I had said those words A LOT! Angrily, I'd said them. Sometimes in tears I'd said them. -If it is true that thought creates (which it is) then those are some pretty scary words to declare into existence - sometimes at really high volume.

I had developed some serious symptoms of what I call 'sitting disease', starting with the weight gain. I even got bursitis from leaning on my left elbow too much in my favorite THINKING position! My left knee would suddenly throb in pain if I sat too long (weird one!)! That, plus the blood pressure and the border line diabetes which I'd gotten inspired to beat back down to a normal number a couple times. But now I feared I might be losing the battle or at the very least, the battle had stepped up a notch. At 306 lbs I now weighed more than I had in my entire friggin life! I felt condensed ....energetically between a rock and a very hard relentless place.

Half way through our mile, emotion welled, my throat tightened and in what sounded like an asthma attack I started to cry. Cardio and emotion don't mix for me! I could barely breathe with all the hurt which kept rising. I wheezed as water rushed out of my eyes and down my face. I sat on a nearby wall in someone's front yard. Berson took my hand and held a silent vigil as my tears flowed hard. While that emotion was a river I listened to the thoughts behind the current so I could fully understand what I was feeling and needed to work on. "I'm not ready to go" I wept, "I have so much to do and ...I love being here". "Then stay", he's always so to the point! My frustration was that, clearly, in order for me to stay, things would have to change. If nothing changed . . .

22

Panic Attacks

December is roaring and we're actually moving gracefully through it. Pretty much all parties were booked in November, now it was just about execution! Piece-uh-cake! My mantra is, "I GOT this".

My Dads birthday was coming up the first week of January so Mom and I were planning to throw him a surprise party. I half kicked myself after suggesting this. How on earth would I fit this in?! Keep in mind, all the while, I'm working on this very book and can't stop, as, it feels like life purpose material. The good news is, weddings had slowed down. My last one was in November and the Bless & Clear phone had gone silent with perfect timing!

After the first blood pressure scare, I proceeded to have a series of very serious panic attacks. While I'd had a few light panic attacks in the past, like, 20 years ago - nothing recently and never anything as severe as what I'm about to explain.

The first one interrupted my morning Jacuzzi ritual one day at about 7am. That one I'm still not sure was completely a panic attack. It felt very other dimensional and simply scared me. I've never jumped out of the Jacuzzi so fast in my life!!!! Took my BP and it was fine. - So...what the hell WAS that??! I then started checking my blood pressure about 10 times a day. Well actually 30 times because each of the 10 times I did it 3 times to triple check the numbers! No exaggeration! In fact, I could very well be under representing the truth on this C.B.P.R.D. - Compulsive BP reading Disorder!! . I even created an Excel spreadsheet! And I learned was that my BP was running higher than it should be. THAT freaked me out and made it higher. I was now in a new realm coupling the C.B.P.R.D. with a psychosis that I'll call 'BP-aphobia'. This new fear didn't help what was about to happen.

My doctor prescribed a beta blocker which was to assist my regular BP medication with one of the side effects being a reduced heart rate. This medication didn't work for my particular body. My heart rate went WAY too low which felt awful physically and then psychologically it seemed to enhance my panic attacks. For the next two weeks I was absolutely terrified my heart would stop completely OR that my BP would peak and I would stroke.

Several of my panic attacks would happen while I was sitting at the computer working. As my thoughts would multiply, to-do lists layering on top of each other, I would feel it starting to happen. The 'it' was almost a sensation in the area of my brain. Pretty soon it would take me over enveloping my whole body. Lungs compressed, it would be pure unadulterated terror. Trying not to get to that point, I could just stand up and breathe it off. But sometimes even that didn't help. One morning around 11am, I stood up in near panic. I knew I had to STOP looking at the computer NOW. I went out the front door thinking fresh air would do the trick. I leaned against the doorway and clearly determined that I was absolutely light headed. Oh no! "Lisa!" I called for Agent Bogenschutz. So glad she was there that day. Sarina was the admin. She's strong enough that I didn't need to worry about the client line right then. I just needed Lisa. I wanted someone to be in my presence and know what was happening.

I took my blood pressure while sitting on the side of a brick planter box next to the car port; it was 157/82 then 161/80 then some other crazy numbers. Dr Lavin could see me at 11:30. Lisa drove. On the way over I felt not only light headed but light bodied. "Oh my God" I said, "I've gotta finish my book first". "Shut up" she fired back, "you're not going anywhere". Thirty seconds later I'm like, "Oh my God... I gotta finish payfrigginroll" (which was due that very day). "Fuck payroll!" Lisa said in my defense. "Oh yeah", I replied, "THAT will go over real well with about 65 people". I was quiet for a moment then surrendered out loud, my voice kind of weak, "I think (sigh) ...maybe I have too much on my plate...." She agreed.

Usually a smidge late to my doctor appointments, I was on time this time! While my BP was too high Dr. Lavin said it wasn't 'stroke' high. What concerned him more was my heart rate, "it's too low" he said, "no more beta blockers". He did an EKG which turned out fine and adjusted my meds again. It would be about a week before I got my real heart rate back. Until then, I was in for several more really awful panic attacks! I'd even have them in my sleep!

One night I sprang from my bed FREAKED out. Butt naked, somewhat delirious and determined to save my LIFE, in the dark I fumbled around the nightstand and grabbed my cell. I clumsily grabbed my purse by one handle and dragged it with me as I hurried from the bedroom out to the dining room table. Why the rush to this destination, IDK but I was like GO!! I made it. The dining room felt like another safe zone. I sat down and was like, "oh shit! What was THAT?" All kinds of thoughts are going through my mind. I took my

BP and it was fine but my heart rate was still about 49-50! During a PANIC! I have rationalized later that some of these attacks were my body trying to spunk up my heart. Honestly, I didn't know WHAT happened and 'just in case' decided to create a cozy bed situation in my couch-less living room using a chaise lounge connected to a big overstuffed arm chair.

Lisa was now very concerned about me. I told her I had a plan. If I was too freaked out and Berson wasn't in town I would just take myself to West Hills Hospital and park in the parking lot. "I'll take my BP gadget with me and if I need them, I'll be RIGHT THERE, already. I'll just walk in. Or worst case scenario, I'll just step out or the car and SCREAM!" A plan with a funny edge but a plan none the less!!

The worst panic attack happened on, ironically, the busiest night of our busiest month, Saturday December 20th. Despite the fact there were nearly 80 Santa Hat wearing valets in the field working about a dozen parking operations, the email and phones were fairly quiet. About 10:15, completely tuckered from the week and day I set up my chaise over-stuffed arm chair bed. The TV was on HGTV - nothing scary there except a little mold in the attic! So that was the channel of choice.

I started to fall asleep and WHAM it hit me. Panic! I'm instantly upright and thinking "WTF"?! At this point I'm like, "oh God is this where I am now? I'm a panic attack person?!" This was awful. I ran for my BP machine- it would give a different reading every time so, you know - I'd do batches of 3 readings and take an average of the last two! Wait, what?! Yeah! Average reading: 158/81/51 (the last number is heart rate).

I sat on the edge of the chair and realized how sad I felt. And I was terrified. I couldn't believe I couldn't get a handle on this. -And that it would wake me from my sleep! And that it happened in the (original deemed safe zone) living room! I didn't know what to do. Of course I prayed and I also cried. In fact I thought "maybe I just need to cry as hard as possible and get this shit OUT!" So, I did. I kinda came down from that for a few minutes and then I checked my blood pressure again; 163/85. Never mind the heart rate I was now in GO mode, again. And... never mind the logic that emotion raises your blood pressure! I was in a different zone. It's called PURE PANIC! You see, back in 2009, the room spun, I dialed 911, simultaneously popped a BP pill and by the time paramedics checked my BP it was 171 over something... I never stopped to realize it was probably much higher when the room started spinning. Taking my BP meds (which I'd forgotten to do in the morning) started working immediately to bring it down. But...I deleted that part of the equation. I just remembered the number 171. *171 is bad.* So when I saw my BP reading 163 – and seemingly on the rise I freaked! I grabbed my cell and texted Agent B "Lucy, I'm going to the ER but I'm actually going INSIDE". I told her I just wanted somebody to know where I was!! I didn't want to freak Berson out since he was out of town so I delayed reaching out to him.

I drove myself to the ER. LOVELOVELOVE the intake system at West Hills Hospital. Props! Love the friendly people, and completely adore Dr. James Buselli. I'm sure he gets that a lot! Handsome multiplied many times over, great big MUSCLES and bedside manner THRU THE FRIGGIN ROOF! I later told Dr. Lavin, regarding Dr. Buselli, "I just wanna go park in the parking lot...and STALK HIM!" Lol! Just kidding, of course! (Kinda. Ha!) But seriously.... DANG!

Ok…

Um...where was I?

Oh yeah -

By the time I got to ER, without tears - just thoughts alone, I had worked my BP up to 183/95- DUUUUDE!

I'm here to tell you, my figurative HEAD caused all that! My THOUGHTS! I was there for about 4 hours. After yet another normal EKG I was monitored (by a team of really fun, friendly staff) as my BP slowly dropped to 144/80. While discharging me, Dr. Buselli gave me a pep talk. While my numbers were a little elevated, I wasn't in stroke zone (Dr. Lavin echoed in my head). He talked numbers with me which set me at ease. "When you get close to 180-200, THEN come see me. And don't take your blood pressure too often", he said. "Blood pressure is like the wind, it can change minute to minute. I even have patients who have created CHARTS to log their blood pressure". I started to laugh, "I have one of those!" His handsome eyebrows bunched like he was trying to figure out whether I was kidding. "Yup, did mine's in Excel" I confirmed. He shook his head, "don't do that!" I laughed harder promising to cease and desist!

I also want to say that I reached out to several people while this was happening, via text; Lori, Justin and once I was all calm n whatnot I texted my beloved Berson. All three were my support team while I went through this but I want to say, especially Lori who I talked to for almost 3 hours during and after. This wasn't the first time we would use our gifts and skills as metaphysicians to energetically diagnose a person's imbalance or ailment. But it was the first time the person was me! The information exchanged and shared was priceless and is part of my wellness today.

Also Justin: I reached out to him because in the last year of our 12 year crazy relationship, he was having panic attacks. During his bouts he always thought he was having a heart attack. When I left the emergency room, still sitting in my car in the parking lot he called me, "here's what I did. I just faced it down". He told me that one day, when he felt it coming on, instead of getting up in a panic he just sat there and said, "Fine! Bring it on, then! Do it! -And it didn't happen. I did NOT have a heart attack and that was my last panic attack 15 years ago, now". I thanked & loved him. I thanked & loved everybody.

Back home alone, Lori kept me company by phone for another couple hours! During that conversation, she told me about a 'Body Building Competition'. At 57 years old, I thought, "oh how COOL would that be?! I'm IN!" My health and fitness was about to begin a serious transformation as I would join this competition in 2015!

Rev. Gillian V. Harris M.S.P.

Energy correcting

I quickly reached out to the USM community for referrals 'Spirit Counselor in need of Spirit Counsel'. Specifically, I needed panic attack counsel! I have much gratitude for Life Coach, Laura Dewey and Spiritual Psychologist, Healer and Shaman Rebekah Vandenberg. Both of these practitioners immediately answered my plea. These sessions were incredibly healing and played into the immediate end of my panic attacks.

To seal it all, God would send another friend to my aid, Light Worker, healer & Shaman Cat Ramos. The also goes by 'La Cat'! I met her in 94 while in radio. I was introducing shows on stage at St Marks, a former night club on Windward Way in Venice Beach owned by a cool guy named Farook Singh. Still a professional dancer/singer as she was then, Cat is also an Urban Shaman. She didn't KNOW how significant her timing was on this visit. She thought we were just getting together because she's interested in also becoming a Bless & Clear Minister and wanted to hear more about the work we are doing. At the same time she wanted to share a healing modality she's providing as a service. She calls it 'Energy Correcting'. I only knew the modality had something to do with severing counterproductive cords/ connections/ agreements. -Connections that were causing more harm than good for me in THIS incarnation. The objective in the work is 'equanimity'. -Non judgment, neutrality. That's all I knew and I was like *BRANG IT*!

In the living room, I sat in the chaise lounge allowing her the big overstuffed arm chair. She started talking, accessing information and using what seemed to be a words and energy based inter-dimensional correcting healing technology. In short, summarized probably WAY too much, to the point of probably doing it an injustice, it is a sound and intention activated modality that works best when the technician is at the least, clairvoyant. She wanted to introduce me to the process "so you can see what it feels like and you may want to start doing it for people. It's amazing". Long story short (so short, there's probably more injustice'), using metaphysical reconnaissance she gathered information regarding three of my other incarnations where the life story is intense and heavy and were affecting my incarnation here! 1) a Cinderella story and I am the Cinderella but there is no fancy 'Ball' to go to, only the unfair amount of work being heaved upon me by unfair people. 2) A life story of false imprisonment. Behind bars for something I didn't do! A serious case of MISTAKEN IDENTITY.

These first two didn't surprise me. #1 was in alignment with the way I used to see the running of Valet Of The Dolls - back when the cart was before the horse. #2... I can only say (for now) is this feels like allowing myself to be misidentified as the one who is supposed to work harder than everyone else!! Both of these, along with the next, were rooted in self-worth issues reflected in my environmental conditions. In a nutshell, that is just me taking responsibility for owning the misinterpretations and mistakenly buying into harmful beliefs that created those circumstances.

The 3rd incarnation of mine that she saw that was affecting this one and needed to be severed was one where I was surrounded by a mountain of paperwork. - SO much paperwork. As she spoke I shared her vision seeing a room full of it - a plethora of ceiling high stacks of paper surrounding me on all sides and with that reality in my mind, a wave of nausea hit me so hard I almost hurled. -Very out of character for me. She quickly moved through the energy correcting process to "disconnect, disassociate, separate you from those experiences and send them off into other dimensions, existence, time and space energy into the black hole and beyond" she kept talking but I noticed that instantly, the nausea dissolved. I emotionally felt nothing about the paper. Equanimity. That's a correction. Incredible work! The session lasted about an hour. It was the perfect clearing after the release of Meredith and what she symbolized for my experience.

23

Lifetime Hallmark

Agent B helped me pull the pieces together for what turned out to be the single most amazing day of my family's history! My Dads surprise birthday party in early January! Sarina, from my office, is also a private organic chef. THIS is truly her expertise. Her company 'Lush Grub' catered the food! About five other Dolls worked as either valet outside to hide the cars or servers inside for the nearly 40 guests. Thank you Uncle Bob & Aunt Shirley (Robert & Shirley Bland), for a job well done. Dad was clueless when these two stopped by and Uncle Bob took him for an afternoon outing which ended with a movie. When they returned Dad walked in from the garage and through the kitchen into a house FULL of love and SURPRISE! So gracious was he, never wiping the tear that fell onto his cheek as he laughed and expressed the true shock and joy at this amazing heartfelt occasion. Momentous! Especially after the scary fainting episode in July, his friends looked forward to honoring him outwardly like this. Once again, love touched me as I watched it unfold and dance that evening. And THIS is what Life is about.

A couple weeks or so later at the end of a visit on the way out the door, I went to hug my Dad. Usually during this embrace, I make up a language and say a sentence to which he responds with the same kind of gibberish and we laugh and may go on for many strange sentences!! This time, in the embrace I quickly told him something like, "boondashdoo, maningkahty bladow bersh don". Instead of responding as he usually does, with the same nonsense...he started *singing*. My Dad has a BEAUTIFUL voice. -Very Nat King Cole. He held me and we swayed side to side while he sang a verse from an old love ballad! I didn't know the song but I was relishing the moment as the words ended, "I have a crush on youuuuuuuu"! "Haha" he laughed, " Ya didnt know your old man could still sing like that, didja"?!

    57 (and a HALF!) years old and my Dad is holding me and serenading me! - I know that there are other wonderful fathers out there so ... please forgive me but… I feel like the luckiest girl in the world!

24

The Island

Just a little side note. I find it so interesting that the LOST Island itself, was a character. There was so much going on there, energetically. So much that couldn't be explained and was simply beautiful. Ironically, the island where they did the filming is full of intense energy and beauty with lots going on outside the physical - just like the LOST Island.

After my trip to Oahu, I was doing some research. I think I must have searched 'Ho`Okupu'. I was thinking of the visit I had to the Hieiu where I'd had the experience of feeling like a "gnat at the dinner table" with Spirits who were hovering on the island! I came across a web site http://www.kaahelehawaii.com/pages/culture_hookupu.htm where the author is writing about Ho`Okupu offerings! Basically it was a warning: *Don't!* Furthermore: *If you already did, you're RUDE! AND you MIGHT be in for it!!* Yes!! They ran down a list of what they considered OFFENSIVE offerings: food (you don't know who/what you're really feeding!), burning money (Pele and others aren't about finances, yo!), GIN and other alcoholic beverages (Teehee!)! WHAT HAPPENED WAS - Apparently there was this guy who used to own the famous 'Volcano House' hotel on Crater Rim Drive in Hawaii National Park Hawaii and he would leave gin in hopes of getting Pele really sloshed so she'd shoot off a fire show which would draw customers to his establishment! SO wrong! Lol!

The web site author goes on to suggest 'curse' like possibilities if you leave hair, a locket you've worn, jewelry or photographs. They wrote that these kinds of gifts entail vows... and that by leaving these kinds of offerings you're making promises you don't know you're making and the promises... (the ones you don't know you're making) could bind you and your family for generations to come!!!!! DUDE!!!!

I'm reading along and I'm like, "phew! Glad I didn't do any of THAT stuff" then I read, "A rock as an offering, wrapped in a ti leaf or not, is offensive"! My eyeballs popped open wide! I'm like "Uh oh!" And now I'm getting defensive, yelling at my monitor "STURMAH MADE ME DO IT!" Ha! According to this author, it's too late to go passing the buck NOW!

So like I said, while at the Heieu, I felt like a GNAT at the dinner table! I GET IT NOW! Lolol! But you know what? A gnat doesn't mean any harm any more than I did. And in fact, where I come from, 'intention' is everything. Now, don't get me wrong, I will no longer leave a physical gift for Spirits in Hawaii. Ever. I will follow this web sites advice and my gifts will be non-physical expressions of gratitude BUT I am NOT cursed! Now, had I been a FLY at the dinner table, I mighta gotten swatted but seriously - how often can ya catch a GNAT!?!

JOURNAL 10 Sunday February 8
TESTING! TESTING 1-2-3...

Last weekend my Dad and this weekend my Mom! Jeesh... WHAT is going on?!

Last weekend, out to dinner with both of them, we were talking about traveling. The good ol' bucket list. My parents have traveled A LOT but they haven't been to Trinidad. I asked why Trinidad? "Because", my Dad said, "that's some place I'd like to go before I die". "You're not gonna die", I told him. "Yes I AM", he was stern. Gently I countered, "your BODY will stop working but the part of you that is talking to me now, will always be alive". His eyes met mine and he was taking in my words. "What fascinates me", I told him, "is how solid this linear existence appears to be - so mesmerizing that this is another layer of the Spirit world cuz we're all eternal Spirits and there are OTHER LAYERS". I turn and touch the wall next to our booth, "it seems like this is all there is. That's amazing to me because we KNOW there's more - or you wouldn't have gone to church this morning". He thought about what I said... It may have been abstract for him on the surface but I know on an inner level he got it... or...wants to get it.

Today, a week later, I'm in the kitchen when my mom says, "let's go sit on the porch". Once there, her conversation was about it being time to sell their dream house and simplify their world. Of all their houses, this was their ultimate. As soon as I went off to college they found the land on the side of a hill and created a master piece. The side with the view is two stories of panoramic glass. From almost everywhere you can see forever. It is the most spectacular house in the neighborhood and my Dad still loves it. It's just hard now. It's A LOT of property requiring a lot of upkeep and cardio (!) "and" she said, "when we go, it would be overwhelming for you as an only child to deal with all of this. I told him, it's not fair to Gill."

I didn't really know what to feel in the moment. I knew I wanted to support her and I wanted to support my Dad. I stayed objective and we talked more...

I left that night thinking about how...*matter of fact*, they had both been about the end of this incarnation, two consecutive weeks in a row. "They've been talking...or something", I thought. Like, as a team, they seem to be...readying themselves or something. Oh God....

25

The Point

What I am doing with LOST is not what normal people do with it. I get that! But I saw such a beautiful opportunity to look at examples of life experiences and then there were the reincarnations. LOST beautifully illustrates the concept discussed here of multiple lives - reincarnation - soul families. Hoping that, as for me, it has opened the part of your mind that is conscious of how much more we really are. How much more there is. Why we, so deeply, love the people we do! I no longer take in stride, moments when I meet someone for the very first time and connect immediately or feel a strong affinity. Those are friends or loved ones from other times and places where we are working life curriculum on other petals. I'm going forward with the understanding that everyone I meet now I may also know ...somewhere else! Makes me think stuff like, what if the person who irritates you today was your loving parent in a previous life who risked their life for you and sacrificed for you all the days of that incarnation? Lol! Makes me giggle cuz face it, you GOTTA be nice to that person! Cuz COME ON! WHAT IF?!

As I said before, I believe that office admin, Sarina, is my daughter in a separate incarnation. I know for sure Rick Bernal, who while on Los Angeles radio went by 'Rick Diego', is my son in a different incarnation. His ex-wife (this incarnation) Ellen is also his wife in the incarnation

Rev. Gillian V. Harris M.S.P.

where he is my son. They were both at my bedside as I transitioned from that incarnation. FYI- In this present incarnation we would meet in 1986 while I was on L.A.'s 1110 AM KRLA and he was on the sister station, at the time 97.1FM. Instant affinity. I became great friends with him and his then fiancé Ellen. It was Rick who introduced me to the book 'Dancing in the Light' by Shirley MacLaine which lead to the trip I mentioned earlier to Galesteo New Mexico – which is where I found out he is my son on another life petal. In fact, prior to this trip…I knew very little about reincarnation. So this was THE pivotal chapter in my spiritual journey this incarnation ending much of the mystery, replacing it with truth about our eternal nature.

Know that when I got to about page 300 (of this book) I also called our then publicist and asked him to switch his vision from Valet Of The Dolls and now focus on 'The Secrets of LOST'! I deployed him to find the LOST creators JJ Abrams, Jeffrey Lieber, Damon Lindeloff and Carlton Cuse for an interview with me. One month later, we've only heard back from JJ Abrams. JJ's agent Brian Kend sent us an email on March 11th thanking us for reaching out but…
"I am sorry to say that Mr. Abrams will be unable to participate due to pre-existing commitments, etc.
That said, he appreciated you thinking of him!
Best,
Brian"

Even though he declined the interview I was absolutely tickled that he responded and that he "appreciated"! :)

Duped for the greater good!

To the creators and writers of LOST, please know that I just want to line ya'll up and hug every last one of you! I am so deeply grateful for how well you DUPED me!!! If you had told us at the beginning that this was a story about …life after life it might have only been popular amongst a small sector of rock totin', sage smudging, crystal gazing Americans like me and maybe doomed to only one season. By being sneaky, you made it so the masses could get an introduction to this truth for years to come. Thank you so much!

26

Check please!!!

Ever notice how often people "die"?! I mean, like, every friggin day! All friggin day and all damn night long! What the..?! - Don't you find this kinda…...*SUSPICIOUS?!!!!* - While part of me is playing, the other part knows I'm kind of on to something. It IS suspicious when you get that, globally, an estimated 56 million people, check out, per year! More than 4.6 million per MONTH! In one MINUTE, it's estimate that 106 people will have "died". I got these numbers from one of many "World Death Clock" type web sites. They are all tick-tocking similar calculations. The most startling one was; every SECOND 1.8 people *die*!

Ok, so, we've got this full on EPIDEMIC with 100% of all humans, at some point, facing this life exit thing! Totally nothing NEW! This has been going on and on FOR EVER!!! 2 every second?! ?! Dude!! Just makes me think the general public is missing something. There's GOT to be more than we can see with our eyeballs on this! And the stuff we're missing has us flippin' out over NOTHING!

Staring at one of the death clocks as the numbers kept growing every SECOND was, at first, startling and dark. One of those things that made me say, 'Oh my God…" But then in the same breath I got a vision. These people aren't dying. As the clock ticked and the count rose, one every almost half a second, I got a picture in my mind of spirit bodies rising from physical bodies… all over the world… one every almost half a second! With the awareness that people aren't dying but instead, transitioning on to more life…watching the clock became lighter, sacred, magical.…

- Now, lots of people classified as 'terminal', eventually stop flipping out and 'come to terms'. But… WHAT, exactly, are they coming to terms with?! My Aunt Jean had come to terms. She knew there were other incarnations to have. She was done with this one. She'd finished swallowing the last bite of this life, not in the mood for more dessert, she was ready to go do something else. *CHECK PLEASE!!*

BRB!! (Be Right Back)

I had a thought the other day as I drove past the gigantic Los Angeles National Cemetery off Sepulveda Blvd in West Los Angeles. As always I was taken by the multitude of headstones.

The neatly filed rows and rows and rows, thousands of headstones perfectly uniformed and at attention as far as my eyes could see. I wondered – "how many of those headstones are for the same soul?!" If a cemetery is old enough, many tombstones could be for the same soul as they ended different incarnations in the same geographical location! And actually, the cemetery doesn't have to be that old for the same soul to have several tombstones from similar time periods in parallel existences happening in the same geographical area!

Because of my awareness of the on-going-ness of life, I am awed by one's entrance into the physical as much as I am awed by their exit. If I ever hear of someone transitioning, I am in immediate prayer for that person and their family. Believe it or not, I get this *opportunity* often because of Valet Of The Dolls. Remember, we valet for private events, only. All kinds. That includes memorials. I have always welcomed each and every such call.

Celebrations of Life are so sacred and special. If I am the one to personally take the quote request, once I've hung up the phone and if I'm not alone, I will go to a quiet, private place. Usually this is my 'healing room', just down the hall where I'm cocooned in the essence of all sorts of energetic healing tools including all of my stones and crystals. And if alone, I'll do it right at my desk. In this space I will commune with Spirit on behalf of the transitioning soul and their family. I will do the same if I become aware of a memorial quote later. But to actually talk to someone related to the disincarnate stimulates an opening for me that makes it easier to connect and even communicate with the deceased. Our valet clients don't know this is happening. (Well…I guess if any are reading this book, they do NOW!) but this is part of what they get with our service! Especially when I know it JUST happened. As we discussed earlier and as we see dramatically portrayed in parts of the LOST TV series, for some people, the period of time between incarnations is a time when prayer and guidance are most needed! There are those who think, "oh well, they're in God's hands now. Nothing I can do". Like it's over! It's NOT OVER! And we're ALWAYS in God's hands yet we can still find ourselves in crazy predicaments!! So, in this critical period of time when one is newly transitioning from their previous physical body, I love to chime in with a much light as I can muster and do my part in blessing their journey.

I don't always try to communicate with the disincarnate. Mostly I'm talking directly to God on their behalf. But sometimes I feel the disincarnate around me or that they are close and I feel like that's for a reason. So if I have time, I do talk to them. One time… I probably shoulda skipped it! Or maybe not! Maybe it's ultimately GOOD that I gave her a moment. But let me just say, this soul didn't want to talk to me. – She didn't have time. She was stuck in the rat race of her previous incarnation.

This was a situation where a would-be client requested a quote while sharing with me the sad story of their sisters passing. After talking to them and quickly sending them a great estimate I went into prayer and felt nudged to go into trance so I did. I knew the transitioned one was nearby and found her easily. She presented herself to me in a busy office building – felt like a government agency. Standing in line and annoyed with the process. She was very unhappy – grumpy – down right pissed off about EVERY thing. And she didn't welcome my communication. This type of reception doesn't happen to me very often. I quickly gave her my blessing anyway to which she looked at her watch and was like, "pff yeah whatever". With that I was on my way. About an hour later, I got an email back from the client – they thanked us profusely but they'd decided to forgo valet service all together! Hm… Coincidence?

In 2008 – 2009 while the country sank into the 2nd Great Depression, memorials saved Valet Of The Dolls from sinking, too. Seriously! When the business volume would fall dangerously low, in the nick of time, a chain of memorials would come our way and save the day! I couldn't help but notice this trend… In trance I asked if this was my imagination or are we actually getting extra help from the other side? I learned that indeed, we do get assistance! My guides in communication with the guides of the transitioned souls – a grapevine of information moves from being to being, from spirit world to physical until finally someone (who unbeknownst to them is creating under the influence – C.U.I.) is now on our phone asking for service!

In training admins for positions in the Doll House, they are guided with how to handle these calls. They learn terms and traditions; what's a 'Shiva', what's a 'Repass'? And so, part of the charm of running this company has been the honor of including these types of life events. I do everything in my power NOT to turn down memorials – even when we're sold out. I will bend over backwards to make it happen if it is at all possible.

As I worked on this chapter, in what I completely get as a re-affirmation, we have been deluged with memorials requests! Out of 15 parties for one week, 5 are memorials! THAT doesn't happen! Not normally! And THEN the most magical of things two days ago. We did a Celebration of Life and at the bottom of her paperwork, the Team Captain wrote, "I was told by the client that her deceased Aunt specifically put Valet Of The Dolls in her will to valet her memorial!! That was an Honor!!!" With a capital H, yes it was! More of an honor than I can find words for! Since learning of this *willed directive to use our service* I have reached into the Spirit world to thank this woman and let her know I'm available to communicate if she needs or wants.

I want SECONDS!!!!!

I'm not ready for the check. I want 2nds, 3rds and then I want dessert! – Just so ya know.

A Thursday afternoon in early spring, finds me blissfully in my parent's home in Riverside and… in a bit of a bicker with my mother. "I KNEW you were gonna interrogate me!" she rebelled. "Hey! Don't get mad at me for growing up to be my mom!" This went on for a few minutes until I gave up. She was just NOT gonna tell me what happened in Palm Springs the previous weekend. "What happens in Vegas stays in Vegas", she said. "But you were in PALM SPRINGS!!!" "SAME TING MON!" she countered with her native Jamaican accent! Finally she told me a snippet. She gave me a couple frames of the most romantic scene ever between her and my dad to which I QUICKLY said, "Ok! That's enough! – What happens in Vegas stays in Vegas!!" We laughed as, simultaneously the phone rang. While she took the call, I felt to go hang with my Dad.

I thought he was outside. As I went out the kitchen door to the garage, I remembered, he's gone. - Already left for his ritual Thursday evening hang out with the guys. Disappointment. Disappointment multiplied… by a sensation that came over me. For a moment, I allowed myself to get lost in a series of thoughts. Depressing unnecessary thoughts because right NOW everything is FINE. That's supposed to be all that matters but here I was hypothesizing … I thought of meeting the same sensation in the future – moving to go talk to Dad only to suddenly remember, he's not here. And then, there's my Mom. My confidant! I talk to her every single day! She's my moral support, my friend, my MOM. She cares like no one else does!

She knows my everything. My journeys, challenges, victories, my do overs and even a few of MY Vegas stories!! The thoughts started to roll (very selfishly, I admit) "when she's not in this incarnation anymore… who will I talk to?" Suddenly I was in a different space, the garden was blurry with my tears as I entered it.

I found the bench and took a seat. I admired my Dads amazing landscaping work. I admired it as I've seen him admire it. I got up and stood where I usually see him standing. I wondered what he thinks about when he's standing there… And then I stood in the spot where he and my mom always stand when they watch me drive away... –Tears. Tears of helplessness at first because, I can't stop this. Then I remembered, this sadness I feel is merely a symptom of Amnesia kicking my emotional b'hind!

It's just that… I am in love with my family. In LOVE with this incarnation. I LOVE being their daughter! I LOVE my Mom being my Mom and Dad being my Dad! This continues to be a very sweet storybook life we've created together! I am so wrapped up in the bliss of it I don't EVER want it to end! - Ever.

And…if it … WHEN it happens – hopefully, like, 15 - 20 years from now (in 20 years Mom would be 103!), our relationship will shift to a multi-dimensional one and in that communication, will I be able to let them go? Will my grief cause either of my parents to stay HERE… with a bad case of Hover Soul Syndrome?! Because of ME!?! Or … will I be able to let them both go…? Will I be able to see them across with grace and joy for the bounty the Light holds for them and their future?

Knowing what I know only makes it a *little* easier. Knowing the bliss they will feel once not limited to the physical, will rest my heart significantly. Being able to communicate with them and feel their presence will also help… But until I leave MY physical body, and join them on the other side, I will miss their touch, their physical sound, the laughter, the sensation of joy that we are when we're together in the same realm.

I acknowledge anxiety right now over the anticipated amount of illusionary *time* I will not be in physical communication with my parents. I've noticed that magically, people survive these transitions of loved ones. I simply trust all will be well…. I know for my parents, there is SO much love waiting for them on the other side. SO much… This truth makes me smile….

There are still tears as I flip the pages on this incarnation but they are much lighter now. Plentiful…but LIGHT as I now know the Spirits playing my mother and father this incarnation are with me forever as part of my Soul Family. I understand why we chose each other. I long for us to do another incarnation together, an even more evolved and blissful one than this. And I wonder who will play which roles or will it be the same set up with my mom being my mom and dad being my dad in other incarnations. Do I get to be the mom or dad in any of these?! I am excited to know that we are an eternal unit and that this is true. -That just like in LOST when Jack and his Dad reunited at the end of (being) lost so will I and my parents. It will feel like the physical again as we embrace and just like Jack, I may say to my Dad, "are you...REAL?!" And after he says yes, I'll punch him in the belly just to make sure he's still got those abs of steel!

The love reunion of me, my mom and Dad one day on the other side is just the tip of the iceberg as there are many, many others who are part of my history of loving on this and other life petals.

March 26, 2015 10:15pm
Great Spirit, Mother Father God...Creator of all there is... great Omnipresence of unconditional love, infinite intelligence and deepest compassion...
I so need you right now...
Always...
Help me....
Help me to, stay with and trust in the truth of your presence in all places, people, things and even situations. Calling myself into your light now to remind me that I am not alone, that I am now and always in your divine flow... and so are my family.....and my friends. Keep me aware that we are guided, guarded and protected in all we do, wherever we are - always.
Thank you for guiding me in this moment...Keep me in alignment with truth...
Wash away my fear. Please transform my tears to mere love...tears because love is so very, very sweet.....
And knowing that it is done, I thank you...

I release my words, thoughts and ideas knowing completely that You, Great Spirit, respond right here and right now and that your Light and Love is shining even more brightly through, to and as me and the people I love. We are safe...

And so it is – *Alem, al meen, a men
(*Aramaic for '*from all ages, throughout all ages, I seal this prayer in faith, trust and truth*)

Journal 11

4-12-15 6:32am...
Hot, blue, 103 degree water embraced my body under the new morning sky. I stretched and exhaled releasing into a relaxed state of being. I stared at the tips of my friends, reaching up

into the sky with all their green glory from a neighbor's yard. "Hello!" Communing from my heart to these three super tall pine trees about four houses away in the distance. They waved back! I looked around at the nature around me, the massive oak tree to my right and the red wood fence in front of me smothered by green vines that will soon burst with purple flowers. "Wow" I thought in appreciation. For once I wasn't claiming inadequacy with words like "but you SHOULD be a homeowner instead of a renter. Buckle down and save a down payment. Stop paying someone else's mortgage, damnit! Blahblahblah". Judgment.Fuel for the *race!* Instead, in this moment, I was looking around in such deep, deep gratitude for everything JUST the way it is. I was deeply HUMBLED by the realization that I needed to applaud myself for *allowing* the reality I am experiencing. In my chosen perspective at that moment - bills and troubles dissolved into nothingness. I was in complete awareness of how perfect my life is. Blissfully aware, so much so, the colors seemed brighter. Everything seemed to pop with animation even my thoughts as I also pictured the people I love and they energetically filed in on the huge redwood deck; Mom, Dad, Berson, Lori, Calvin, David, Randy, Cliff, Justin, Cindy, Stephanie, Angie, Jackie, Debbie, June, VOTD, Bless & Clear, O M G! In my mind's eye there was an army of love on the terrace with me. Salty bliss tears fell into the Jacuzzi as I realized the majesty of Life/Gods plan RIGHT NOW and how thankful I am for everyone and everything.

There is just SO much going on. There are other layers and dimensions the regular human eyes just don't see. But it's still there. -The reality of it all. I changed positions to look out the other side of the yard which overlooks a bit of the world. Taking in this fragment of a smaller fragment of a dot on the globe, knowing it's only a micro-speck of a micro-speck of the whole. The Magnitude... Taking it all in... There were no words behind my emotion...only awe. And more salty bliss tears as my thoughts come back to this book. 'The Secrets of LOST' has been an extraordinary project, process, growth opportunity that will continue to transform me long after the pages are done and in ways for which I continue to find I have no adequate vocabulary. Let's just say every day and every moment is richer now than I ever thought it could be as I can't help but live every day in awareness of myself as a multi-dimensional being. Simple thing like...grocery stores or gas stations are magical to me now. Driving down the street is magical. I look around at other commuters knowing we are all Spirit Beings and the whole trip becomes exhilarating as I factor in our multi-dimensional truth!

I will so miss swimming in the world of this TV series! It has meant so much to me to delve into our multi-dimensional present tense realities and related areas and to bring everything I know about it all to the table. What I originally intended on behalf of others has been surprisingly priceless for me. Transitioning is scary because we have friggin amnesia. And even without amnesia, I still want to live this joyful life experience out until I'm done with it! Like my Dad said that day, "I'm not goin' anywhere til I'm ready". :)

Rev. Gillian V. Harris M.S.P.

Originally, I mostly wanted this book for other people which fulfills a lifelong intention for me. I want to help as many people as I can - get through the moments when our loved ones leave and we feel like we're the ones who died as the pain is seemingly unbearable and we are …at least for a time, *lost* without them. The pain is worse when we have amnesia. Amnesia creates a HORRIBLE misperception indicating erroneous finality. At least knowing that what you're feeling is merely a SYMPTOM of the amnesia, can help!!! Knowing the truth, our tears don't go away BUT they can be different once we understand life transitioning for what it truly is. It's really NOT death. Still sad though…*missing the good times* is putting it lightly.

Looking up at the clouds I suddenly was aware of the cords of love connecting me to people who have already transitioned from this incarnation. I thought about how every time a loved one transitions before us, a cord is cut to our existence in this incarnation. The cord is still connected to us but it's flipped around and instead of being anchored to a point in this dimension, it's now anchored to a point in the spirit world. As they go, we're less and less connected here and more & more connected there.

The seeming state of memory loss about this URGENT, SACRED and IMMINENT process is the leading cause of the fear of transitioning from one life to the next. Hoping you are now realizing a greater state of ease on this inevitability than when you began reading these pages. Personally, while I am more and more at ease… I am also - oh so tearfully in wonder and amazement…

The most significant thing I've learned is that from our current perspective anchored in THIS incarnation, THIS incarnation is the most important one. We must give the life we're conscious of, right here, right now - 100%. The rest (parallel lives n whatnot) is the rest. Like, it is what it is. Know that and then trust the process! Trust that this knowingness is bleeding over to your other selves and that you are realizing the need to give 100% in all of your incarnations. This evolution can bring you an abundance of all that is good, everywhere.

As I've been writing, trying to explain the workings of this life - a little Spiritual Anatomy 101 - a little orientation into what we really are and why when a loved one transitions it isn't separation but instead it is a new form of the relationship - I've also realized that… I want to switch my focus, for a while, from transitioning to, just being! Enjoying life as it is miraculously gifted to me today thereby enhancing my experiences in this dimension rather than focusing on what happens 'when'. What happens when our bodies *die* is interesting but pales by comparison to what happens when we LIVE! I'm getting in ***<u>bold italic underlined</u>*** energy that the trick to our evolution is in the focus and attention on LIVING - in the NOW. In the now while being simultaneously conscious of our *authentic state* as eternal spirit beings just here for a figurative minute - having a temporary and hopefully very cool, very fulfilling human experience. THAT is what time it truly is.

My plan as I close this project is to find my friends and family and love them like I never have before! People who irritate me - look the hell out; I'm gonna be showing you love, too! Somehow! Meredith, Meredith, Meredith..... I actually AM sorry for the energy exchanged that day and especially for my part in it. And Thank you! From the bottom of my heart - I love you and I am so grateful for you! All that stuff coming to the surface was part of a healing/detox I desperately needed on behalf of my wellbeing and future productivity.
By spring of the following year, the Doll House was bustling with BRILLIANT minds! Multiple! A couple of them are, without question, smarter than ME! I so embrace this! Life is good!

My gratitude today is for the gift of knowing, as Sun & Jin did, that I'm safe. I'm always safe. And more than that - much more than that - I am loved and ...I love BECAUSE ...I AM Love. Wishing that reality for everyone. That or something better for the greater good... All of the illusionary chaos - the emotional undercurrent to the modern day rat race - as we figuratively push that damn button every 108 minutes - is not the end all.
    I leaned completely back, hot water wrapped around my neck as my toes reached for the opposite wall. I was face to face with the scattered clouds pink from the waking sun. It was chilly out but I was protected, wrapped warmly in this early morning water blanket ritual. -Realizations of my part in the whole of life continued to flood my space. As a unique expression of our Creator, I am basking in the radiance of a core knowingness that lifts me and will carry me all the rest of my days. Eternity...

THE END (Almost)

Appendix A

Dissolving Contracts

I usually say I'm gonna "Kill a Contract". Lol! I'm so dramatic. Its most commonly called "Burning a contract". Look it up through an internet search engine and you'll find that there are many ways to do it but the end result is the same!

Light it up and then... burn it - literally! Energetically, I like the idea of dissolving the contract back into the nothingness from whence it came. It's a victory and an absolute knowingness that subsequent to this action, that agreement no longer exists. If the other party with whom you made that agreement still needs a partner in the situation, they are welcome to find one elsewhere. In LOST, Kate coulda killed her contract with Wayne without actually killing Wayne!! She could have also killed at least PART of the contract she had with her mother. It was a contract to feel a certain way as she witnessed her mom's CONSCIOUS CHOICE to be in a brutally violent relationship. That's a hard one, indeed. But everything is connected to everything else. Different agreements might have meant different solutions; therapy for mom, jail for Wayne. ...Just a thought.

Everyone is connected to everyone else. Our physical bodies give the illusion, in this dimension that we are separate but we are connected to everything which is connecting all of us. And we are not bodies, we are energy fields of consciousness!

Everybody who went to the island had a contract with it! Jack seemed to be the last one to let go of his agreement and that was only after certain tasks were handled as he proved to 'himself' that he is capable. The black smoke jungle monster - poor guy! I just wanna give him a more optimistic name! Lol! But anyway, he had a contract with the island mother lady and another separate contract with Jacob. He also had a contract with each person who's body he used to fake other folks out! And he had a contract with everyone he scared and tossed around on the island. - That's messed up, I know but...

How to kill a contract

Get centered with a short quieting meditation. I love what I call the following; a 'nostril meditation'! Lol In truth it's not just about your nostrils. Air is coming in and going out all kinds of different directions!!!

Usually in a chair, I sit upright with my feet flat on the floor. I close my eyes and begin to focus on my breathing. Noticing everything there is to notice about my breath as it goes in my nostrils and out my mouth.... in my mouth and out my nostrils, in my nostrils and out my nostrils, in my mouth and out my mouth. Then I might keep it the same; in my nostrils and out my nostrils noticing how cool the air is coming in, how warm the air is going out. Then I might change to; in my nostrils and out my mouth for a while and 'Belly Breathe'.

For Belly Breathing you simply observe the movement of your belly and chest as they rise and fall to the motion of your inhale....exhale... peace. Ultimately remember to inhale Love.... let it fill up your body and then exhale LOVE...

Now, with every breath - focusing on love, watch it fill you up, inhale as it fills your body, it stays and multiplies within as you exhale love. Inhale more love expanding it into your aura; breath Love out, breathing Love in....; circulating the essence of God through your being.

I can hold this type of meditation for about 20 minutes but even if you only do 2 - 3 minutes, you'll feel the effect of the intention which is to quiet the mind. Your chatter is reduced to belly, nostrils, breath.

I recommend starting this process with a prayer or invocation that includes your ultimate intention with the process. Setting a clear intention is urgent. You don't want to march aimlessly in! Give gratitude for this moment and opportunity! Ask the Source of all Life to bless your process. I also like asking that God's "Love and Light fill my space, fill the aura of my home and saturate my being so that we are protected and orbiting in the realm of pure Love.

Then I might say, for example, "MY INTENTION: is to release the obligation and guilt I feel regarding Beula. It has served its purpose in my learning. I release it now to return to my authentic state of peace and joy within. This or something better for the greater good of all concerned. And so it is."

Now you're ready to begin the contract burning process!

1. This is not a buddy process. While I have seen this done in a group, the individuals in the group are not to SHARE what they're writing and burning. Further, make sure you've got time to do this process to completion without interruption.
2. S C A M: Yeah. A positive spin to the word SCAM!
Stop - Contemplate - Acknowledge - Move
STOP to get quiet enough to go within where you will
CONTEMPLATE what contract/agreement is up for official termination
MOVE: Let it OUT! Write what's on your mind. - Let it flow, baby! There is no right or wrong. It doesn't have to be grammatically correct or sensible! It can be fragmented and incomplete - the urgent part is to get what you are feeling about this agreement OUT.
3. Write the wrongs, my friend! Write for a while! 20 -30 minutes is typical. You can even go longer! I've learned that we should limit the writing to 2 hours max. The trick is to do it 'til you're complete. You're complete when you don't feel the charge anymore!
4. This is a purging exercise. You are getting it out and claiming the disconnection and dissolve of the previous agreement to experience this condition. Ultimately - after

raging for many pages, I might say something like, "Here's the bottom line Mr. Paperwork Piles - You don't get to rule me anymore!! Thank you for the lessons you've given me, valuable lessons and you forced me into a corner where for the sake of my wellness I changed my priorities and found tools and support for the needed transformation. I no longer need you to imprison or COCOON me – if that's what you were doing. What purpose that served for a time, is no longer fruitful. We're done. I am breaching this contract agreement RIGHT Now! Forever. Peace – Out!"

5. LET IT GO- that means once you write it don't take it in again by reading it. This process is a DETOXING. You don't want to re-ingest the toxin!!! Ew! You are DONE with this now. Don't reprogram it in!!!
6. I love metal buckets! With one of these I can immediately and safely burn the document I've written. Outdoor fire places and barbeque pits are also nice! If you're like me, you type faster than you write and it's very natural and effortless for you to emote this way. If so and you did your writing on a computer you must A) PRINT the document you created B) DELETE the writing from your entire computer and then empty the computers deleted items. C) Burn the document.

If you cannot BURN - SHRED! If you can't do either, tear it into the tiniest pieces you can and dispose of it. You can also bury it! If you bury it - go deep! Know that it is biodegradable and will eventually dissolve into the earth. Whether you've burned, shredded, torn and buried, walk away knowing IT'S DONE.

Peace, Bliss & Blessings in your multi-dimensional journeys....

Appendix B

Bibliography

-Anita Moorjani, 'Dying to be Me: My Journey from Cancer to Near Death, to True Healing'

-Eben Alexander, III MD.., 'Proof of Heaven: A Neurosurgeons Journey into the Afterlife'

-Jane Roberts, 'Seth Speaks: The Eternal Validity of the Soul (A Seth Book)'

-Marcus J. Borg 'Reading the Bible Again for the First Time; Taking the Bible seriously but not literally'

-Marianne Williamson, 'Illuminata; Thoughts, Prayers and Rites of Passage'

'-Micheal Newton, 'Journey of Souls; Case Studies of Life Between Lives'

-Rhonda Byrne, 'The Secret'

-Shirley MacLaine, 'Dancing in the Light'

-James Von Praagh, 'Talking to Heaven; A Mediums Message of Life After Death'

-Michael Nahm, Ph.D., 'Terminal Lucidity in People with Mental Illness and Other Mental Disability: An Overview and Implications for Possible Explanatory Models' in Volume 29 of The International Institute of Near-Death Studies

Web sites
http://www.kaahelehawaii.com/pages/culture_hookupu.htm
http://www.flixxy.com/world-war-ii-fighter-pilot-reincarnation.htm
https://www.youtube.com/watch?v=I9u2EpK35PY
http://www.medindia.net/patients/calculators/world-death-clock.asp

(The web site links above are provided for informational purposes only. They do not constitute endorsement of any products or services provided by these websites and the links are subject to change, expire, or be redirected without any notice.)

Disclaimer

There are a few places in this book where names and character details of a few people have been extensively disguised so that any resemblance to any person, living or dead, is coincidental. The intention is to protect the identity of certain people yet authentically share the story while preserving the essence of truth in the events.

Neither the publisher nor the individual author shall be liable for any physical, psychological, emotional, financial, or commercial damages, including, but not limited to, special, incidental, consequential or other damages by way of information in this book. Our views and rights are the same: You are responsible for your own choices, actions, and results.

This book is designed to provide information and awareness on the validity of multi-dimensional existence and/or life, after life. This book does not contain all information available on the subject. Every effort has been made to make this book as accurate as possible. However, there may be typographical and or content errors. Oops & Sorry! Therefore, this book should serve only as a general guide and not as the ultimate source of subject information.